YALE AGRARIAN STUDIES SERIES

James C. Scott, Series Editor

The Agrarian Studies Series at Yale University Press seeks to publish outstanding and original interdisciplinary work on agriculture and rural society—for any period, in any location. Works of daring that question existing paradigms and fill abstract categories with the lived experience of rural people are especially encouraged.
—James C. Scott, *Series Editor*

James C. Scott, *Seeing Like a State: How Certain Schemes to Improve the Human Condition Have Failed*

James C. Scott, *The Art of Not Being Governed: An Anarchist History of Upland Southeast Asia*

Timothy Pachirat, *Every Twelve Seconds: Industrialized Slaughter and the Politics of Sight*

James C. Scott, *Against the Grain: A Deep History of the Earliest States*

Jamie Kreiner, *Legions of Pigs in the Early Medieval West*

Ruth Mostern, *The Yellow River: A Natural and Unnatural History*

Brian Lander, *The King's Harvest: A Political Ecology of China from the First Farmers to the First Empire*

Jo Guldi, *The Long Land War: The Global Struggle for Occupancy Rights*

Andrew S. Mathews, *Trees Are Shape Shifters: How Cultivation, Climate Change, and Disaster Create Landscapes*

Francesca Bray, Barbara Hahn, John Bosco Lourdusamy, and Tiago Saraiva, *Moving Crops and the Scales of History*

Deborah Valenze, *The Invention of Scarcity: Malthus and the Margins of History*

Brooks Lamb, *Love for the Land: Lessons from Farmers Who Persist in Place*

Jamie Sayen: *Children of the Northern Forest:* Wild New England's History from Glaciers to Global Warming

Michael R. Dove, *Hearsay Is Not Excluded: A History of Natural History*

Gregory M. Thaler: *Saving a Rainforest and Losing the World: Conservation and Displacement in the Global Tropics*

Lee Sessions: *Nature, Culture, and Race in Colonial Cuba*

Brian Donahue: *Slow Wood: Greener Building from Local Forests*

Merrill Baker-Medard: *Feminist Conservation: Politics and Power in Madagascar's Marine Commons*

James C. Scott, *In Praise of Floods: The Stake of All Creatures in the Freedom of the River*

For a complete list of titles in the Yale Agrarian Studies Series, visit yalebooks.com/agrarian.

Feminist Conservation

Politics and Power in Madagascar's Marine Commons

MERRILL BAKER-MÉDARD

Yale

UNIVERSITY PRESS

NEW HAVEN AND LONDON

Published with assistance from the foundation established in memory
of Philip Hamilton McMillan of the Class of 1894, Yale College.

Yale University Press books may be purchased in quantity for educational,
business, or promotional use. For information, please e-mail sales.press@yale.edu
(US office) or sales@yaleup.co.uk (UK office).

Set in Electra type by IDS Infotech, Ltd.
Printed in the United States of America.

Library of Congress Control Number: 2024938748
ISBN 978-0-300-26542-2 (hardcover);
ISBN 978-0-300-26541-5 (paperback)

A catalogue record for this book is available from the British Library.

10 9 8 7 6 5 4 3 2 1

For my mothers, Ann and Folovelo, and grandmothers, Selma, Esther Sophia, and Soavy, thank you for the strength and wisdom embedded in your lineage. Thank you to Mike, Theo, Myron, Morton, and Sousa Medard for also living and loving in support of your partners and children.

For my hearts Louva, Soa, and Naunau—lovey-dovey time, dance parties, and your kisses have helped this project come to fruition.

And to the coastal communities that give life to these pages. I am indebted to the many individuals who fished, talked, fetched water, pounded rice, shared a meal, and responded to my perpetual inquisitiveness with kindness.

And to the superbly complex and wonderfully curious ocean, which binds us and brings so much meaning to our lives.

I believe in
intergenerational becoming
like coral
radically rebuilding
from the rubble left by crumbling capital
I believe in
caudal fins
winged propellors forged from watery resistance
fanlike bones of history
righting our relations
stabling us in tempestuous tides
I believe in
commoning
grouping like groupers
collective liberation
in deep waters sacral
I believe
as we evolved from the expansive blue
we can return again
humble
grateful

CONTENTS

PREFACE

It's early morning in a small fishing village in southwestern Madagascar. In the subtle light of dawn, roosters crow as fishers emerge from thatched houses to walk to the crest of the sand dunes that overlook the ocean. Enveloped in blankets or colorful wraps, the fishers gaze out at the vast expanse—dark navy in the distance, bright white where waves break against the reef, and deep turquoise near the shore. Surveying the waves in the distance, the clouds in the sky, and the direction and strength of the wind, they decide where they will fish and what gear they will bring. There is a slight onshore wind today that will pick up by the afternoon, so those who have sails will bring them along in their boats to quicken the journey home from the reef.

Yawning into the green wrap draped over my head, I follow Lesta Kely up the sandy slope near our house. She has brought two buckets for us to fetch water from the well on our way back from the dune. Pointing toward the white foam of the waves, she says to me with a smile, "It's a really low tide today," which I have learned means that we'll head out to the reef early, paddling with four or five other women in one of the larger dugout canoes, to fish on the reef flat until noon.

I began the research that led to this book in order to understand how international conservation organizations such as the Wildlife Conservation Society, Conservation International, and others based in my country of origin, the United States, helped to create community-based conservation in Madagascar, considered a hotspot for biodiversity conservation. I had worked in Madagascar for several years as a consultant for international conservation organizations, collecting baseline social and ecological data from which conservation organizations could assess the impact of new terrestrial and marine protected areas. In this role, I attended many presentations, community meetings, ceremonies, and workshops run by governmental or nongovernmental conservation organizations. At these events, even the seemingly mundane choice of where to sit was fraught. If other foreigners, generally white male foreigners, were present, village leaders would lead me to sit with them on chairs in the shade. If I was the only foreigner in the crowd, I would sit next to the other women present and nobody would object, although frequently someone would bring me a chair, upon which I would perch awkwardly while all the other women sat on the ground around me. It was clear that my whiteness and my femaleness were in conflict within the hierarchical space of these meetings. Men often sat closest to the center or front of the space, whereas women often sat on the outside or near the back, making it harder for them to hear the presentation. These experiences, among other observations of gender, ethnic, and class-based hierarchies, attuned me to the complexity of intracommunity dynamics in conservation projects.

This book took shape in the many conversations I had while heading in boats out to the reef, sitting in smoky kitchens, cleaning and salting fish, gutting and boiling sea cucumbers, pounding rice, standing in line to fetch water, peeling manioc root, and waiting for afternoon heat to dissipate under the shade of a tree. In these moments conversation flowed, and I was able to listen more deeply. As I listened, the worldview that had wrapped around me from birth began to unwind. The dichotomies that I was born into—nature/culture, female/male, private/public, local/global, victim/perpetrator, emotional/rational, experience/knowledge, tradition/modernity—dissipated and were reshaped themselves through these conversations.

The sea, far from being a passive recipient of conservation, is I learned, quite the character: one day a wily partner who undermines one's efforts fishing or traveling, the next an eager and helpful friend who provides a calm surface and plentiful catch. The sea can also be a ruthless arbiter of rules bent or broken, taking the lives of fishers, both young and old, who have transgressed taboos or wronged ancestors or local spirits. Depending on how you treat it, the sea can bring luck and wealth by revealing the hiding spots of octopuses or by offering a steady breeze to fill one's sail on the way back home. I learned that the sea, and the spirits that work in relation to it, such as *vorombe*, *angatra*, or *lolon-drano*, are part of conservation decision-making in ways I could have never imagined before the slow unwinding of my worldview. From a young age, I'd been taught that nature was something "out there," needing isolation from humans to be healthy. In focusing on protecting nature from humans, Western conservation has often ignored or erased the reciprocal, mutually reinforcing relationship that has long existed between humans and the more-than-human world in Madagascar and beyond.

When I began working in Madagascar in my early twenties, I regarded the coastal places I visited—the reefs and villages—as remote from the rest of the world. I have since come to learn how deeply connected Madagascar is to locales around the globe through networks of trade, aid, and information. My colonial mindset—seeing the cosmopolitan cities and areas of the West as center and rural coastal Madagascar as periphery, remote, or untouched—unraveled as my research progressed. I dug into precolonial archives in Madagascar that showed long histories of trade with East Africa, the Middle East, East Asia, and beyond. I traced where marine exports have gone when they leave Madagascar both today and historically, and I investigated the vast number of conservation and development projects funded by dozens of countries. As I became increasingly aware of the array of links between fishing villages along the Madagascar coast and hundreds of faraway places, I have grown to understand place as relational rather than local and isolated. Similarly, rather than regarding the Malagasy people I visited primarily as victims of the big, bad Western world, I have come to see them as agents of their own fate and participants in shaping their future within the uneven economic and political terrain they navigate daily. They choose where and how they fish (for example, legally or illegally), where and on what they spend their money, time, and organizational power, and whom they esteem,—or ignore.

The processes of learning and unlearning during the twenty-plus years I've spent in Madagascar have also shown me how my position as a formally educated, white, able-bodied, American-born, queer woman shapes how I make sense of what I observe and experience while doing research. My identity and position influence the vocabulary and terms I use in this book, which often do not have the same resonance or significance for the people with whom I work most closely in Madagascar. For example, I write about a feminist approach to conservation, yet the word *feminism* doesn't directly translate into Malagasy, although some Malagasy scholars, activists, and NGO workers use the French word *féminisme*. However, the notion of *mira zo, mira lenta* for women, roughly translated as "the same rights, the same value," is something that many women I interviewed or lived with in fishing villages both understand and desire. Although I am not advocating for universal sisterhood, I do see the importance of adapting the quest for gender, racial, and class-based equity, representation, and justice to the sociopolitical and cultural context of Madagascar and of finding ways to collaborate with similar movements beyond Madagascar. As a Malagasy colleague put it, "The word *feminism* is alienating, it doesn't fit here [in Madagascar], but of course we need to fight for gender-inclusive conservation. Many women want a voice. We need a movement so women's voices are heard." In this book I try to meet people where they are, to use the language they use, one embedded in their worldview and connected to their values. I am interested in understanding how all fishers, especially Malagasy women fishers, think about—and act to bring about—change in their lives.

By untangling some of what makes conservation introduce or entrench existing gender, class, and race inequities, I hope to identify paths toward a more just form of conservation. Some might consider the term *feminist conservation* an oxymoron. I question whether conservation can be just, given the imperialist and masculinist history of big *C* conservation and the capitalist goals and interests of the large international nongovernmental organizations that sponsor conservation projects. Can conservation be feminist? Ultimately, I argue that conservation can be feminist if it centers reciprocity, accountability, and care both within and across human and nonhuman communities through collective action. I believe that, by focusing on this process of commoning rather than primarily on the material resources of the commons—community-based conservation driven by smallholders and informed by their worldviews—little *c* conservation is not only possibly but necessarily feminist. With a focus on reciprocity, accountability, and care, on coming together to solve how best to work with and relate to the more-than-human natural world, a reconfigured approach to conservation can attend to intracommunity stratifications and injustices.

What, then, should be the role of international conservation organizations that currently dominate conservation funding and projects globally? For my many friends and colleagues working in conservation organizations, I posit that if they truly care about community-based conservation, they need to trust that greater representation of fishers, farmers, and smallholders, who have a different set of experiences and knowledge than those in power, will lead to ideas better suited to the values and goals of these communities and, by extension, to a more just form of conservation. When systems center smallholders' voices, including those of women, the influx of new knowledge and interests can help existing systems shift and thus ensure that smallholders maintain access to places and resources where they live. As many political ecologists, anthropologists, critical conservation scholars, and cultural geographers have shown, from its colonial origins, top-down conservation has not been just nor can it be. Sustainable and just conservation must arise from people situated at the frontlines of shifting ecological systems who are bearing the brunt of the problems generated by our current political economy—in short, from those who have the most at stake and the most to lose from the current configuration.

With this book I hope to do justice to the stories, experiences, and visions of those I observed, conversed with, and lived with over the years. My hope is that the laughter, anger, dreams, and tears shared with the many friends, colleagues, and coconspirators I found in my research reverberate through these pages and help people forge new paths of feminist collaboration and solidarity within and beyond Madagascar. I am humbled by how much people know in living with and from the sea, how people every day affirm their own dignity and agency amid immense economic, environmental, and social change, and how some of my Malagasy colleagues, by engaging in the slow and hard work of coalition building, have begun to shift the winds of conservation and fill the sails of boats previously tacking upwind.

ACKNOWLEDGMENTS

This research would not have been possible without the generous support of the households and communities that opened their doors to share food, wisdom, laughter, anger and hope with me. I am especially indebted to all the people in Madagascar who welcomed me into their homes, took me out on the reefs, patiently answered my questions, and showed me a new way of seeing the world. Mahavelo bevata an'i mpikaroka mahafinari-tra tena mahavita raha baka atimo: Miza Pierette Razafindravelo, Charlotte Lahiko Nagnisaha, Gabriel Rahasimanana, Felicien Eloi Gauthier, sy Emma Tinahindrazany. Fisaorana koa aminareo jiaby baka avaratra Hortensia Raso-ananandrasana, Abdou (Boomer) Mitsounga, Floris Saula, Rolande Fagnahy, Gaustin Ramamonjisoa, Silvère Ravelomanana, sy Olive Rafidison. Misaotra tamin'ny fanohananareo, ary indrindra ny fitondranao am-bavaka ny fikaro-ana ambanivolo. Misaotra mandray ahy an'tranonareo i Totoa Mence, Tatie Vola, Solange, BeLeonor, sy Lolo sy Ludo Tilmazana. Tsy manadino le raha tsara vitanareo tamiko. Lasa longoko, havako ianareo e!

Thank you also to my incredible research assistants in the United States who are a group of hard-core, generous, and brilliant folks: Ellie Kroger, Diego Rey, Courtney Gantt, Gabe Lefkowitz, Ivonne Juarez Serna, Jake Faber, Katie Concannon, Maria Celes Abragan, Valeriia Vakhitova, Tara Santi, Becca Brown, Isaac Danuloff, Tatum Peskin, Matia Whiting, Victoria Andrews, Meïssa Atmani, Aiden Acosta, Emily Ray, Maddie Lehner, Caroline Daley and Reilly Isler.

This research also would not have been possible without the help of my intellectually stimulating and incredibly supportive mentors and colleagues. Thank you to Mary Mendoza, Kathy Morse, Mike Sheridan, Sujata Moorti, Dave Allen, Dan Suarez and Jess L'Roe. Since my move to the Green Mountain State you have been my intellectual family, thank you for all that you are and all that you have done. Thank you to Anne Goldman and Lisa Beard for your love and for keeping me centered enough to finish this book despite big life events that threw me for a loop.

Thank you Louise Fortmann for your unwavering intellectual and emotional support throughout my journey as a scholar. Thank you for your insights on gender, on property, and on interdisciplinary and participatory research. You are an incredible mentor and an incredible convener—the Louise crew rolls deep and wide! Claire Kremen, thank you for your excellent mentorship and guidance. Your encouragement, timely advice, and critical comments were key my development as scholar and as a human. Nancy Peluso, you have deeply influenced my intellectual identity. Thank you for always pushing me to dig deeper in my research. You have helped me think like a political ecologist and tackle taken-for-granted aspects of socionatural processes. Thank you for your patience and your laughter.

My intellectual trajectory was also deeply informed by my UC Berkeley mentors and colleagues, including Gill Hart's insight on critical development theory and space, Justin Brashares's perspective on protected area effectiveness, Marissa Baskett's knowledge on marine conservation, and Carolyn Finney's insight on identity, representation, and difference (grateful you are in VT now!). I'd also like to extend a warm thank you for the excellent feedback on early drafts of my work, including: Derek Hall, Christian Lund, Leonardo Arriola, and Elizabeth Havice. Also, misaotra betsaka amin'i Tendro Tondrosoa and Chris Golden for being my Gasy brothers from another mother.

There were several people who spent extra time helping me develop this work, including Mehana Vaughn, Jade Sasser, Catherine Corson, Clare Gupta, Margot Higgens, and the other half of (M)alice . . . Alice Kelly Pennaz. Early drafts were also commented on by Caro Prado, Ashton Wesner, Beth Rose Middleton-Manning, Megan Ybarra, C. N. E. Corbin, Esther

Conrad, Sharon Fuller, Kevin Woods, and Aghaghia Rahimzadeh. You are all incredible folks, and I am inspired by your brilliance and generosity. An extra thanks to the bighearted Sibyl Diver for excellent help on my conclusion. And to Mary Woolsey, who was in it for the long haul and helped me through long and laborious revisions, thank you for all your generous comments, insights, and incredibly helpful edits. I would be remiss if I didn't also extend a warm thanks to the patient and wonderful Jean Thomson Black, and to Laura Jones Dooley and Margaret Otzel, detail-oriented editors extraordinaire from YUP.

I am also grateful for the help and guidance of many other people embedded in conservation organizations in Madagascar, including the one and only Bemahafaly, whose advice early on set shaped my work in Madagascar and the other WCS crew: Francisco, Bebe Jean, Santisy, Ravo, Tantely, Dimby and Ambroise. Thanks to WWF crew: Tantely, Vola, Eulalie, the CI crew: Frank, Ando, and Boris and the MIHARI crew: Vatosoa Rakotondrazafy, Marianne Randriamihaja, Prisca Ratsimbazafy, and Guy Rakotovao. I am deeply thankful for your warmth and generosity.

This research was also made possible by funding from the National Science Foundation Graduate Research Fellowship Program, Andrew and Mary Rocca Fellowship for African Studies, UC Berkeley Center for Race and Gender, Foreign Language and Area Studies IIE, and the Fulbright Fellowship.

Endless thanks to my rock, my father, Mike, my mother, Ann, my sister, Esther, my brother-in-law, Olivier, my niece, Windega, and Papi Theo, Neny Folovelona, Bebe Soavy, Tatie Chantal, Titi Nirina, Clô, Pres, Marostara, Yann, Aiko and Kenzo. Oroka mamy be.

. . . and last but not least my lovey-doveys my KunaTata Beloha, Soa and Louva. Thank you for your heroic support over these many years and making me laugh and dance when I needed it most.

ONE

Introduction

Gendering the Commons

Sure, many of us [women] used to go out there. I would go with my
husband; he'd drop me off and I'd fish on foot while he went by boat
to line fish near the big island. You can see everything through the
water at low tide. . . . I would get octopus, shells, all sorts of things
when I fished on foot out there. Sometimes we'd spend the night
out there if a storm came in. That was a long time ago; I'd be
thrown in jail if I went out there now.

—*Zara, retired fisher, northeastern Madagascar, October 27, 2010*

Zara, at age sixty-three, is one of just a handful of women I met in Kobalava who vividly remembers fishing. Kobalava is a village in northeastern Madagascar where the tapestry of rainforest, rice fields, clove trees,
and vanilla vines meets a bright blue ocean spotted with coral, offshore
sandbars, and small islands whose trees stretch out over the water.[1] Large
white-capped waves roll in off the Indian Ocean, churning along the shoreline and leaving but a few points for boats to launch. Once out to sea, most
fishers, of all genders, used to focus their efforts a few kilometers offshore
around a cluster of three islands.

No women fish anymore in Kobalava. As I learned in my time as a participant observer there, women collect, process, and sell fish—but do not
catch of their own. The shallow areas where women used to fish, around the
cluster of islands, are now part of a no-take zone of a marine protected area
(MPA). This no-take zone was created as part of an international conservation, institution–driven trend toward area closures to conserve marine biodiversity, restore fragile ecosystems, and stabilize fisheries' production. A

world-renowned biodiversity hotspot known for high species endemism coupled with increasing anthropogenic threats, Madagascar receives millions of dollars each year, funneled through governmental and nongovernmental conservation organizations, intended for marine biodiversity conservation and fisheries management. The pressure to protect biodiversity in Madagascar and elsewhere, moreover, is likely to become even greater with the launching of the 30×30 global campaign to conserve 30 percent of land and ocean by 2030.

Zara's husband, Bakely, continues to fish from his boat in the deeper waters beyond the reserve. Like most men in northeastern Madagascar, men from Kobalava fish from small dugout canoes propelled primarily by paddle instead of sail. Zara, however, like all the other women in Kobalava and in most coastal villages across Madagascar, fished on foot. With spears, sticks, and bare hands, women across Madagascar wade into shallow waters during low tides, especially the lowest tides, called spring tides, that occur several times a month. These extra-low tides make accessible coral reef crests, seagrass fields, and mudflats that are otherwise too deep to reach on foot. Before the establishment of the MPA near Kobalava, women harvested shells, octopus, sea cucumbers, fish, and other organisms during spring tides in the shallow waters of the small islands offshore. The steep shoreline near Kobalava prevented women from fishing from shore; when their island fishing ground became a reserve, women thus stopped fishing, not only changing their daily practices and livelihood opportunities but also reducing their contribution to household food.

The MPA at Kobalava had its origins in the late 1980s, when a large international conservation organization arrived with a project in mind. Project personnel presented the idea of establishing a comanaged MPA to the villagers. Fishers were told that the MPA would improve catch, safeguard coral reefs, and protect unique marine biodiversity in the area, including sea turtles, dolphins, and dugongs; conservationists were particularly concerned about the impact of fishing on foot on the reefs. The Malagasy government and international conservation organization saw the proposal for comanagement as an enlightened alternative to top-down conservation. Conservation organization workers explained comanagement to Kobalava villagers as shared decision-making between the Malagasy government and the people of the four villages (Kobalava being one) next to the proposed MPA. As planned, the international conservation organization departed several years after the MPA project was up and running, leaving the Malagasy government and village leaders to navigate management of the MPA. Via village fishing associations and local management committees, Kobalava villagers were supposed to be involved with all aspects of marine resource management, including decision-making, monitoring, and enforcement.[2]

Unfortunately, the community-based element of MPA management never came to fruition. A report written for the Malagasy government by a consulting agency in the late 1990s attested to the lack of local input and agency in MPA management, arguing that "the local management sector of park operations has long been tenuous and in the shadows of the technical operations of other park sectors" (protected source, 89). The authors of this report then called for "increased attention to local participation," noting that "the sustainability of the project depends on the dynamic input of local associations" (90). Despite this call for change, according to an internal government report written a decade later, local involvement in marine resource management was reduced to a total of three representatives across the four villages adjacent to the MPA. Currently monitoring and enforcement of the MPA relies on two government-salaried park guards, who stay in a cement house on one of the three islands in the MPA. Corroborating this decline, both park agents and key informants from Kobalava told me that although the project at first facilitated some community involvement in MPA management, by early 2000 Kobalava's fishing association and local management committee were functionally extinct. Former members of the Kobalava association complained to me that they had been duped by the governmental and nongovernmental officials into thinking they would have equal control over the project. A decade after the MPA's establishment, villagers had almost entirely ceased attending comanagement meetings in Kobalava because, as the village president exclaimed, "We didn't want to hear lies anymore."[3] Whereas the Malagasy government and the international conservation organization had initially attempted to engage the whole village, community involvement in MPA management had been reduced to one middle-aged man hired by the government to represent Kobalava. Although this man was formerly a respected leader in the village, his involvement with the MPA turned villagers against him. In an interview he lamented the loss of local buy-in and the decline of community comanagement, noting that someone had even poisoned his dog to punish him for his alliance with governmental MPA workers.[4]

Approximately 60 kilometers north of Kobalava is the small coastal village of Hoalankara, where an MPA similarly encloses several small islands. The women in Hoalankara, as in Kobalava, have a long history of fishing on foot in the shallow waters around the islands; unlike at Kobalava, however, they can also access the shallow waters of the coral reef fringing the coastline by foot from the village. Hoalankara's reef attenuates the impact of the big swell and choppy seas, enabling women to fish without a boat. In the early 1990s, an internation conservation organization initiated an integrated conservation and development project there; certain sections of the barrier reef and a few small islands became strict no-take zones, where fishers were not allowed to fish or even to cross in their boats. Based at a guard station adjacent to the village of Hoalankara, one or two park guards survey the no-take zones with binoculars from shore and patrol the area in kayaks.

Although park guards were to monitor and enforce MPA rules, the now government-managed project claimed to integrate local people into its planning and management and to establish local laws, called *dina*, to restrict the harvest of certain organisms such as sea turtles, dugongs, sea cucumbers, and numerous kinds of shells during certain periods of the year. As in Kobalava, the conservation organization working with the Malagasy government to establish the area considered fishing on foot highly destructive and banned all fishing on foot except for in the few feet from shore to allow individuals to harvest small bivalves, oysters, and crabs for home consumption.[5] Although the MPA did not eliminate the women's fishing area, women from Hoalankara told me that they now fish much less frequently than before due to the shrinkage in legally fishable area. In fact, half of the women interviewed said they no longer fish because of the MPA restrictions. As one interviewee explained, "Before, many women were enthusiastic to take

Pulling up the sail in northeastern Madagascar. Photograph by author.

bivalves [*tekateka*] and small fish [*ampiny*], but now most have stopped because we will be punished if we do." According to another woman, "When
the [MPA] project came, women were not allowed to fish anymore because
it ruins the reef; now men only fish."[6]

One evening after I had been living in Hoalankara for several months,
someone knocked on the door of my palm-thatched house. It was my neigh-
bor Maman'Gary, a woman in her mid-thirties. Beckoning me close, she
whispered that the low spring tide was that night: I was invited to go fishing
with her. Over the preceding months, she had been kind enough to let me,
a young white American woman, do participant observation research and
accompany her as she farmed and fixed food; occasionally we had collected
quarter-sized oysters together along the rocky shore. I helped her children
with their homework on most evenings, and we cooked meals together.
However, she had never whispered to me before. I stood there for a moment, unsure why we needed to collect small oysters on the shoreline in the
dark, but I agreed to go. Before leaving, she added, "Bring a flashlight and
your shoes."

That night, Maman'Gary and I walked from the village out to the reef with
another woman and her husband. I was thrilled but also terrified because by
then I understood that the four of us were doing something illegal—going
into a part of the reef where fishing on foot was not allowed. I also realized
that what we were doing was not an uncommon practice for fishers in
Hoalankara. With a full moon providing enough light to see the reef through
the water, Maman'Gary lifted a large dark sea cucumber from a sandy spot,
and then ten minutes later turned over a dead, flat piece of coral to find three
more sea cucumbers, two light-colored and another dark one with large white
bumps along its side. She smiled at me and said, "I'll get good money for this
one."[7] She threw her catch into the woven basket slung around her waist and
waded into slightly deeper waters, leaving me to fumble my way over exposed
coral rubble and wade through sandy passages looking for sea cucumbers and
shells. Even though sea cucumbers are relatively sedentary, I found only two
small ones that night, but Maman'Gary came back with more than a dozen,
plus several large shells and one octopus. We ate the octopus for lunch the
following day, and she sold her sea cucumbers to a local collector who

brought them to a Chinese trader in the regional port city. Several of her sea cucumbers fetched US$5 apiece, double the average daily income for a household in Madagascar.

After the nocturnal fishing trip, I figured out that a small cohort of women in Hoalankara who had fished during the day before the establishment of the MPA still fished out on the reef, but at night. This form of resistance, cloaked in nocturnal secrecy, was enabled by the fact that some women still fished alongshore close to town; women could thus openly claim that they fished or could be seen with their catch without being suspected of illegal activity. Moreover, people on foot can fish during low tides in the relatively shallow lagoon area protected by the barrier reef that flanks much of the coastline. The different physical risks associated with transgressing MPA rules in Kobalava and Hoalankara illustrate how both the biophysical features of the marine environment and the size and location of the marine protected area strongly shaped gendered access to marine resources in each village. The opportunity afforded by Hoalankara's physical setting to evade MPA rules combined with the lack of local buy-in to these rules clearly reduced the ecological effectiveness of the marine conservation strategy.

As the pressure exerted by governments and international conservation organizations to protect biodiversity and natural resources becomes more intense, the stories of Zara in Kobalava and Maman'Gary in Hoalankara offer a warning and illuminate a postmodern paradox: even though conservation institutions have moved toward more collaborative, context-specific, and community-based strategies, approaches consistent with a postmodernist framework, their projects have exacerbated divisions of labor and deepened inequity of access to natural resources, thereby undercutting both their engagement with the whole community and ultimately the efficacy of their conservation intervention.[8] In each locale the creation of an MPA reconfigured the risks and benefits of fishing along gendered lines. With the arrival of MPAs, women's access to marine resources was either significantly reduced or eliminated altogether. Beliefs about the distinction between what women and men already do or should do were rendered concrete through conservation interventions deemed collaborative.[9]

Extending beyond gendered disparities, so-called community-based conservation also reinforced the stark differences in decision-making power along axes of race, class, age, and nationality. Despite the good intentions of international conservation organizations guiding the implementation of these MPAs, the community-based paradigm was hollowed of its ideological core as local involvement waned, revealing the complexities of executing goals established by international conservation institutions in a postcolonial context.[10]

This book explores the origins and consequences of this paradox. What occurs when a conservation agenda is not attentive to intracommunity divisions or to hierarchies within and across national boundaries? What is obscured when conservationists and governments focus primarily on local or community—rather than global—drivers of ecological decline? What are the causes and impacts of marine enclosure in the name of conservation? The stakes of marine conservation interventions are high, both for people whose livelihoods depend on the areas where uses are restricted and for the goals of sustaining food networks, preventing species extinctions, and adapting to and mitigating climate change. It is thus particularly important to think carefully about what it will take to create more just and effective outcomes for conservation projects. A crucial question emerges: What is the relation between self-determination and an ecologically viable future?

Ultimately, in this book I aim to advance a conservation framework where social justice and sustainability are seen not as mutually exclusive but as co-constitutive, a framework I am calling feminist conservation. In doing so, I draw on critical feminist scholarship concerning international development and on the burgeoning field of feminist political ecology. To date, numerous studies of marine protected areas around the world have focused on the human dimensions of marine systems (Bennett et al. 2017; Rasheed 2020). Yet although this literature is sensitive to some power differentials among different stakeholders, it has paid less attention to analyses of intra- and intercommunity power differentials across lines of gender, class, age, and race. A small but growing number of scholars of marine conservation around the globe have demonstrated the importance of understanding the dynamics of marine resource use across gender and other axes of difference (Di Ciommo and Schiavetti 2012; Gissi, Portman, and Hornidge 2018; Harper et al. 2020; Kleiber, Harris, and Vincent 2018; Lynch and Turner 2022; Máñez and Pauwelussen 2016; Pike, Jiddawi, and de la Torre-Castro 2022; Walker and Robinson 2009; Wosu 2019). They argue that by understanding how these intersecting and overlapping differences affect participation in, control over, and impacts of marine resource management, we can improve both the ethics and the outcomes of conservation projects.

Feminist Conservation

Feminist conservation seeks to center an ethic of self-determination and a commitment to the eradication of domination in conservation practice.[11] Instead of focusing on the notion of equality, feminist conservation privileges the pursuit of mutual respect and accountability across geographic and social difference. It is a framework both to understand our social and ecological interdependence and to hold our differences, differences that shape and have been shaped by deep histories of theft, violence, and trauma stemming from imperialism, white supremacy, capitalism and patriarchy.[12]

The concept of self-determination does not have a single agreed-on definition. Within the field of psychology, self-determination focuses primarily on agency and power at the individual level, asserting that autonomy, competence, and relatedness to others are three intrinsic psychological needs for humans (Deci and Ryan 2004, 235). Social relations across difference, however, are central to a transnational feminist understanding of self-determination. Feminist scholar Chandra Mohanty warns that self-determination's focus on the individual cannot come at the expense of collective self-determination. Mohanty (2003, 8) emphasizes that although "autonomy and self-determination are central to the process of liberation," they can be achieved only through "self-reflexive *collective* practice."

A feminist approach to conservation is therefore one that embraces distributive, procedural, and transformative justice as avenues to work toward enabling self-determination and eradicating dominance within the increasingly complex and interconnected goals of sustainable resource use and biodiversity conservation. Distributive justice, or the equal distribution of benefits and burdens in a society, is a helpful framework to understand how to redress disproportionate access to marine resources in Madagascar because it does not focus primarily on guilt or innocence but instead centers the notion of entitlement and fairness (Harris 1993). Achieving the fair share ethic embedded in distributive justice underscores the importance of distributive justice's twin: procedural justice. Procedural justice refers to the idea of a fair process—fair consideration and treatment of individuals and communities by the institutions that structure society. Participation in deliberation and decision-making features prominently in procedural justice (Young 1990), a critical focus of this book, given the community-based paradigm that informs marine conservation in Madagascar. Increasing the participation of people previously underrepresented in marine resource management, however, also requires systems transformation to address or prevent potential backlash from those who oppose changing the status quo.

Although no conservation intervention that I explore in the following chapters has explicitly aimed to marginalize women's access to marine resources, marine protection projects nonetheless have reduced the ability of women and the poorest in a community to fish. Feminist conservation therefore serves to disrupt the allegedly gender-neutral, race- and class-blind programming that pervades many conservation efforts.

At a broader scale, I take a postcolonial intersectional approach to understanding how marine conservation emerged and still operates in Madagascar. Rather than assuming a tidy end to the colonial period, scholars of postcolonialism examine the political, economic, and sociocultural relations that sustain colonial and neocolonial power. In doing so, postcolonial research explicitly engages an anticolonial framework that decenters hegemonic masculinist and Eurocentric ideas and ideologies and works to reclaim and rethink the history and agency of individuals, communities, and nations shaped by imperialism (Kothari 2002; McEwan 2001). Postcolonial intersectionality, as defined by feminist political ecologists and cultural geographers Sharlene Mollet and Caroline Faria (2013, 117), "moves beyond US based racial and gender hierarchies to acknowledge the way patriarchy and racialized processes (including whiteness) are consistently bound up in national and international development practice." A postcolonial intersectional analysis is particularly important in Madagascar given how colonization shaped and continues to mold conservation processes (Campbell 2005; Tucker et al. 2021). Although I center gender and class in my analysis, I also illustrate how colonial and more recent conservation agendas and projects shape race and ethnicity in Madagascar, which overlap and intersect with gender, class, and age differences.

In addition to advancing a core ethic of (collective) self-determination and a commitment to the eradication of domination in conservation practice, this book engages other principles of feminist conservation. A necessary first step toward Malagasy self-determination in this realm, I argue, is stopping the widespread enclosure of the marine commons that has characterized colonial and postcolonial conservation. Moreover, MPAs enclose key areas accessed by women and people with lower socioeconomic standing, thereby impairing access to common pool resources by gender and class. Managing marine resources without requiring fixed spatial enclosures will reduce gender- and class-based restrictions of access to marine resources and recenter Malagasy worldviews and desired marine-based socioenvironmental futures. Resisting enclosure is thus an important feminist principle for marine conservation.

I further contend that the narrow focus on local drivers of marine decline places a disproportionate burden on women and the poorest within coastal communities in Madagascar, and elsewhere in the Global South, instead of on the communities and corporations in the Global North that drive the insatiable demand for seafood internationally. The greenhouse gas emissions of the Global North, moreover, have and continue to devastate coastal and marine ecosystems in Madagascar and elsewhere. Therefore, addressing the root drivers of natural resource use and degradation is an important feminist conservation principle that can push back against regressive and myopic solutions to problems that are in fact multifaceted, temporally complex, and multiscalar.

As I explore in this book, customary laws in Madagascar, called *dina*, have been invoked by marine conservation organizations and have ultimately favored Eurocentric and patriarchal conservation strategies. Another principle of feminist conservation I advance, therefore, is to identify and resist the invocation and cooptation of customary law and traditional rules that supplant participatory and iterative decision-making. When conservation ceases to rely on imposed conceptions of tradition, local cosmologies and ontologies, notably those that challenge the human-nature divide, can become central guides for conservation intervention.

Last, I argue that a feminist approach to conservation should not require formalization and modernization of resource-based livelihoods. Processes to formalize small-scale fishing in Madagascar were one of the most insidious ways in which international and national conservation and development organizations restricted marine resource access for women and the poor. Embedded in the logic of modernizing and professionalizing fisheries in Madagascar was a neocolonial project to make fisheries more so-called rational and organized. These framings disparaged existing Malagasy fishing practices as irrational, disorganized, and decidedly not modern. The discursive and material strategies conservation organizations used pushed

Three generations of women in a family heading out to fish on foot, southwestern Madagascar. Photograph by author.

women's and poor fishers' fishing practices to the political margin, ultimately rendering their activities illegal.

All in all, these principles form a preliminary framework for what a more feminist approach to conservation might look like. The principles outlined here, however, are not exhaustive; rather, they emerge from the stories, experiences, and opinions of those I observed, interviewed, and lived with in specific places in Madagascar during particular moments in time. These principles are thus a heuristic tool more than a definitive list. Given different historical, ecological, and social contexts, I imagine feminist principles for conservation could—and should—look quite different globally.

The Roots of Feminist Conservation

The notion of feminist conservation is rooted in political ecology, which focuses on understanding the complex relations between nature and society, and specifically how knowledge, power, and practice shapes forms of access to and control over resources.[13] Feminist political ecology explicitly addresses how gender and other intersecting axes of difference such as race, class, caste, and nationality shape human-environment relations as well as resource access and control at local, regional, and global scales (Agarwal 2010; Elmhirst 2011; Harcourt et al. 2023; Leach and Green 1997; Leach, Mehta, and Prabhakaran 2015; Mollett and Faria 2013; Resurrección 2017; Rocheleau, Thomas-Slayter, and Wangari 2016; Sasser 2018; Shiva and Mies 1993; Sundberg 2017). Foundational scholarship in feminist political ecology by Dianne Rocheleau, Barbara Thomas-Slayter, and Esther Wangari in 1996 showed through numerous case studies the variety of ways in which human-environmental processes are gendered. Their work, echoed in other scholarship at the time, illustrated that women not only use different parts of the environment than men—as in Kobalava and Hoalankara—but often have different knowledge of and access to natural resources than men (Fortmann, Antinori, and Nabane 1997; Harrison and Watson 2012; Rocheleau 2008; Walker 2002). These scholars argued that we must push beyond analyzing the power dynamics between local and extralocal actors in order to examine how, within a given community, ethnicity, race, class, age, and gender shape access to, control over, and benefit from natural resources (Agarwal 2010; Davis and Nadel-Klein 1992; Leach, Mearns, and Scoones 1999).

Increasingly, feminist political ecologists are rethinking how we can individually and collectively move beyond capitalist forms of interaction and value. Their frameworks, which dovetail with the degrowth movement, reconceptualize labor and work in terms of care, or providing for the human and nonhuman worlds through webs of reciprocity, accountability, and repair (Harcourt et al. 2023; Puig de la Bellacasa 2017; Singh 2019). These frameworks are essential to combating current political economic systems that perpetuate gendered, classed, and raced hierarchies globally.

Feminist political ecology is thus increasingly informed by postcolonial and transnational feminist scholarship that analyzes hierarchies of knowledge and systems of dominance and subordination embedded in postcolonial development (Gago 2020; Marchand and Parpart 2003; Mohanty 2003; Radcliffe 2015; Spivak 1999). Intersectional impacts constitute an important and underresearched area of global environmental justice and critical conservation studies. Two scholars working to bring critical race theory into conversation with critical conservation studies are Sharlene Mollet and Caroline Faria. Drawing directly from the foundational work of feminist scholars of color, including Kimberlé Crenshaw, bell hooks, Patricia Hill Collins, Ania Loomba, and Chandra Mohanty, Mollet and Faria (2013, 2018) bring a deeper understanding of how multiple interacting and overlapping historically situated social and political identities create disparities in access to and control over natural resources. Their work illustrates how racism, classism, patriarchy, colorism, and capitalism are intimately bound up in nation building, in which conservation initiatives have been central.

In line with other transnational feminist thinkers, Mollet and Faria also challenge the common misconception of a single or universal woman-environment relationship, as well as the assumption that gender difference is the primary origin of a woman's environmental oppression. Their work directly contradicts some of the early ecofeminist scholarship that emerged in the late 1980s and early 1990s. That gender-environment scholarship argued that women and nature shared a history of oppression by patriarchal institutions and by a colonizing Western culture that understands human-environment relations in narrow mechanistic ways guided by scientific and capitalist rationality (Merchant 1980; Plumwood 1986; Shiva 1989; Shiva and Mies 1993). While expanding on the intellectual project of early ecofeminists, most feminist political ecologists reject the essentialist idea that women are naturally or spiritually closer to nature than men. Instead, feminist political ecology favors analyses of how sociopolitical and cultural institutions determining tenure, property, access, and labor shape peoples' environmental interests, knowledge, and opportunities (Elmhirst 2011; Kerr 2014; Leach 2007; Mollett and Faria 2013; Nightingale 2011; Ojeda, Sasser, and Lunstrum 2019; Resurrección 2017; Rocheleau, Thomas-Slayter, and Wangari 2016; Sultana 2011; Sundberg 2017).

Early ecofeminist frameworks that critiqued gender-neutral conservation and development programming were simplified and absorbed into international conservation and development agendas in the early 1990s. As a result, institutions proclaimed "women's empowerment" and "women's participation" as key objectives in their conservation and development portfolios (Cornwall and Rivas 2015; Leach 2007; Leach, Mehta, and Prabhakaran 2015; Ogra 2012, Schroeder 1999; Wilson 2011). The idea that women are important vehicles through which international organizations can achieve conservation and development goals was epitomized by Women in Development (WID) and Women Environment Development (WED) initiatives embedded in international organizations such as the World Bank, United Nations Development Programme, United Nations Environment Programme, and the International Institute for Environment and Development (Braidotti 1994; Jackson 1993; Leach 2007; Resurrección 2017). WID and WED projects tended to focus on the gendered division of labor and had a static conception of women's roles in society and in the environment. In these programmatic strategies, women were seen not only as victims in need of protection but also as uniquely positioned stewards of the environment and key agents of development (Resurrección 2017; Sasser 2018).

WED and WID initiatives in the 1980s led to a series of commitments by the United Nations, International Union for the Conservation of Nature,

US Agency for International Development, and other organizations to mainstream gender, as it was termed, in their programs and policies (Ogra 2012; Moser and Moser 2005). Defined as a process in which organizations evaluate their programs and policies in terms of gender equality and orient programs and policies to achieve this goal, gender mainstreaming became a norm in most international conservation institutions at the turn of the twenty-first century.

Feminist scholars have shown that the substantive change in women's lives did not match the so-called discursive landslide concerning women's rights and women's empowerment in these realms (Cornwall, Harrison, and Whitehead 2007; Ellerby 2017; Ogra 2012; Westberg and Powell 2015). Women's empowerment in these interventions was thus hollowed of its political weight. Instead, gender-specific programming became instrumentalized in very narrow and technocratic ways by international conservation and development organizations to achieve development and environmental goals instead of equity and transformative justice (Sasser 2018).

Concurrent with the efforts to mainstream gender in international conservation and development institutions, a new conservation paradigm was taking hold. In the late 1980s and early 1990s, bottom-up or decentralized conservation became a popular resource management strategy in many developing countries (Adams and Hulme 2001; Leach, Mearns, and Scoones 1999), advanced by scholars and conservation practitioners because it helped solve key challenges conservation organizations were experiencing with top-down models, including poaching, local resistance, and continued loss of biodiversity within protected areas. If conservation organizations worked directly with people living next to conservation sites, it was thought, local ecological knowledge could inform management decisions and local people would be intrinsically motivated to protect the ecosystems on which they rely, thus leading to more effective and efficient conservation (Adams and Hutton 2007; Agrawal and Gibson 1999; Brosius, Tsing, and Zerner 2005; Ostrom 1990). Gender mainstreaming and community-based conservation efforts, while seemingly separate endeavors, were born from the same framework where female and "the local" are held in ontological opposition to male and "the global" (Freeman 2001).

Ostrom's Principles and Feminist Critiques

Elinor Ostrom, the first female economist awarded the Nobel Memorial Prize in Economic Sciences, is the most famous intellectual architect of the community-based conservation paradigm. Ostrom was best known for her analysis of common pool resources (CPR) governance, and common property regimes. More than thirty years have passed since she wrote *Governing the Commons: The Evolution of Institutions for Collective Action* (1990), her foundational work on this topic. In this book she drew on case studies from around the globe to illustrate how natural resource management can be locally conceived and executed to prevent depletion without government intervention. Ostrom's work in *Governing the Commons* thus disproved Garrett Hardin's (1968) tragedy of the commons theory, based on the economic model of the prisoner's dilemma, which asserted that rational, self-interested individuals will necessarily deplete a common pool resource unless the commons is privatized or the government intervenes. Ostrom's CPR theory challenged the long-standing notion that individuals only act in utility-maximizing, rational, and self-interested ways with common pool resources and are unable to cooperate and collaborate without state rule or privatization. According to Ostrom, collective action and collaborative management were not only possible but desirable in most circumstances. Disrupting the predominately masculine spaces of political science and economics (Wall 2014), Ostrom promoted a paradigm shift in environmental management and transformed conversations across multiple disciplines, including political science, economics, geography, and sociology. Ostrom's work also inspired and intellectually legitimized grassroots resource-rights movements and community-based self-governance (Brosius, Tsing, and Zerner 2005; Forsyth and Johnson 2014; Wall 2014). With its emphasis on cooperative behavior, her research challenged the foundations of the neoliberal economic paradigm (Forsyth and Johnson 2014).

Ostrom's CPR theory appealed to conservationists because it seemed to solve a crisis in both efficiency and legitimacy that conservation institutions were facing. It would be more efficient for them to work directly with local resource users than to work through governmental institutions, thus speeding up the process of project implementation and reducing overhead costs

(Salafsky and Wollenberg 2000; Shackleton et al. 2002). Additionally, conservation organizations were increasingly worried about so-called paper parks, protected areas that were not adequately monitored and enforced or, worse, protected areas where outright local resistance undermined environmental conservation (Brosius, Tsing, and Zerner 2005; Pimbert and Pretty 1997). Ostrom's model solved these issues by placing the onus and opportunity of managing natural resources on the local communities most reliant on these resources for their livelihoods and subsistence. In Ostrom's work, conservationists saw a potential model for controlling the use of and, in their eyes, preventing overexploitation of natural resources in places that lacked enduring CPR management of the sort Ostrom described.

To return to Kobalava and Hoalankara: before the imposition of the MPA, village residents had fished around the islands and on the reefs. Although colonial and postcolonial governments had made efforts to manage fisheries, local fishers' practices were shaped primarily by taboo (*fady*), various cultural practices (*fombafomba*), folklore/stories (*tafasiry/angano*), and the presence of ancestors (*razana*) and spirits (*lolo/angatra*) in terrestrial and marine spaces. In other words, no formal, clearly codified, and organized common pool resource management rules of the sort Ostrom had studied existed there. Although a suite of locally specific marine resource use practices existed before colonization and persist to this day, they are rarely legible to nonlocal organizations and individuals as meaningful fisheries management or biodiversity conservation strategies.[14] Furthermore, taboos, cultural practices, folklore, and spiritual beliefs vary substantially by region in Madagascar and are defined largely by ethnicity, gender, and livelihood.

Through her research on communities that successfully managed grazing land, fisheries, and irrigation in different areas of the world, Ostrom extracted eight design principles for "enduring common pool resource institutions."[15] The first three of these eight principles, and ones that I would argue form the foundation of Ostrom's logic, are deeply important to the communities and places included in my research. For example, in chapter 2, which focuses on the concept of decentralization or localization, I illustrate how Ostrom's first principle of "clearly defined boundaries" is not only difficult to establish in the settings I have studied but also belies the social and ecological entanglements a given community and seascape has with people and places across the globe. The applicability of Ostrom's second principle, which insists on "congruence between appropriation and provision rules and local conditions," is also challenged in chapter 2, where I show that one's worldview, or cosmology, ultimately determines one's understanding of the conditions for which rules are created. This principle is explored in chapter 4, in which I outline the history of dina, illustrating that there are clear differences between how conservation scientists understand and make rules to manage marine resources and how some fishers understand and follow particular rules related to marine resource conditions. Ostrom's third principle, the necessity of "collective-choice arrangements," is the focus of chapter 3, where I argue that the MPAs I researched lack procedural justice: women and the least wealthy in a community are nominally and effectively underrepresented in decision-making despite community involvement. Thus, even in situations that might appear to be well suited to the implementation of Ostrom's principles, my research reveals both how problematic it may be to meet at least some of her prerequisites and how her principles, even if fulfilled, may fall short.

Nevertheless, Ostrom's eight design principles for enduring common pool resource institutions have been widely circulated and cited in both development and conservation literature (Berkes 2004; Forsyth and Johnson 2014). Although Ostrom's impact was profoundly political and helped to justify and shape the broad application of community-based conservation, from a feminist perspective it did not critically engage power differentials in CPR management. Even though Ostrom herself was acutely aware both of class differences, given her very modest upbringing, and of gendered inequalities, given her experience in the male-dominated fields of economics and political science, for the most part she did not interrogate gender and class power dynamics in her work.

Later in Ostrom's career she pivoted back to earlier work she had started with her partner Vincent Ostrom, analyzing polycentric governance, especially as it related to climate change. In this later work, scholars have noted, she also failed to attend to issues of equity and historical accountability in her otherwise creative and flexible framework for governance of our global atmospheric commons (Forsyth and Johnson 2014). In the year before her death, Ostrom was asked specifically about the lack of gendered analysis in her work. She replied, "While I have not made gender a major factor affecting my analysis of common-pool resource situations, I have been very interested in observing the diversity of roles that women play in many different settings" (May and Summerfield 2012, 31). Indeed, some of Ostrom's collaborators and students have built on her work to show why gender and other axes of difference matter to common pool resource governance (Mwangi, Meinzen-Dick, and Sun 2011; Westermann, Ashby, and Pretty 2005).

The central concept around which the Ostrom-inspired community-based conservation strategies pivot is community. In practice, however, decentralized conservation strategies have failed in many cases to fundamentally shift the terms on which power is negotiated among the state, nongovernmental organizations (NGOs), and resource users (Borrini-Feyerabend and Tarnowski 2005; Chhotray 2004; Flint, Luloff, and Finley 2008; Kellert et al. 2000; Li 2002; Ribot 2003). Feminist scholars have shown that narratives of decentralized management and women's empowerment both obscure important drivers of environmental change and resource degradation and erase critical power relations among people within a community, across class, gender, race, caste, and age, as well as across communities at different scales of political and economic organization (Arora-Jonsson 2012; Leach, Mearns, and Scoones 1999; Mollett 2010; Mollett and Faria 2013; Sasser 2014, 2018).

Feminist economist Zofia Łapniewska (2016) conducted a discourse and content analysis of more than a hundred of Ostrom's publications, not only scholarly writings but also other works such as interviews. According to Łapniewska, Ostrom fell into a common gender-neutral trap, relying on descriptions of actors that flattened differences across gender, age, class, caste, ethnicity, race, and ability.[16] With this flattening, Łapniewska (2016, 143) argues, Ostrom opened the door in resource management practice for institutions to avoid accountability for their racist and sexist practices as long as they contribute to the long-term goal of sustainably managing a common pool resource. Thus, because Ostrom's actors are not differentiated by degree of access to power, women can conveniently be counted on to change practices deemed destructive in order to solve a "community" or even a "global" problem. In the case of marine conservation in Madagascar, changing, or in some cases extinguishing, the highly gendered activity of fishing on foot was advanced by conservation organizations as way to protect a resource (such as reefs and fish) that they saw as both a local and global commons. This framing of both the problem and solution echo the ideas common in many WED projects where "women" and "the community" were positioned as both the source and savior of environmental problems, thus ultimately preserving instead of upending the power geometries that these community-based institutional configurations purportedly aimed to address (Arora-Jonsson 2011; Leach 2007; Sasser 2017; Schroeder 1999; Wilson 2015). The community-based paradigm thus shifts the responsibility for intractable transnational political and economic problems onto women, the poorest and least politically resourced people in the Global South (Cleaver 2007; Wilson 2015).

Because of its local orientation, Ostrom's framework for commons governance fails in important ways to adequately consider political economic relations such as global markets, multilateral aid, and trade networks that cross multiple scales, thus leaving local power differentials that emerge from these relations unassessed and unaddressed (Bardhan and Ray 2006; Goldman 1998; Horning 2009; Saunders 2014). Feminist geographer Kalpana Wilson's work in Bihar, India, shows how resource management and development strategies reliant on "community empowerment," "women's empowerment," and local "participation" ultimately further advanced global capital accumulation (Wilson 2006, 2011, 2015).[17] Wilson (2015) argues that this framing conceptually individualizes and localizes the drivers of poverty and resource degradation, thus erasing structural injustices created by colonization, imperialism, and capitalism. Exacerbating the erasure of these historical and ongoing structural injustices are the self-referential methods and metrics through which the biggest funders and institutional proponents of the community-based model evaluate a CPR management project's success. Multilateral development institutions and international conservation organizations often sideline the worldviews, values, and goals of local resource users, the so-called beneficiaries of CPR management, in the pursuit of broader institutional mandates such as production intensification, capitalization, and formalization (Goldman 1997, 1998).

The issues regarding the practice of Ostrom's CPR principles are in part rooted in key assumptions underlying the theory. Several scholars argue that Ostrom's reliance on rational choice theory, institutional economics, and methodological individualism means that spatially and temporally complex socioenvironmental relations are necessarily rendered static and mechanistic (Forsyth and Johnson 2014; Mosse 1997). The concepts scarcity and fairness, for example, change over time and are understood differently by people both *within* a given locale (read along such axes of difference as gender, race, class, age, and ability) and across different locales. Yet these two concepts are the unquestioned foundation on which conservation and development organizations operate when working with communities to devise community-based commons management (Cleaver 2002; de la Torre-Castro 2006; Forsyth and Johnson 2014; Mosse 1997; Prakash 1998; Saunders 2014).

It is precisely because Ostrom's common property theory is rooted in rational and mechanistic theories of collective action and institution building that so many conservation and development organizations, informed by similar theories of social and ecological change, eagerly adopted Ostrom's framework. Although Ostrom herself pushed back against the idea of using the eight CPR principles as a blueprint, they have become just that for many organizations globally. In Madagascar, for example, researchers for the United States Agency for International Development (USAID 2016, 7) applied a "modified set of Dr. Elinor Ostrom's (1990:90) eight common pool resource design principles" to improve marine biodiversity conservation and fisheries development in Madagascar. USAID's instrumentalization of Ostrom's work is by no means unique. A wide variety of governmental and nongovernmental organizations and institutions use Ostrom in similar ways to locally craft commons institutions (Agrawal and Gibson 1999; Dressler et al. 2010; Esmail 1997). However, as I shall demonstrate, the implementation of at least some of these principles in marine conservation projects in Madagascar could be incomplete and problematic.

Conservation Frontiers and the Rise of Marine Protected Areas

A postcolonial and intersectional analysis of marine conservation in Madagascar requires that I historicize and deconstruct dominant colonial and neoliberal frameworks that perpetuate injustices in marine conservation work. Briefly here, and more fully in subsequent chapters, I trace the genesis of marine conservation in Madagascar across multiple geographic and temporal scales.

Marine ecosystems provide food and income for billions of people and have immense cultural and social significance for coastal people globally (FAO 2020). Many marine systems are under mounting pressure from the enormous demand worldwide for marine products, the impacts of climate change, and other such factors as pollution, invasive species, and unsustainable fishing practices. Due to rising concern over declining fisheries production and the degradation or loss of marine biodiversity, marine conservation efforts since the early 2000s have garnered increased global interest and funding (Berger, Caruso, and Peterson 2019; Worm 2016). Much of this interest and funding focuses on increasing the area of marine ecosystems under protection (Maestro et al. 2019; Rees et al. 2017; Venter et al. 2014). In particular, governments and conservation organizations around the world have embraced MPAs as a panacea to address both fisheries decline and ecosystem degradation (Laffoley et al. 2019; Topor et al. 2019).

Conservation scholars and practitioners sometimes describe the marine environment as an "emerging frontier" (Toonen et al. 2013), an "open access frontier system" (Norse 2005, 434), or "Earth's last conservation frontier" (Gjerde et al. 2016). This evocative language positions those venturing into the watery realm of ocean conservation as intrepid explorers, poised to bring stability and order to an otherwise chaotic or unruly space. Frontiers are colonial constructions in that they are conceived as spaces beyond state or statelike (nongovernmental or corporate) power, whose materiality (open ocean) and/or people (fishers) are resistant to state hegemony.[18] Enclosure, which includes the imposition of colonial property regimes and legal structures, is therefore a fundamental feature of frontier exploration and control.[19]

The rise of marine conservation is tied to, yet distinct from, the origin of terrestrial conservation. Whereas the rise and proliferation of terrestrial protected areas in sub-Saharan Africa emerged during a colonial context that favored centralized governance (Brockington 2002; Brockington and Igoe 2006), the expansion of marine protected areas has occurred when decentralized governance was the dominant management paradigm (Berkes 2007;

Ferse et al. 2010). Ostrom's legacy has in turn deeply shaped marine resource management strategies, embedded in a suite of categories including community-based marine resource management (CBMRM), community-based marine conservation (CBMC), locally managed marine areas (LMMAs), and territorial use rights for fishing (TURFs). Broadly, these terms refer to areas of nearshore waters and coastal resources that are partly or entirely controlled and managed by coastal communities, often in collaboration with governmental and nongovernmental organizations (Afflerbach et al. 2014; Govan et al. 2009; Johannes 2002; Rocliffe et al. 2014). The efforts of marine conservation organizations in Madagascar to reinvigorate decentralized marine conservation management run parallel to broader efforts globally to decentralize conservation.

Unlike terrestrial spaces, once the primary focus of most international conservation work, marine property is much less visible and institutionally legible as property (Diver et al. 2019; West, Igoe, and Brockington 2006). The specter of the lawless open-access marine environment, characterized in this narrative by overfishing and habitat degradation, is thus frequently used to legitimize efforts to enclose marine areas. This framing has contributed to the rapid increase in total marine area under protection globally (Fairbanks et al. 2018; Gray, Gruby, and Campbell 2014; Kelly 2011; Ramesh and Rai 2017; Raycraft 2018; Silver and Campbell 2018).[20] In the past two decades marine protected areas have increased from 2 million square kilometers to more than 27 million square kilometers (UNEP-WCMC and IUCN 2020; Venter et al. 2014). Most community-based conservation efforts (CBMC, CBMRM, LMMAs, and TURFs) focus entirely on or include some element of marine enclosure.

MPAs, Property, and Access

Before the establishment of MPAs, restrictions on gear, season, species, total allowable catch, and time spent fishing were the most common strategies of fisheries management (Hilborn and Ovando 2014). Although MPAs are an obvious form of spatial enclosure, gear, season, and other restrictions, known as "creeping enclosure," reconfigure and limit who has access to and control over marine resources through time (Apostle, McCay, and Mikalsen

2002; McCay 1999). This is especially true in shallow areas dominated by reef, seagrass, and mangroves where fishers become deeply familiar with the underwater terrain, clearly delineated fishing spots have place-names, and intimate socionatural relations endure (Diver et al. 2019). Unlike landed property, where people are dispossessed of or barred from parcels of land, the enclosure of marine areas pertains to people's access not just to marine spaces but also to primarily fugitive (mobile) resources such as fish.

Around the world, many fishing societies have deep histories of spatially specific restrictions on fishing behavior based in taboos, cultural traditions, and systems of reciprocity with local organisms and ecosystems (Berkes 1994, 2007; Johannes 1978; Thorburn 2000; Vaughan 2018). In Madagascar there is evidence of the use of marine spatial enclosures, including marine protected areas and private marine concessions during the French colonial era. However, a new era for marine enclosure began in 1982, after the United Nations Conference on the Law of the Sea (UNCLOS) became effective. UNCLOS formalized and expanded national jurisdiction over territorial waters from 3 nautical miles to a 200-nautical-mile exclusive economic zone and thus served as the foundation for all future nationally designated MPAs (Humphreys and Clark 2020). In 1994, a little over a decade after UNCLOS, the International Union for Conservation of Nature (IUCN) established six protected area designations that applied to both terrestrial and marine protected areas.

The IUCN defines marine protected areas as "any area of intertidal or subtidal terrain, together with its overlying waters and associated flora, fauna, historical and cultural features, which has been reserved by law or other effective means to protect part or all of the enclosed environment" (IUCN General Assembly 1988). The six IUCN categories for MPAs range from the least restrictive Category VI, which allows for a variety of types of "sustainable use" or "non-industrial natural resource uses," such as fishing, deep sea mining, and oil and gas exploration to more restrictive Category II Marine National Parks, where visitors can observe "large-scale ecological processes" protected in their "near natural" state, and to the most restrictive Category I, where "human visitation, use and impacts are controlled and limited to ensure protection of the conservation values" (Dudley, Shadie, and Stolton 2013, 2).

In this book, I use the umbrella term *MPAs* for marine protected areas as well as the more specific term *reserve*. All marine conservation areas considered here contain at least one marine reserve, a zone where no fishing or any other type of extraction is allowed and, in most instances, through travel is not permitted. Also, most of the marine reserves described here are contained within broader marine protected areas that vary in designation from least restrictive multiple "sustainable use" Category IV areas to more restrictive Category II National Park areas (REBIOMA 2023).

In theory, all categories of MPAs contribute broadly to marine conservation and benefit humans in a variety of ways, including stabilizing or enhancing fisheries production (Ban et al. 2019; Lubchenco and Grorud-Colvert 2015). Marine reserves, no-take zones that generally fall under IUCN Category I, are considered by marine conservation scientists to be the most beneficial to biodiversity conservation and fisheries production (Edgar et al. 2014; Lester et al. 2009; Sala and Giakoumi 2017). However, marine scientists debate the conditions in which any given marine reserve can successfully contribute to *both* biodiversity conservation and fisheries production (Giakoumi et al. 2018; Pendleton et al. 2017).

The boundary setting required to establish MPAs affects not only legal rights to fish but also broader mechanisms of access to marine resources. MPAs are particularly complex property regimes, produced not only by state laws and local norms and rules but also by international regulations.[21] Franz von Benda-Beckmann, Keebet von Benda-Beckmann, and Melanie Wiber (2006, 3) argue that contemporary states, especially in postcolonial contexts, have a plurality of property ideologies and legal institutions. Each legal institution may have a different source of legitimacy, such as local or traditional law, religious laws, the official legal system of the state, and international and transnational law. The relative security of one's property rights, however, is contingent on the power of the politico-legal institution sanctioning the right (Lund 2002). In the case of community-based MPAs in Madagascar, the politico-legal institutions sanctioning marine property rights include the Malagasy government, international NGOs, and community-based institutions that either existed before the establishment of MPAs or were imposed by the Malagasy government and international NGOs. Given the lack of private title to marine resources, peoples' right to harvest resources is predicated on the relative power of the politico-legal institution upholding that right. Many Malagasy fishers consider it their right to harvest marine resources but may halt fishing, shift their efforts seasonally and spatially, or shift the gear they use while fishing according to restrictions on those rights established by fady (personal or communal taboos), fombafomba (local practices), cultural expectations, governmental laws, and international conservation organizations' projects.

Intersecting the complexities of institutionalized rights in the marine realm are broader mechanisms of access that shape how, where, and what people fish in the ocean. While property is broadly defined as the *right* to benefit from things, Jesse C. Ribot and Nancy Lee Peluso (2003, 153) define access as "the ability to benefit from things." In Ribot and Peluso's framework, access is made up of the full range of social relationships that constrain or enable people to *benefit* from resources, including but not limited to institutionally legitimated rights (such as property).[22] They argue that a broad suite of social-relational mechanisms (including the influence of technology, markets, and identity) directly influence an individual's or community's ability to access natural resources—even without a shift in formal property rights. The distinction between *rights* and *access* forms an important conceptual groundwork for a more feminist approach to conservation. It helps to trace the intersecting and overlapping ways in which power operates in human-nature interactions. For example, in Kobalava, although Zara technically had the right to fish beyond the reef in a boat, her sociocultural location as a woman prevented her from acting on this right. Similarly, although the right to fish on foot was heavily diminished in Hoalankara, Maman'Gary's ability to fish at night was enabled through her social relationships with other fishers who were also willing to transgress resource management rules, as well as by specific environmental conditions such as the reef being walkable from shore and the moon being bright enough to see into the shallow water but dim enough to hide the transgressive behavior. These mechanisms highlight the porous nature of resource rights and illustrate the broader suite of tools and processes through which resource users move beyond a mere *right* to benefit from marine resources to the *ability* to benefit from marine resources.

As the above examples indicate, gender, like race, ethnicity, and class, is a key factor shaping people's rights and abilities to access natural resources. The inverse is equally true: people's negotiation of access to natural resources helps to form their identity. Internationally driven conservation projects shape individual and collective identity by shaping access. Conservation projects thus operate as important sites through which identity comes to matter (Agarwal 1994; Escobar 2006; Nightingale 2006). Juanita Sundberg's (2004, 44) work in the Maya Biosphere Reserve in northern Guatemala shows how identity is not a preexisting and static category but is instead formed by resource users' encounters with international conservation projects, where such binaries as men/women, modern/traditional, and north/south are "brought into being and enacted in time and place."

Similarly, ethnicity shapes how gender is understood and operates in relation to livelihoods and conservation projects in Madagascar. There are distinct dialects in Madagascar where gender categories, albeit still within a binary, have different names, for example, *ampela* (southern region) and *vaiàvy* (northern region) for women, and *lehilahy* (highland region) and *lahy* (coastal regions) for men. Moreover, social relations regarding gender differ across regions of Madagascar based on daily practices of social reproduction. Ethnicities along the arid southwestern coast of Madagascar tend to rely on the marine environment for their livelihoods and sustenance. Ethnicities in rainy northeastern Madagascar tend to rely on a mixture of subsistence agriculture, cash cropping, and marine fishing. The two regions have different gendered divisions of labor and social relations as a result. Expectations put on me as a young female, albeit foreign, researcher in each region differed. Household chore expectations were similar across regions; however, where and how these chores occurred were shaped by weather, fuel type and availability, and food availability and preference, among other factors. For example, in southwestern Madagascar I was able to socialize and share information with women from many different households in the village while waiting in line to fetch scarce water, whereas in northeastern Madagascar smaller groups of women, often related, would chat while planting rice, harvesting corn, or sorting cloves. Daily practices of farming and fishing were vastly different across regions, shaping both social and socioecological relations and thus understandings and definitions of gender and ethnicity.

In seeking to understand the intersecting and overlapping nature of social and political identity, I have examined how the legacy of colonial narratives advancing European superiority has affected current marine socioecological relations in Madagascar. My archival research, explored in chapter 4, reveals that French colonial conservationists viewed Malagasy fishing practices as ineffective and backward. Traditional Malagasy methods of fishing on foot with spears or from boats with small nets are framed in these narratives as both "lazy" and "fiercely destructive." The perceived inferiority of Malagasy fishing practices was used as a rationale for colonial marine conservation policies that would help "modernize" and "civilize" Malagasy fishers and thus "scientifically" manage Madagascar's marine resources (Baker-Médard 2020, 5). Ideas of race are woven into the fabric of these colonial conservation efforts. In fact, the prominent conservationist Georges Petit, who worked as a naturalist in Madagascar for the colonial branch of the National Museum of Natural History (Muséum nationale d'histoire naturelle), referred to colonial marine policies as *racial* policies. Petit argued that "fishing policy is at the same time a race policy" and asserted that by shaping fishing practices, the colonial government could codify and control different coastal ethnicities across the island.[23] Petit further reasoned that by introducing European fishing gear and techniques and working to extinguish Malagasy "inefficient" and "traditional, fishing practices, colonial conservation policies would encourage a thriving colony."[24] French colonists established a hierarchy of fishing practices that were simultaneously racialized and gendered. Fishing on foot and fishing with traditional gear such as spears or small nets became feminized, and categorized as decidedly nonmodern or traditional Malagasy. Thus it was through colonial conservation policies that gender as a category came to matter in relation to marine resource access. The privileging of boat-based fishing with so-called modern gear in colonial conservation policy and rhetoric both shaped and gave new meaning to Malagasy racial and gender categories.

An additional component of Petit's fishing policy as race policy focused on nation building via improved fertility. The logic Petit advanced was that French colonial marine conservation policies would help Malagasy fisheries be a more reliable source of nutrients across Madagascar, thus improving

Poster from 1897, advertising political journalist Henri Galli's book *The War in Madagascar*. A soldier from the colonial troops plants the French flag in Antananarivo, the capital of Madagascar.

Malagasy fertility, which would increase the country's population and thus enhance the overall productivity of the colony.[25] French colonizers saw
Madagascar as a "civilization of death" (Feeley-Harnik 1995, 47); pronatalism,
an approach encompassing attitudes and policies that encourage reproduction, was a core component of the French colonial project. While the colonial
government advanced pronatalist policies explicitly to help solve their press-
ing need for workers, historian Margaret Andersen shows that these policies
were also motivated by sexism, queer fear, and ableism. Andersen (2010, 424)
argues that colonial pronatalists "saw [in Europe] supposedly immutable gender identities break down as growing numbers of women postponed or re-
jected motherhood, pursued careers, demanded political rights, and benefited
from legislation granting them greater independence" and that some single
men "seemed to lack essential masculine qualities," including "men who as-
pired to little more than the sedentary life of a bureaucrat, were homosexual,
or were in poor physical condition." Heterosexual reproduction and a family
unit defined by the gender binary were thus woven into the fabric of imperialist racialization. The categories of "healthy," "heterosexual," "man," and
"woman" were constructed and reified by colonial policies that positioned
Malagasy "race" as "chaotic and promiscuous," "morally depraved," and in
"need of French guidance." Colonial conservation policies and practices were
core to the broader processes of gender categorization and racialization.

The imprint of these colonial policies can be seen in conservation strategies and law today, including the continued disfavoring of fishing on foot,
the reclosure of colonially established MPAs, the reestablishment of an array of marine resource use policies (gear, seasonal restrictions, and so on),
and the continued focus on the nexus of population, health, and environmental sustainability. Key facets of these policies and strategies disproportionately impact women and poorer fishers.

The Politics of Marine Conservation in Madagascar

The material and discursive legacies of the colonial period point to the need
for a postcolonial intersectional analysis of conservation. Madagascar has
a long and ongoing history of foreign-driven conservation and external

interest in preserving its unique species, a history shaped by race and gender in important ways.

As an island that separated from the African continent approximately 88 million years ago, Madagascar is home to an unusually high number of endemic plant and animal species that have evolved in isolation (Ganzhorn, Wilmé, and Mercier 2014). As early as the 1600s, a French enclave governed by Étienne de Flacourt concerned itself with documenting the unique fauna and flora of Madagascar, making a case for their protection (Deschamps 1961; Flacourt 1661). Madagascar became a French protectorate in 1882, with the French violently establishing colonial control in 1896 (Brown 2002). During the French colonial era, more than forty terrestrial protected areas were established, and many laws regulated both the terrestrial and marine environment in the name of conservation (Corson 2016; Kull 1996; Scales 2014a).

Although Madagascar gained independence in 1960, some scholars mark the early 1970s—with the rise of nationalist pride, protests against the dominance of French nationals in Madagascar's political economy, and a turn toward socialism—as the point at which Madagascar took key steps to decolonize the state's administrative apparatus. A socialist Second Republic dawned in 1972 under President Didier Ratsiraka, and little foreign conservation funding entered the country. Not until the early 1980s, when the island transitioned from an isolationist socialist regime to one oriented toward neoliberalism, did foreign loans, private investment, and foreign conservation aid pour back into the country (Brown 2002; Horning 2009; Kull 2014). An important facet of Ratsiraka's popularity was that he was not Merina, an ethnic group from the highlands (*haut-plateaux*) but rather Betsimisaraka, one of the seventeen ethnic groups from the coastal (*côtier*) region. The highlander-coastal ethnic divide, which has immense salience both politically and economically today in Madagascar, was heightened during French colonial rule when Merina people were heavily recruited as colonial administrative personnel, but that divide had emerged, several historians argue, at least fifty years earlier (Campbell 2005; Rakotondrabe 1993). Before French colonization, the Merina had violently established a Malagasy empire, maintaining economic and political relations with both Britain and France and asserting political and economic control over most areas of the island. Gwyn Campbell (2005) describes this dominance as the "internal colonization" of Madagascar before the French colonial period.

The political and economic history of ethnic divides in Madagascar continues to shape who is educated in environmental fields and who is employed by governmental and nongovernmental conservation organizations in Madagascar. Coastal ethnicities tend to be underrepresented within governmental and nongovernmental conservation organizations, notably at the highest levels (directors, ministers, and administrators), but also at the regional and subregional level, including the agents charged with working most closely with farming and fishing communities. Therefore, both highlanders and foreigners, who represent the vast majority of conservation administrators and hold several country director positions for international conservation organizations, have important influence on the orientation and implementation of conservation projects across the country.

After the Cold War, Madagascar was one of the first African countries to create an environmental charter and a national environmental action plan, or EAP. These efforts occurred in 1990, two years before Earth Summit, the United Nations Conference on Environment and Development in Rio de Janeiro in 1992, at which all signatories were mandated to create EAPs. Madagascar was ahead of the curve owing to pressure from and oversight by international conservation organizations working in the country, such as the World Wildlife Fund, as well as bilateral and multilateral donors and creditors, including USAID, World Bank, and the International Monetary Fund (Corson 2016; Horning 2009; Hufty and Muttenzer 2002).

Given that international meetings prioritized terrestrial conservation, most nations' early environmental action plans focused on land rather than oceans. By the early 2000s, however, marine conservation emerged as a priority in international conferences and congresses such as the Convention on Biological Diversity (CBD) and the World Parks Congress. In 2003, at the World Parks Congress, Malagasy president Marc Ravalomanana committed to tripling the land area under protection in Madagascar in eight years. It was one of the largest expansions in the postcolonial period of

Madagascar's terrestrial protected area network. This commitment, deemed the Durban Vision, also included a goal to put 1 million marine hectares under protection (Allnutt et al. 2012; SAPM 2009).

As political ecologist Catherine Corson shows in *Corridors of Power: The Politics of Environmental Aid to Madagascar* (2016), the hasty timeline of Ravalomanana's Durban commitment in 2003 precluded meaningful engagement with local resource users in the establishment of new parks in the forested region of northeastern Madagascar. Mayors were brought to large regional meetings at which they were encouraged to accept protected area boundaries established by largely nonlocal and non-Malagasy scientists, with little to no consideration for traditional users, sacred sites, or the potential socioeconomic impacts of the new protected areas on local people. Corson argues that the network of international conservation organizations, donors, and private companies not only took decision-making authority away from local resource users but also diverted funding that should have been used for community-based conservation and capacity building in rural communities to fund the salaries and bureaucratic work of those organizations both nationally and internationally. Corson illustrates how financial and technical expertise concerning natural resource management was concentrated at the highest levels of governance, with meetings that took place primarily internationally or in Madagascar's capital city, Antananarivo, instead of on the ground with broad participation from local stakeholders.[26]

In the 2000s, catch across multiple fisheries in Madagascar was notably declining (Le Manach et al. 2012). Given the status Madagascar holds internationally as a biodiversity hotspot, international conservation organizations in conjunction with the Malagasy government called for increasing marine conservation funding and effort (Ratsimbazafy et al. 2019). By the early 2010s, governmental and nongovernmental organizations collectively turned toward marine protected areas as the solution to fisheries decline and marine biodiversity loss.[27]

Whereas terrestrial protected areas in Madagascar had a ninety-year history of periodic additions, the total marine area under protection in Madagascar increased dramatically from 2005 to 2018 (see accompanying illustration) (Marine Conservation Institute 2023). In the early 2000s there

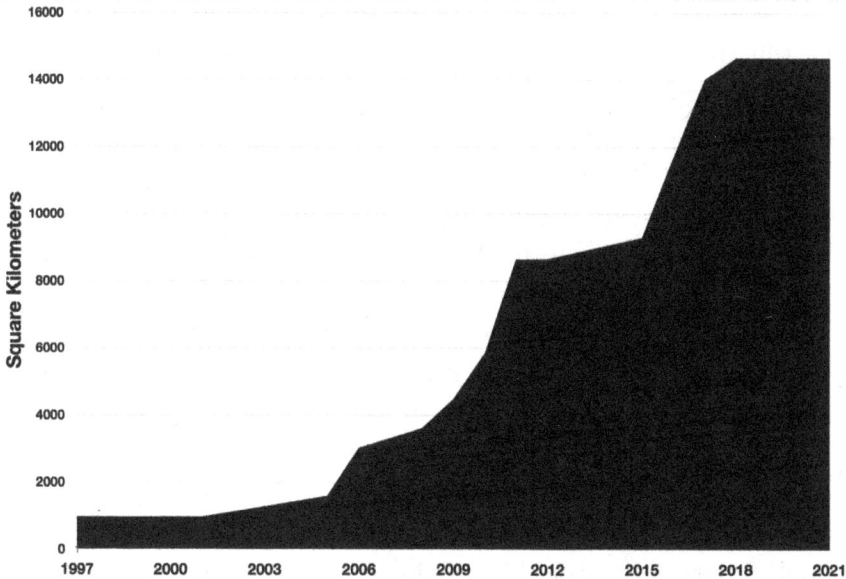

The cumulative marine area under protection in Madagascar, 1997–2021, highlighting
the rapid increase during these years. Not shown here is the long history of marine
area under protection, which started during the French colonial period.

were four nationally recognized MPAs covering 3,250 square kilometers
(Mansourian and Dudley 2008); by 2019 there were more than fifty nation-
ally recognized MPAs covering approximately 54,000 square kilometers
(UNEP-WCMC and IUCN 2020; Venter et al. 2014).

Before the considerable expansion of MPAs in Madagascar, the
Malagasy government banned certain types of fishing gear, restricted key
fisheries seasonally, and prohibited the extraction of endangered marine organisms. However, according to both governmental and nongovernmental
marine conservation organization representatives interviewed regarding
this era, these management strategies were seen as relatively "ineffective." A
senior official at Madagascar's Ministry of Fisheries and Marine Resources
(now the Ministry of Fisheries and the Blue Economy) cited lack of funding
and personnel dedicated to monitoring and enforcement as a key reason for
the laws' ineffectiveness in managing fisheries.[28] Other issues, note scholars,

such as fishers' lack of alternative livelihoods and incentives to stop fishing illegally (Bruggemann et al. 2012; Chaboud 2006; Davies, Beanjara, and Tregenza 2009), as well as the high cultural importance (incongruent with a Eurocentric perspective) of consuming certain endangered species (Humber et al. 2015; Lilette 2006), likely contributed to the ineffectiveness of particular marine conservation measures.

Following the previous president's Durban Vision, in November 2014 President Hery Rajaonarimampianina advanced his Sydney Vision at the World Parks Congress, in which he committed to tripling Madagascar's protected areas by 2020, but this time exclusively in the marine realm. The Sydney Vision set Madagascar on course to reach the Convention on Biological Diversity's global Aichi Biodiversity Target of protecting at least 10 percent of coastal and marine areas by 2020 (CBD 2010). The Malagasy government codified Aichi goals into national commitments, copying nearly word for word: Target 6, focused on eliminating destructive fishing practices and sustainably managing fisheries; Target 10, on reducing anthropogenic impacts on coral reefs and other fragile marine ecosystems; and Target 11 for protected areas, which Madagascar changed slightly to be 15 percent by 2025 instead of the original 10 percent by 2020 (CBD 2015).

Rajaonarimampianina's Sydney Vision gave the Malagasy government, in collaboration with marine conservation organizations working in Madagascar, approximately five years to implement the commitment. The president's vision to facilitate this ambitious expansion included a commitment to establish a legal framework to protect community management of fishing grounds (Amia 2014). The focus on community management was, as one marine conservation director at an international conservation organization explained, intended to help Madagascar "avoid the lack of stakeholder input" that defined the implementation of the Durban Vision a decade earlier.[29]

Despite intentions to bestow greater rights to coastal fishing communities in Madagascar through Rajaonarimampianina's Sydney commitment, the ambitious time-sensitive goal of tripling marine protected areas in Madagascar resulted in the rapid implementation of MPAs. However, there were many cases of inadequate engagement with local fishing communities. As with the earlier terrestrial protection effort, the goal of expanding

MPAs was advanced at the highest level of government, and the urgency embedded in the timeline similarly undermined meaningful community participation, thus leading to outcomes such as a lack both of buy-in from fishing communities and of adequate consideration of whole-community needs. Rushed timelines meant not only that few resource users were involved in decision-making regarding location and management practices of new MPAs but that those involved tended to be already politically powerful, wealthier, and male. These results are one reason why a feminist approach to marine conservation in Madagascar includes resisting enclosure of the marine commons.

Although it is beyond the time frame of this book, the upcoming CBD Conference of the Parties will consider the 30×30 target of protecting 30 percent of the world's lands and oceans by 2030. As protection efforts continue to accelerate in response to an increased understanding of environmental crises, the importance of ensuring justice and self-determination in conservation projects becomes ever more urgent.

Gathering Information

When I set out to design my research, I knew that a single methodological approach would not be sufficient to understand both intracommunity processes and historical dynamics in relation to the establishment and maintenance of a given marine conservation project, as well as trends across ethnic and regional differences and across gender, class, education, age, and other axes of difference.

I focused on three regions of Madagascar (southwest, northeast, and northwest) because they represented a diversity of marine environments and of fisher harvest techniques and frequency. These three regions also contain the vast majority of MPAs across the island. Ecologically, southwestern Madagascar is dominated by fringing reefs and shallow backreef areas that are protected from big swell and heavy winds. Fishers in the southwest are heavily reliant on fishing as their main source of income. Ecologically, the northwest is characterized by numerous small islands and some atoll reefs, with a mixture of protected backreef areas and more exposed higher-swell deeper water fishing. Fishers in the northwest are partially reliant on fishing as their main source of income but also tend to have a variety of other land-based livelihood options, including cash crops and tourism. Ecologically, the northeast has fewer fringing reefs and is characterized by a steep drop off the continental shelf, and thus waters tend to be rougher than off the west coast of Madagascar. Fishers in the northeast tend to split their time between fishing and farming or husbandry. As in the northwest, cash cropping is also very common in the northeast.

I was interested in obtaining information that could summarize trends across multiple regions and communities but also retain my ability to "thickly describe" processes and events—that is, to analyze the interconnected cultural, economic, and political context that give meaning to people's actions and words at a given moment in time (Geertz 2008). Ultimately, I used a mixture of semistructured interviews, survey data, archival research, and participant observation. The bulk of my ethnographic data draws from more than thirteen months of participant observation (Aktinson and Hammersley 1998) primarily in four fishing villages in the three regions from 2009 to 2019 (see map). As a participant observer, I experienced some of the hardest, most illuminating, and most rewarding times in my research. I lived and worked with fisher and fish trader host families in each of the four villages. I fried fish in pans of sputtering oil, pounded rice until my hands were blistered and then calloused, fished on foot with a spear, dug my toes into sand to find bivalves while chest deep in water, fished from boats with a line and a net, fetched firewood in the dry forest as well as the rainforest, collected water from streams and deep wells, mended hand-woven nets, swept compounds with grass brooms, sat with people as they sold their goods in the village market, attended meetings about both village and marine conservation business, attended educational films screened by governmental officials and international conservation organizations, listened to stories told at night around smoky fires in small thatched kitchens, and lived and breathed and listened to the rhythms of coastal life in Madagascar. The more ethnographic portions of my research relied on an extended case method approach to draw macro-level conclusions from in-depth micro-observations rooted in place-based histories and observations (Burawoy 1998).

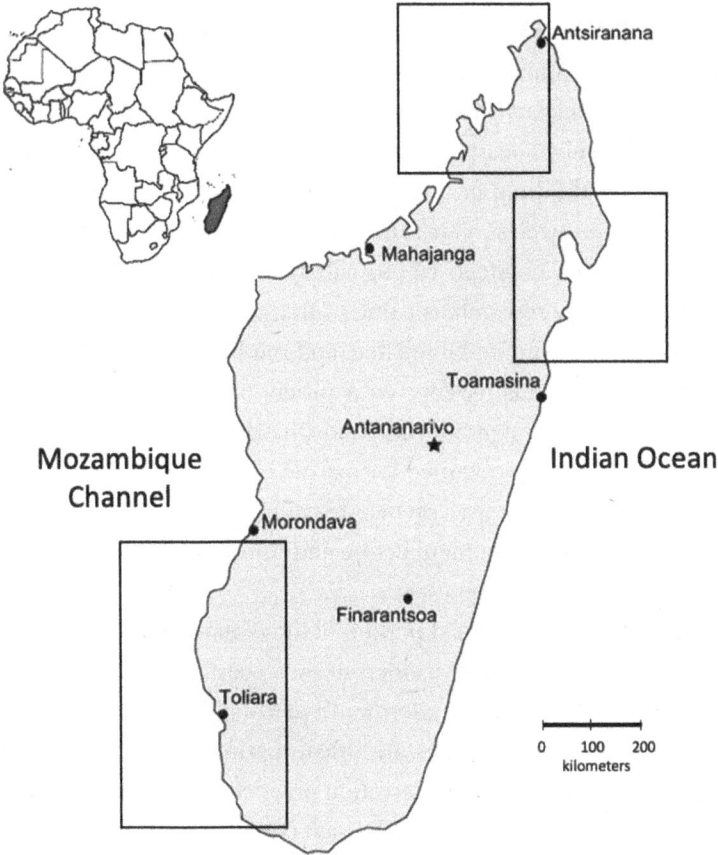

Map of Madagascar with the northwest, northeast, and southwest research regions sectioned.

In addition to participant observation, I conducted ninety-two semistruc-tured interviews from 2009 to 2022, where predetermined open-ended ques-tions oriented an otherwise free-flowing conversation about an individual's perspective on a variety of topics relating to the marine environment, fisher-ies, trade in the area, the MPA and other conservation initiatives in their area, and the history of marine use and restrictions. I interviewed fishers as well as local, regional, and national government officials in Madagascar, fish collectors and exporters, and nongovernmental conservation organization personnel. I used snowball sampling to identify key informants in six cities and large towns in the three regions: Toliara, Antsiranana, Nosy Be, Toamasina, Maroantsetra, and Mananara. I also interviewed key informants in ten coastal villages in southwestern Madagascar, eight coastal villages in northeastern Madagascar, and eight coastal villages in northwestern Madagascar.

In 2011, with the help of a team of eight Malagasy researchers, I conducted 889 randomized surveys (Olsen 2004), stratified by gender (431 men, 458 women) across nineteen fishing villages located adjacent to MPAs.[30] The eight Malagasy researchers came from a variety of disciplines, including geography, environmental science, and marine science.[31] The survey, a standardized questionnaire, covered a variety of topics, including fishers' demographics, assets, migration, and trade, marine harvest practices, uses of marine products, prices obtained for marine catch, and destinations of the catch. The survey also focused on people's perspectives on and participation in marine resource management before and since the adjacent MPA was established.

For the field-based historical portion of the research I conducted twenty-six oral histories with one to two elders in each coastal village. Each oral history interview focused on the informant's personal history, origin stories of the village and adjacent villages, historical marine resource use practices, and traditional and colonial conservation practices. I also spent three weeks conducting archival research at the French National Overseas Archives (Archives nationales d'outre-mer) in Aix-en-Provence, as well as four weeks at the National Archives of Madagascar (Tranobokin'ny Arisivam-pirenena) in Antananarivo. I collected documentation concerning marine resource use and conservation efforts both before and during the French colonization of Madagascar. I also read both internal and public-facing reports generated by governmental and nongovernmental conservation organizations over the past thirty years. Most of these reports were in the organizations' regional or national headquarters in Madagascar.

The latter part of this book, especially the final chapter, is deeply informed by a conversational method approach to research, which as Indigenous scholar Margaret Kovach (2010, 40) explains, "involves a dialogic participation that holds a deep purpose of sharing story as a means to assist others." Conversational method, at its foundation, is collaborative, dialogic, and reflexive. Many of my close colleagues and friends have deeply shaped the ideas I have written on these pages. Although I express gratitude to these incredible people in the acknowledgments to this book and cite their work where appropriate, single authorship of this book belies the deeply relational thinking and collective experience that underpin the heart and soul of the work presented here. The exact words (in Malagasy or French) and some of the nuance related to words and ideas that were shared with me go beyond what is conventionally placed in the documentation, so I have made the original texts and additional context related to the conversations available at mezmedard.com/publications.

Each chapter that follows is guided, in part, by key principles advanced by commons scholars, most notably Elinor Ostrom. These include establishing "clearly defined boundaries" in CPR governance (chapters 2 and 5); ensuring that the "individuals affected by the operational rules can participate in modifying the operational rules" and are involved in "monitoring" (chapter 3); and making sure there is "congruence between appropriation (use) rules and local conditions" or that these rules and local institutions are not "challenged by external governmental authorities" (chapter 4). I also investigate obvious as well as more insidious ways in which gender disproportionately affects participation and inclusion in—and impacts of—marine conservation efforts. Although gender is a primary analytic throughout the chapters, I also explore class, age, and education as well as the broader racial and ethnic power differential influencing where, how, and why marine conservation occurs in Madagascar.

The stories and statistics offered in this book illustrate key dynamics shaping the establishment and governance of marine common pool resources in Madagascar. The delineation and management of these common pool resource management strategies have been heavily influenced, if not outright imposed, by international conservation organizations. How, then, did this process transpire, and more important, what have been its outcomes?

TWO

Enclosure

Localizing Degradation

> There used to be rules here in the ocean. When? During
> colonization. We weren't allowed to harvest oysters over there
> [pointing south], and there was a time we weren't allowed to fish
> for lobster. Now? They are making this whole island into a marine
> park. I don't know why, but foreigners [of European descent] have
> always wanted this island.
>
> —*Elder fisher, northwestern Madagascar, August 10, 2011*

In a small village in southwestern Madagascar, it is opening day for a temporary marine reserve—fishing is now permitted. Women walk in small
groups on the beach, spears in one hand and buckets or burlap bags in the
other. As they venture south from their village along a stretch of white sand,
their colorful wraps fly like serrated flags in the light breeze. Once closer
to the reserve, the women wade into the ocean, tying their wraps higher on
their waists and peering through the shallow water, ready to harvest octopus,
sea cucumbers, and shells. Dozens of boats are also in the water, each with
two to three men steadily paddling toward the reserve to catch their share of
octopus, sea cucumbers, and fish. Men lower their snorkeling masks as they
enter the water. They, too, wield spears, and some carry nets. Several men
brandish a less common tool, a fish gun.

Standing on the beach is a field agent from an international conservation
organization that has worked for the past four years to establish this temporary reserve, a small area (1 square kilometer) within a 400-square-kilometer
multiuse MPA—approximately four times the size of Paris. Peering through
his binoculars, the field agent marvels at the sight: "Lots of people out there.

Imagine in ten years it might be triple the number. They will destroy everything."[1] He shakes his head in dismay at his own projection.

The temporary reserve has been closed for three months, and now fishers are eager to see whether the waiting was worth it given promises of improved catch, and just how large their catch will be today. Later in the afternoon, the fishers will return to their village. They will bring their catch to collectors waiting in the shade of thatched huts with handheld scales, pens and papers, and large boxes of ice. That evening the collectors will load their ice boxes onto dusty trucks that will bring the catch to processing facilities in a city five hours away. From there, the octopus will likely end up in the frozen food section in Spain, the sea cucumber in a dry goods shop in Hong Kong, and the fish in a French supermarket (OEC 2021).

Four years later, I stand with Maman'i Onja, a well-known spear fisher from the village, on the same spot where the agent surveyed the scene through binoculars four years prior. Now the temporary reserve is a permanent reserve. Nobody is allowed to fish there. Looking out at the reserve, Maman'i Onja says, "I don't understand why they made that spot a reserve. That spot was great, we could access it by foot."[2] In fact, the area was one of the only regions of the barrier reef near the village that was walkable from shore during low tide. When the area became a permanent no-take zone, most women saw the marine area accessible to them by foot cut by a third. Women who had access to boats, however, were able to maintain access to other parts of the reef. The stakes of this closure were significant. Women contribute significantly to household food provisions. In this village in southwestern Madagascar, nearly three-quarters of what women catch (74 percent) is brought home to feed their families. In contrast, just 43 percent of what men catch is brought home for consumption, the rest sold for export. These numbers are similar to trends across the nation (see accompanying illustration). The decrease in the area where women fish undoubtedly changed household food consumption patterns, potentially exacerbating food insecurity. Why then was the marine reserve placed there? On whose terms were decisions made to create the marine reserve?

Reports show a decline in fisheries production across Madagascar (Gough et al. 2020; Le Manach et al. 2011). Similarly, multiple reports indicate a

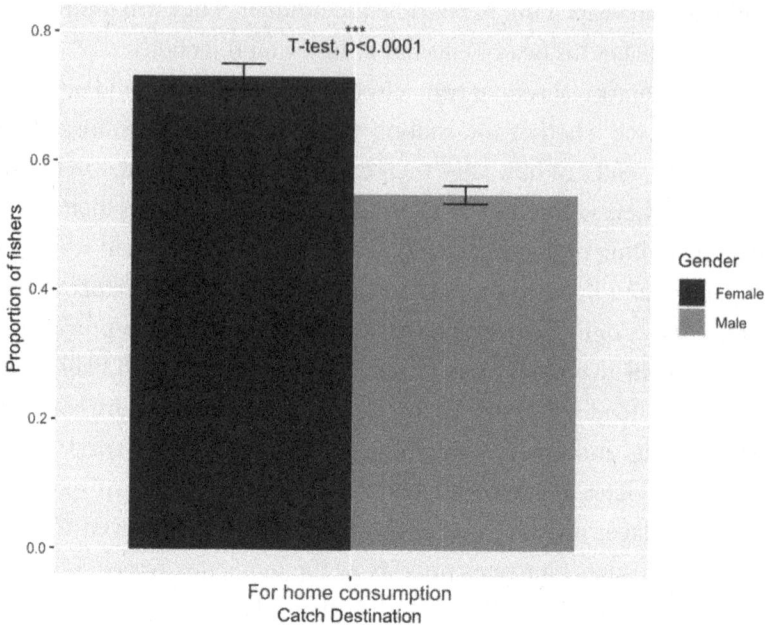

The proportion of catch brought home for consumption versus sold across gender categories. Although some *sarindahy* and *sarimbavy* were included in the survey, they chose to identify along the gender binary.

decline in the health of coral reefs around the island (Botosoamananto et al. 2021; McClanahan et al. 2014). Why this decline has occurred and who or what is to blame are important questions to answer for fishers, conservation organizations, researchers, and the Malagasy government. Despite the complex suite of drivers at multiple social and ecological scales that underlie declines in fisheries production and marine habitat change, conservation organizations working in Madagascar define the problem in narrow terms. The field agent's assumption that local population growth and local fishers are the source of decline in the marine environment echoes a familiar narrative among Western conservationists. In Madagascar as well as in other developing countries, population, and particularly the population of people near resource-rich areas, are often framed as a primary source of ecological decline (Baker-Médard and Sasser 2020). The field agent's conclusions that day reflect a problematic framing in which small-scale fishers and marine reserves feature prominently, whereas consumers of seafood and fossil fuels sitting comfortably in their high-rise apartments in Beijing, restaurants in Spain, seaside hotels in Mauritius, and gridlocked cars in Boston are tacitly absolved of their role in the depletion of marine resources and the deterioration of marine ecosystems.

In this chapter I advance a key principle of feminist conservation, which asserts that conservation interventions should address underlying drivers of ecological decline. I argue that international conservation NGOs' and governments' focus on marine protected areas led to a disproportionate emphasis on local drivers of marine degradation without adequately considering more distant causes of marine systems change and fisheries decline. This principle dovetails with the observation that the emphasis on local causes placed a disproportionate burden on women and the poorest inhabitants of coastal communities in Madagascar, something I call a low-hanging-fruit conservation politic. By focusing on changing or stopping fishing methods used by women and poor fishers, conservation organizations relinquish responsibility to address larger systemic drivers, which tend to be politically fraught, multiscalar, and temporally complex.

Further, I critique framings of the "local" as something separate from "global," instead emphasizing a feminist approach to analyzing the structural webs of political and economic relations that favor some people's claims to natural resources over others. I analyze how a hyperlocal framing of marine degradation unduly emphasizes the role of women fishing on foot in the depletion of marine resources instead of tackling the more complex and powerful influence of global seafood markets. The ecological and political paradox of conservation organizations' focus on the local as a priority site of conservation intervention is laid bare by the reality that nearly four-fifths of marine products are exported from some regions of the island. International conservation organizations persist in depicting fishers as harvesting for subsistence even though small-scale fishers in Madagascar export much of their catch to more than forty countries globally (Breuil and Grima 2014; UN Comtrade 2023).

In addition, I show that while governmental and nongovernmental organizations are motivated to establish marine protected areas due to international commitments to conserve biodiversity and increase the total number and size of marine areas under protection, this mandate is hidden in narratives promoting MPAs to fishing communities at the local level. Instead, conservationists frame marine protected areas primarily as a fisheries management tool that will improve local catches. Many international conservation organizations base their policies on the unquestioned belief that marine enclosures are a panacea for both biodiversity conservation and fisheries management. The use of MPAs as a catchall solution belies the uncertainties and concerns researchers share in scientific studies of MPAs. This research shows that there are important differences between MPAs designed primarily to conserve marine biodiversity and those intended to improve catch for local fisheries. Moreover, even with MPAs designed specifically to manage fisheries, there are many caveats and contingencies concerning the conditions in which marine protected areas will actually enhance fisheries.

Opening day for a temporary marine reserve in southwestern Madagascar. Photograph by author.

Last, I explore stark differences between how some Malagasy fishers understand the marine world and drivers of change in the marine environment and how international conservation organization workers understand them. These differences expose the primarily foreign-driven framing of both the problem of marine resource decline and the solution: marine protected areas. Ultimately, despite working closely with fishers and coastal communities in Madagascar, conservation organizations impose the commons in ways that undermine broader community participation, specifically the participation of women and poorer people in the community, thus hollowing community participation of its political weight. The lack of a feminist approach to conservation intervention, one that takes seriously the process of collective decision-making, not only misconstrues the values of local marine resource users but also disproportionately burdens some fishers.

Weaponizing Scale: Hyperlocalizing Intervention and Blame

Marine conservation in Madagascar is deeply shaped by questions of scale: hyperlocal drivers of environmental change are framed as problems to be solved by global capital and expertise. Political-economic restructuring and rescaling of authority under neoliberal capitalism, or "glocalisation" (Swyngedouw 2004), enables transnational resource managers (international conservation and development organizations) to define local ecological crises in ways that legitimize conservation interventions developed in a global context.

These framings are based on a narrative that environmental degradation is primarily a local issue amenable to local solutions, which shifts attention from the broader (nonlocal) political-economic drivers of poverty and environmental change (Lambin et al. 2001). In addition, they play on gendered and racialized global discourses wherein black and brown fishers of the Global South, and what turns out to be primarily women's fishing practices, are blamed for resource depletion (Hartmann 2014; Peluso and Watts 2001). These framings demonstrate a "hegemonic production and representation of 'the local' " (Mohan and Stokke 2000, 249) to advance the spread of MPAs as the dominant marine conservation strategy—which is based on an international conservation paradigm that operates through national-level commitments.

Erik Swyngedouw (2004) explains how, at the turn of the twenty-first century, development discourse and practice increasingly focused on the local as a site of intervention even as governance authority was simultaneous scaling up. He explains this dynamic, called "glocalisation," as the "twin process whereby, firstly, institutional/regulatory arrangements shift from the national scale both upwards to supra-national or global scales and downwards to the scale of the individual body or to local, urban or regional configurations" (25). This reorganization of institutional arrangements creates "geographies and choreographies of inclusion/exclusion and domination/ subordination which empower some actors, alliances and organizations at the expense of others, according to criteria such as class, gender, race/ethnicity and nationality" (Brenner 2001, 608).[3] This dynamic is apparent in marine conservation interventions in Madagascar. Conservation efforts have moved away from being solely under the purview of centralized state institutions and into the hands of international conservation organizations or private institutions that work at the regional or local level with resource users. The shrinking role of the state in Madagascar, as in many other nations globally, stems from core neoliberal processes such as privatization, marketization, deregulation, and a reconfiguration of the public sector (Castree 2008). These processes have opened up spaces for NGOs to define conservation and development agendas in conjunction with networks of other international conservation organizations, industry actors, and donors, as well as to orient the strategies and tactics of conservation on the ground (Brockington, Duffy, and Igoe 2008; Corson 2016). Born from neoliberal processes, the power that international conservation actors have to shape governance in Madagascar is then used in numerous ways to entrench a neoliberal approach to conservation such as enclosing common pool resources through the establishment of MPAs, working closely with the private sector to expand and improve marine resource exports, and privatizing access to marine spaces. By focusing on the local, moreover, international conservation organizations can better control donor and foundation funding. According to my interviews with conservation organization agents and directors in Madagascar, working with local fishing communities is more efficient and effective than working with the Malagasy government. As one senior international conservation organization representative put it, donors would "rather have their funds go through us who work at the local level than the corrupt and ineffective Malagasy government."[4] This sentiment was echoed by numerous other conservation organization representatives, who broadly saw themselves as more capable than the Malagasy government of both preserving marine biodiversity and managing marine fisheries at the local level.

As Leila Sievanen, Rebecca Gruby, and Lisa Campbell (2013, 207) argue, "The struggle to define the scale at which marine management should be planned and implemented is inseparable from the struggle over who should define, inform, and conduct the governance process." Scale-specific frameworks lead to funding particular resource management activities, such as the expansion of MPAs, over other approaches, such as restrictions on marine product exports or foreign industrial fishing. Although some conservation organizations work at the national and international level to address multiscalar drivers of marine resource decline such as consumption, trade, and advertising (examples are detailed below), the scope and scale of these programs remains limited. Instead, most conservation organizations focus their funding and personnel on projects implemented with marine fishers at the local level.

By politicizing the notion of local, we can better analyze the relationships between people and place across different scales of social, political, ecological, and economic organization.[5] Each MPA connects fishers, international conservation organizations, Malagasy governmental offices, regional and local authorities, consumers, donors, and a suite of other people and organizations. Furthermore, these connections not only operate in the current moment but are threaded through time, transposing historical relations, trauma, and memory onto the current moment. The deep history of Malagasy marine resource use and exports includes historically coercive and unjust colonial conservation and development practices (Baker-Médard 2020).

As feminist geographer Doreen Massey (1994, 3) argues, people in a given locale interact with "the outside" in different ways across time, meaning that "social relations of place are experienced differently, and variously interpreted, by those holding different positions as part of it." She explains that the identity of place "does not derive from some internalized history" but rather comes "from the specificity of its interactions with 'the outside' " (169). Anna Tsing (2011, 122) articulates a similar argument as it relates to culture and place: "Even the most out-of-the-way cultural niches are formed in world crossing dialogues. Cultures are always both wide-ranging and situated. . . . The challenge of cultural analysis is to address both the spreading interconnections and the locatedness of culture . . . the inextricability of interconnection and location."

Boundaries, of marine protected areas as well as what counts as a local community, are ongoing expressions of political processes. What each MPA means, or how it is understood as a place, changes as the social, political, and environmental relations change around it. As the elder quoted at the beginning of this chapter suggested, MPAs represent a type of ongoing colonization in the eyes of some fishers even when they were established as recently as five years ago. Although the actors who govern the marine area have changed, a similar dynamic of control and prohibition between conservation agents and resource users persists. As I discuss below, there is a long history of foreign intervention in Malagasy fisheries.

People's ties, political and economic mobility, and ability to benefit from relationships in distant locales, moreover, are refracted through their gender, class, educational background, ethnicity, and other axes of difference. A wide variety of relations create a patchy and uneven web of connections among people living in a fishing village in rural Madagascar and those in distant as well as not-so-distant locales. Every individual I surveyed, interviewed, or observed had a unique set of ties with other people in their village as well as with an array of outsiders, including fish collectors, export company representatives, traders of other goods, tourists, conservation personnel, distant family members, and researchers.

From physical displacement such as in- and outmigration and travel to material exchange of goods or money and to the exchange of knowledge, people's experience with the "outside" also varies widely. These differences are deeply gendered. Men not only travel longer distances but they travel more frequently than women across the three regions I researched.[6] These differences in turn shape men's and women's abilities to access and control natural resources through a variety of structural and relational mechanisms that are created through travel such as improved knowledge and perspective, access to nonlocal markets, and the creation of a wider network of social and political relations.[7]

Fishing on Foot: The Politics of Picking the Low-Hanging Fruit

Who then benefits from or bears the cost of a hyperlocalized framing of marine resource degradation? Analyzing how gender, specifically gendered marine resource use practices, intersects with the conservation strategies employed at the local level allows us to start answering this question.

Surveys conducted across nineteen villages in the three regions of the island demonstrate that although both men and women participate in the global marine product trade, the means by which they obtain marine products differs significantly (table 1). Fishing on foot was the dominant fishing mode reported for all women across Madagascar (98.9 percent). Although some men also fished on foot (35.3 percent), all men surveyed used a mixture of fishing methods that shifted depending on the weather, tide, temperature, and season.[8] This gendered division of labor, which corresponds to both the equipment people use as well as which marine products they harvest, extends back as long as the people I interviewed could remember (see accompanying illustration). Generally, women lacked flexibility in fishing methods due to cultural norms around fishing practices, lack of training in boat-based fishing techniques, and lower levels of boat ownership compared to men.

Table 1. Gendered distribution of fishing methods across study sites (n=889)

	Men (%)	Women (%)
Boat: net fishing	84.3	2.8
Boat: line fishing	69.6	0.5
Boat: diving	56.6	1.9
Fishing on foot	35.3	98.9
Beach seining (boat and foot)	26.8	4.3

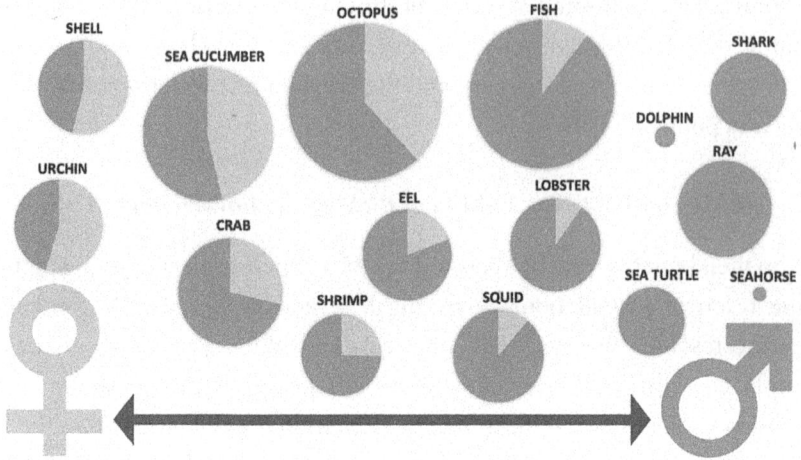

Marine products targeted by fishers according to respondent-identified gender category. Each pie chart illustrates the relative proportion fished by men and women for each organism. The size of each circle corresponds to fishing frequency, calculated as the proportion of all fishers surveyed who reported harvesting each marine organism type.

Even though women have fished on foot across the island for centuries and the practice *remains* the dominant mode of fishing for women, it is a particularly maligned practice in marine conservation discourse in Madagascar. In some marine protected areas fishing on foot is allowed yet discouraged. In other areas conservation organizations have outlawed the practice entirely. Just as conservation organizations across Madagascar disparage *tavy* (swidden, or fire-based, agriculture) in the terrestrial realm, so they also disparage fishing on foot (Kull 2004). As Christian Kull (2000) and others (Corson 2011b; Jarosz 1996; Pollini 2010) argue, one cannot understand any resource use practices absent the broader ecological, socioeconomic, political, ideological, and historical context in which a practice occurs. In some ways, fishing on foot is Madagascar's tavy of the sea.

Both governmental and nongovernmental conservation organization reports on MPA management contain sections dedicated to addressing the "problem of fishing on foot." For example, in a report by the Ministry of Water and Forests (MEF 2010, 219), one of the air clearest stated objectives is to extinguish the practice of fishing on foot: "The degradation of the coral reefs that protect the MPA to its marine limit will be avoided when the coastal population no longer tramples on the reef, and no longer practices fishing on foot [*ne pratiquent plus la pêche à pied*], nor fishing that harms corals within a radius defined by the new delineation." In the same report, fishing on foot is the only example used to illustrate what constitutes "destructive activities" (42). Similarly, in a report on the UNESCO Biosphere Reserve of Mananara in northeastern Madagascar, a section entitled "fishing on foot" (*la pêche à pied*) describes the practice specifically as "the task of women" (*la tâche des femmes*); the following section is entitled "real fishing" (*la vraie pêche*), or fishing from boats. The framing of fishing on foot underscores the importance of fishing practice and gender performance. Fishing on foot is a way that individuals perform femininity and thus are legible socially as women. The practice of fishing on foot is explicitly feminized, even though some cisgender men regularly fish on foot, especially those without boats who therefore are of lower socioeconomic status. As with the idea of "true" fishing, another report for the same region cited fishing on foot as the main "disruption of the ecological niche."[9]

Fishing on foot was similarly framed as "a key issue" plaguing marine conservation in multiple interviews with conservation agents. One conservation agent emphasized that he wanted to see the practice stop altogether, across the whole island if possible.[10] Conservation organizations worked hard to educate local fishers about the problems associated with fishing on foot through meetings, workshops, conferences, brochures, illustrated signs erected near the ocean, and one-on-one conversations. One director of a conservation organization working in southwestern Madagascar explained that their environmental education strategy tried to induce a psychological change concerning what is right or wrong and that "they [fishers] need to come to their own understanding of the problem of fishing on foot, see what we already know as true."[11]

Why is fishing on foot such a target for conservationists? Without deeper examination, it might seem obvious. The vast majority of MPAs in Madagascar are concentrated on protecting coral reefs. Coral reefs, like tropical rainforests, harbor crucial habitat for a wide variety of marine species and provide a large suite of ecosystem services ranging from provisioning fisheries to protecting coastlines from erosion and storm damage. As one international conservation organization agent in northeastern Madagascar asserted, "Coral reefs are sensitive; they are the most important piece of the ecosystem. So it's only normal that we want to stop all forms of fishing that ruin the reef."[12] This desire to extinguish the practice of fishing on foot seems logical from the perspective of a Western-trained conservation biologist: because coral reefs are a key habitat for many marine organisms and take many years to regrow once broken, fishers should not walk on them or disturb them (move or turn pieces over) when fishing.

Fishing on foot, however, is not inherently destructive. Instead, it depends on where fishers walk, how they walk, what organisms they harvest, and how they harvest these organisms. While some artisanal fishing gear such as beach seins and other small-mesh bottom dragging nets have been found to negatively affect coral growth (Mangi and Roberts 2006), the long-standing practice of fishing on foot has not specifically been shown to drive biodiversity loss. In more than eighteen months of participant observation in three coastal regions of Madagascar, I observed that most fishing on foot took place either on the reef flat or the shallow intertidal zone along the coast. The reef flat, or the highest point of a fringing reef, is the zone most heavily used by fishers on foot. This zone is also one of the densest parts of the reef, where coral has accumulated to form a plateau that marks the boundary between the forereef (extending toward the ocean) and the back-reef (extending toward shore). Although live coral, sponges, algae, and other marine organisms are alive in lower layers in this zone, much of the top layer of this zone is already dead due to heavy wave action and exposure to the sun during low tide. The shallow intertidal zone hugging the beach is the other most popular place for fishing on foot. It is an area where coral and other fragile benthic organisms are present, but the habitat is often dominated by sand, mud, rock, or seagrass, not coral. Based on my observations as well as my participation in fishing on foot, walking on the reef crest as well as in the shallow coastal intertidal zone contributes little to coral damage. Similarly, the practice of digging into the sand in and around seagrass beds to find and harvest macroinvertebrates such as bivalves or sea cucumbers may not be destructive, depending on the technique. Generally, when a fisher uses a spear or a thin piece of metal to find and then remove the macroinvertebrate, they tend to uproot fewer seagrass fronds than if the harvester uses their toes or heel. Few fishers I observed relied only on their feet for harvest, and few if any seagrass fronds were dislodged.

The other practice often associated with fishing on foot is the act of flipping loose pieces of coral over or moving a piece of coral to find sea cucumbers and other organisms under it. The living parts of the coral, if left upside down in the sand, will eventually die due to lack of light. However, if the coral is not broken and is flipped back over, it will survive. In almost all the fishing on foot I observed, when fishers flipped over a piece of coral, they flipped it back so that the piece would continue to provide refuge for the sought-after organisms. I did observe a few people fishing on foot who left coral pieces upside down to die or flipped over staghorn or another type of coral that breaks off when flipped. Yet this behavior was not typical of the practices of most people I observed in the field.

The nuances of how people actually fish on foot, however, did not matter to the larger quest of marine conservation organizations to find and address a local cause of marine degradation. Nor did it matter that women's work in the ocean would be marginalized by eliminating this fishing practice. It is crucial to understand the gendered stakes of focusing on this local driver of ecological decline. When I asked governmental and nongovernmental conservation organization workers specifically why women's fishing practices seemed to be disproportionately affected by conservation rules and restrictions, the answers I received tended to fall into two categories: (1) coincidence or (2) women are not professional fishers (see chapter 4). In dozens of conversations with organization directors, regional coordinators, and field agents involved in the establishment and management of marine protected areas, I was told that the disproportionate effect of MPAs on women's marine resource use was by chance. Women walk on reefs as their primary mode of fishing. Men walk on reefs but they also fish from boats; therefore, banning or discouraging the practice of walking on reefs affects women's more than men's work in the ocean. Because coral reefs harbor high amounts of biodiversity (the primary interest of many conservation efforts), it seems that banning a resource use primarily employed by women was simply an unintended consequence of biodiversity conservation.

In the marine protected areas included in my research, the no-take zones enclosed, in part or in full, the regions of reef that were shallow enough to enable fishing on foot during low tide. Because most men practiced diverse fishing methods, partial or complete closures of shallow regions in the ocean did not prevent them from fishing despite the establishment of no-take zones within the broader MPA. Yet again due to gender norms or how gender was performed through fishing practices, if an MPA enclosed most or all of the shallow reef areas near a village, women would have to stop fishing altogether, fish illegally at night in the shallow areas within the MPA, or decrease their fishing efforts given the new spatial constraints of the MPA (Baker-Médard 2017).

The gendered inequities resulting from these changes is apparent. What is less visible but nonetheless significant, however, is how these shifts might affect nutrition and food security in villages near these MPAs. As mentioned, women bring home a statistically significantly higher proportion of their catch to feed their families than men. While some marine organisms did not display gendered differences in destination, such as sea cucumbers, which were always exported by both men and women, other organisms had strong gendered differences. For example, 88 percent of shrimp caught by women versus 63 percent of shrimp caught by men was brought home for consumption. The most striking gendered difference in destination pertained to gastropods and bivalves, where 68 percent of shells harvested by women versus 5 percent of shells harvested by men were brought home for consumption.

Even though a few conservation organization informants argued that the gendered consequences of MPA establishment were simply coincidental, the location of each MPA was not preordained but instead determined through a process that favored some voices over others. Women's exclusion from MPA decision-making has had a profound impact. For example, in an MPA in northeastern Madagascar, women no longer fish because the protected area enclosed all shallow areas amenable to fishing on foot. In a focus group I conducted there, women said that, if given control over the MPA limits, they would have kept some of the reef now enclosed in the MPA open to fishing on foot.[13] Given that gendered fishing practices correspond to particular benthic geographies, it is likely that a critical mass of women at the decision-making table would have changed the MPA boundaries in this area.

If we broaden the scale at which we analyze the efficiency, effectiveness, and fairness of efforts to decrease the practice of fishing on foot for the sake of fisheries management and biodiversity conservation, we see that this strategy is just one option in a much wider array of possible solutions, given the web of ecological, economic, and political connections. In fact, the overfocus on local marine resource use practices reinforces the conception that these MPAs are locally bound, instead of places inextricably linked to and produced by a broader political economy (Blaikie and Brookfield 1987; Massey 1994). Spatial narrowing creates the postmodern paradox where decentralized so-called collaborative interventions ultimately further entrench the hierarchies of gender, status, and wealth they theoretically aim to dismantle.

The History of Foreign Interests in Madagascar

The consensus by international and national marine conservation organizations that fishing on foot was a key problem plaguing biodiversity conservation and fisheries development in Madagascar has legitimized external intervention to extinguish the practice. Moreover, heaping blame on this practice made it unnecessary to engage critically with the longer history and broader political economy of fishing in Madagascar. The focus on fishing on foot as a problematic local practice was part of a broader assertion, despite strong evidence to the contrary, that small-scale fisheries in Madagascar were primarily subsistence driven. In fact, in some coastal villages, more than two-thirds of marine products harvested were exported (detailed below).

Interestingly, according to oral histories I gathered in three regions in Madagascar as well as written accounts from early French, Portuguese, and English explorers, Malagasy women and men have fished on foot in Madagascar for at least five hundred years—and likely much longer (Darboux et al. 1906; Grandidier et al. 1903; Petit 1930). Clearly, then, women's fishing techniques per se are not the source of marine degradation. However, to echo colonial conservationists' claims that ecological destruction in the marine realm is rooted in local fishers' "lazy" and nonmodern "destructive" fishing techniques is to erase the underlying historical and political-economic processes that have driven the increase in marine resource extraction in Madagascar.

Framing Malagasy fishers as primarily subsistence fishers justifies a particular kind of conservation intervention, one that aligns with Elinor Ostrom's common pool resource management regime. For example, a USAID report (2016, 24) states, "Most fishers in Antongil Bay [northeastern Madagascar] are traditional fishers using dugout canoes and nets. They have no real access to external markets and fish almost exclusively for subsistence." (Two pages later, under a section on their theory of change, USAID lays out Ostrom's approach to CPR management, citing each of the eight principles in turn, and suggests embedding these principles into "local laws based on traditional social code" (26). Similarly, the website of Reef Doctor (2023b), an international marine conservation organization working in southwestern Madagascar, frames the situation similarly in "Issues We Address": "Current fisheries catches are now exceeding sustainable levels, pushing small-scale fisheries increasingly closer to the verge of collapse. Over-exploitation of fish stocks has resulted in an increase of fishing effort in order for communities to sustain a subsistence lifestyle. This has consequently exacerbated the problem, condemning many marine resources to exhaustion." "Issues We Address" goes on to clarify exactly who Reef Doctor sees driving "marine resources to exhaustion," stating that "Madagascar experiences an annual population growth rate of 2.8%, one of the highest in Africa. This has led to an increase of both native coastal Vezo populations and also inland populations in the region. The rapidly expanding population is increasing the pressure on the remaining marine resources and habitats, and making it more difficult for traditional Vezo fishing communities to eke out an existence dependent on the sea." Elsewhere, similar to the USAID report from the northeast, Reef Doctor (2023a) states, "The intensive exploitation of the reef fishery in the Bay of Ranobe and the high level of community dependence on these resources prompted us to implement a sustainable community-led management system. In 2006, we brought together the local fishing communities of the bay to form a marine conservation and management organisation with elected representatives to work with us." Taken together, these narratives localize the marine conservation problem and solution and position Reef Doctor as the initiator and engineer of the community-led approach.

These tidy narratives of local subsistence fishers exhausting their own resources, thus necessitating intervention from international conservation organizations, belies the historical and ongoing foreign demand for Malagasy marine products. Interviews with elders as well as archival documentary evidence also underscore the deep history of foreign interest in Malagasy marine products as well as marine conservation. Colonial documents from the early 1920s illustrate the presence of a well-established and robust marine export market. For example, a first quarter report of exports from Madagascar in 1920 indicates exports for 10.8 metric tons of sea cucumbers, 6.8 metric tons of dried fish, 0.4 metric tons of shark fins, 9.5 metric tons of diverse shells, 11.1 metric tons of mother-of-pearl shells, and 1.3 metric tons of sea turtle shells, among others (Archives nationales d'Outre-mer, 1920). Although all of these products continue to be harvested and exported, sea cucumber, fish (primarily frozen and/or processed), and shark fins remain most prevalent in current day exports.

Despite the long histories of export, the end use of some of these marine products remains a mystery to many of the fishers who target these resources. Shark fins, sea cucumbers, and fish maw (swim bladders) prompted particularly interesting theories from some Malagasy fishers. In one focus group conducted in southwestern Madagascar, fishers suggested that shark fins were used for wires in airplanes because the fibers are so strong. Another said that he had heard that Chinese eat shark fins but didn't believe it. He explained that he and four other fishers were so hungry during one fishing trip to a remote island that they cooked a whole shark. They all tried eating parts of the dorsal and pectoral fins, but he reported that "it wasn't good" (*tsy soa*) and that he didn't believe that the fins were consumed because they had no taste (*matsatso*). Instead, this fisher surmised that shark fins were probably used to build clothing for people who do deep-sea exploration (*maniriky lalina mare*) or perhaps used in rockets (*sambon-danitra*) or something technologically advanced (*teknolojia avo lenta*).[14] In another fishing focus group conducted in northwestern Madagascar, one fisher suggested that shark fins were used to make bombs, and sea cucumbers were used to make special furniture or shoes. Another fisher added that he heard that sea cucumbers made men strong "down there," signaling toward his groin (*mampahery ambany*) and thought that it might be true given the shape of sea cucumbers. A third fisher said that he still has no interest in eating them, plus he didn't know how to cook them.[15] A fisher in northeastern Madagascar had been harvesting and selling fish maw (*salavatraka*) for more than six years but asked me what it was used for. When I answered that I genuinely did not know, he speculated that perhaps it's used in organ transplants.[16] Yet even though many fishers, most of whom had no direct contact with exporters, did not know the end use of the products they extracted, they knew that many of the marine resources have been part of international trade for a long time.

In the early twentieth century, Madagascar acquired a reputation as a region with an abundance of sharks and other marine organisms that were of particular interest to the French colonial government (Deschamps 1961; Petit 1930). Interviews conducted with village elders in southwestern Madagascar indicated that a small hub of shark liver oil production existed near the village of Tsiandamba in the early 1920s. From this hub, French colonists hired Malagasy fishers from the area to fish shark, extract the shark livers, and boil the livers to make oil to export to France.[17] In Europe, shark liver oil was used in cosmetics, perfume, skin lighteners, lamps, leather tanning, metallurgy, and as a dietary supplement (Lagoin 1961; Petit 1930; Vannuccini 1999). In the early 1900s, marine products from Madagascar often passed through Zanzibar, a long-established port for all goods leaving southeastern Africa for Asia and beyond (Deschamps 1961; Laurent 1906). Dry shark meat, fins, and shark liver oil from Madagascar brought to Zanzibar were eventually exported to Canton and Shanghai (Barnett 1996; Laurent 1906). In addition to Zanzibar, shark fins, oil, and meat were also exported to the Mascarene Islands (Mauritius, Réunion, and Rodrigues), French territories that were hubs for trade between Europe and the East African coast (Deschamps 1961; Petit 1930). Direct export from Madagascar to East Asia likely started in the early 1900s as more Chinese merchants settled in Madagascar and started purchasing directly from fishers, and in this era between two thousand and five thousand fins per year were exported to Zanzibar,

China, and Reunion Island (Petit 1930). Since the mid-1900s, shark product exports have narrowed to primarily fins (Cripps et al. 2015).

Sea cucumbers have also been harvested for a century. In his two-volume study of the Malagasy fishing industry, French colonial naturalist Georges Petit reported that a sea cucumber industry was well established and running at full yield (*en plein rendement*) in northwestern, northeastern, and southwestern Madagascar (Petit 1930, 144). While accurate numbers of sea cucumber exports remain elusive, current documentation shows that through most of the twentieth century, dry sea cucumber exports ranged between 50 and 140 tons per year (FAO 2008).

The later colonial period into the early 1970s marked the introduction of new fishing gear such as stronger and larger nylon nets, oxygen tanks for diving (although this technology was not widely disbursed until the early 2000s), better communication technology, more reliable inland transportation—and an increase in foreign demand for marine products such as shrimp, lobster, octopus, and tuna. As a result, even more Malagasy fishers engaged in export-oriented fishing (FAO 1982; Iida 2005; Le Manach et al. 2011). Although marine resources such as sea cucumbers, anchovy shoals, and sharks were abundant and easily accessible near villages in the early 1970s, by the early 2000s many resources declined significantly. For example, sea cucumber exports peaked in 2002 at 980 tons (FAO 2008), bringing in approximately US$3.1 million that year. Since then, however, sea cucumber exports have steadily declined (Baker-Médard and Ohl 2019; Louw and Bürgener 2020). As export-oriented marine products became less easily accessible, many fishers in the most heavily fished regions, such as southwestern Madagascar, began making seasonal trips to remote islands and fishing grounds where these lucrative marine resources were still plentiful, while others supplemented fishing with seasonal urban work (Cripps and Gardner 2016; Iida 2005).

The rise and subsequent dominance of commercial export-oriented fishing in numerous regions of the island persists today. In two villages in southwestern Madagascar, for example, longitudinal data for the years 2011–2018 from intermediary buyers working for marine product exporting companies in the region indicate that the majority (78.8 percent) of small-scale fisheries

An oxygen tank used as a church bell, southwestern Madagascar. Photograph by author.

catch was sold for export, a finding that corresponds to other research in the region (Barnes and Rawlinson 2009; Westerman and Benbow 2014). Malagasy marine product exports have increased steadily from US$40 million in 1990 to just under US$120 million in 2022 (see accompanying illustration). These numbers, through helpful in showing trends, are very conservative given that they do not contain any illegal exports, which have been docu-

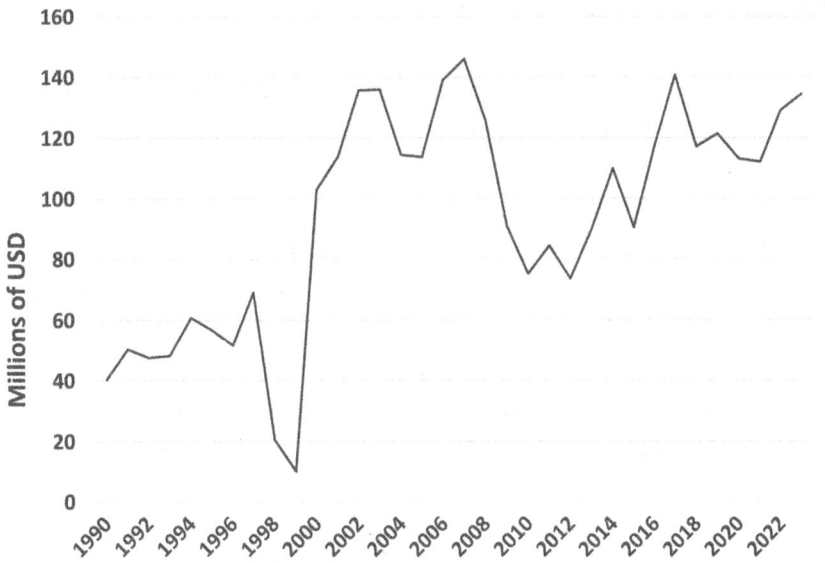

The total export value of fish, crustaceans, mollusks, and other aquatic invertebrates from Madagascar, 1990–2022. Source: https://comtrade.un.org/data/. The dip in 1998 and 1999 corresponds with a change in industrial fishing licensing. Based on an FAO report, it is likely that fishing occurred at a similar level, but exporters found other mechanisms to export their products that year (Soumy 2004).

mented to be substantial; underreporting is a significant problem in Madagascar fisheries statistics (Le Manach et al. 2011).

The increased dominance of export-oriented fishing in numerous regions of the island aligns with the neoliberal turn of Madagascar's political economy in the late 1980s (Corson 2011b, 2016; Kull 1996). The steady commercialization of small-scale fisheries in multiple areas of the island, unacknowledged by the conservationists' subsistence fishing discourse, undoubtedly contributed to the need for greater fisheries management.

The history of marine markets in Madagascar, as well as the current scale and scope of exports, provides an important context to understand the rise in number and intensity of marine conservation and fisheries management projects across the island. International conservation organizations point to a local decline in fisheries production in order to legitimize their work in the marine realm. These fishery collapses are the discursive foundation on which marine conservation organizations and development agencies build their argument for why small-scale marine resource users need their aid and assistance and why addressing the issue at the local scale is necessary.

Similarly, only in the context of the long history of fishing on foot in coastal regions of Madagascar can the professed unsustainability of this particular fishing *practice* be called into question. Instead, it is clear that the broader commodity chain and end use of marine products deserve much greater attention.

Although some conservation organizations work at the national and international level to address multiscalar drivers of marine resource decline such as consumption, trade, and advertising, the scope and scale of these programs is limited. One notable initiative is the World Wildlife Fund's collaboration with the Marine Stewardship Council to "harness consumer and retailer purchasing power" to promote the sustainability of eight artisanal fisheries (WWF 2016).[18] Another was Blue Venture's work in Madagascar with the Marine Stewardship Council investigating the feasibility of octopus fishery eco-certification in the Velondriake locally managed marine area (Blue Ventures 2019). Other examples include the Wildlife Conservation Society's and WWF's work with governments to strengthen trade control measures concerning endangered sharks and rays protected by the Convention on International Trade in Endangered Species of Wild Fauna and Flora (CITES) (Bräutigam et al. 2015), and Conservation International's Center for Environmental Leadership in Business, which has forged partnerships with companies like McDonald's to encourage greater sustainability in marine resource purchasing practices (CI 2016). Although these efforts move in the right direction, they are mired with challenges given the technical and financial burden of certification for small-scale decentralized fisheries (Gardner et al. 2020). Furthermore, these approaches do not rise to the level of engagement necessary to create greater accountability across the variety of formal and informal networks through which Malagasy marine products flow.

Just as Malagasy marine resource users have been connected to the interests of distant shores through markets for centuries, marine conservation efforts also have a long history in Madagascar. The notion that a conservation organization can start from scratch and introduce new local marine fisheries rules, whether spatial, temporal, or gear-focused, belies the deep history of foreign intervention and interest in managing Madagascar's marine resources. Unaware of this history, most marine conservation agents interviewed who were working in Madagascar generally believed that efforts only began in earnest in the past twenty years, with a steady increase in the number of MPAs. Although governmental and nongovernmental interviewees acknowledged that some marine conservation occurred before the late 1980s, most said that all early efforts were "minimal" and that relevant state agencies such as the Ministry of Production, Waters, and Forests, the marine portion of which is the Ministry of Fisheries and the Blue Economy, were until recently "powerless" and "underfunded."[19] However, foreign-led marine conservation had started during the colonial period, where spatial and temporal enclosures were established, gear and species restrictions were instituted, and foreign marine concessions were granted.

Beyond the important influence of marine product exports on marine socioecological systems, global climate change is a critical nonlocal driver of change in Madagascar's marine ecosystems and coastal fisheries. Climate change effects—specifically ocean acidification, rising ocean temperature, and increasing frequency of storms—have already harmed coral reefs and the lives of people who depend on reef ecosystems in Madagascar (Sumaila et al. 2014; Weiskopf et al. 2021).

Shifts in the Indian Ocean Dipole (sometimes called the Indian Niño because it is akin to El Niño cycles in the eastern Pacific Ocean) and an increase in frequency and strength of cyclones are occurring in the southern Indian Ocean due to climate change. The increased severity and frequency of storms damages fragile reef structures; changing and more severe weather also forces fishers to shift where and how frequently they fish (Bruggemann et al. 2012; Salinger 2013). For example, fishers in Ambodivahibe in northeastern Madagascar report that their fishing season has been shortened by three months annually because of strong wind conditions (Weiskopf et al. 2021). Moreover, rising air temperature and diminishing rainfall make agriculture and livestock production less viable, leading Malagasy farmers to depend more on coral reefs for food, especially as a source of protein (Bruggemann et al. 2012).

The western Indian Ocean has been warming at a rate faster than any other region of the tropical oceans, with an anomalous warming of 1.3°C in summer sea surface temperatures (Dueri 2017). Ocean warming is linked to coral bleaching and reductions in coral cover in Madagascar, which harm coral-associated marine organisms and thus marine fishers. According to a study focused on global mollusk-based exports (bivalves, gastropods, squid, octopus), Madagascar emerged as one of the top five exporting nations most susceptible to mollusk harvest declines from ocean acidification (Cooley et al. 2012). Similarly, sea cucumbers, which have important ecological and economic roles in Madagascar, are also sensitive to acidification (Collard et al. 2014).

The long history of marine product exports from Madagascar and climate change disruptions to Malagasy marine systems discredits both the narrative that growing numbers of isolated subsistence fishers are the main culprit of declining marine fisheries production and the related contention that marine conservation intervention is new, a response to the needs of a subsistence fishery in crisis. The twin forces of foreign demand for marine resources and foreign intervention in marine conservation now converge on a so-called local strategy to conserve biodiversity and improve fisheries output: marine protected areas. Although MPAs are often advanced as a cure-all, research about their effectiveness is not conclusive. And yet, the cautions and caveats that marine scientists include in their research are absent in the narratives fishers and even governmental officials receive from conservation organizations eager to help expand marine protected areas in places such as Madagascar.

Framing and Fisheries Production: Linking MPAs and Catch

We have ecological data that we will never share because it shows the opposite of what we are trying to do. It could mess up funding and fishers' confidence in us. Fish abundance is crazy low in some MPAs, and we don't know why. We hope it changes.

—*Foreign scientist working for an international conservation organization in western Madagascar, August 25, 2020*

Marine protected areas, and specifically marine reserves (or no-take zones), are often framed as a panacea that will safeguard marine biodiversity, stabilize or increase fisheries production, prevent local extinction of culturally or economically valuable species, and restore marine habitats for long-term ecosystem stability (Abesamis and Russ 2005; Di Lorenzo et al. 2020; Green et al. 2014; Lubchenco and Grorud-Colvert 2015; Sala et al. 2021). Despite evidence that some MPAs have achieved a subset of this list, considerable debate remains in the marine conservation literature concerning the conditions under which a reserve can meet both marine biodiversity protection and fisheries objectives that relate to goals such as food security (Cabral et al. 2019; Hilborn and Kaiser 2022; Kerwath et al. 2013; Thorpe, Bavink, and Coulthard 2011). For example, one of the more direct mechanisms by which MPAs may benefit fisheries is a process called spillover, where marine organisms grow in abundance and size inside a no-take zone and venture into zones where fishing is allowed, thus improving harvest. However, spillover is also one of the most hotly debated topics within the marine conservation literature (Di Lorenzo et al. 2020; Micheli et al. 2004).

Conservation organizations implementing MPAs in fact often play down debates in the marine science literature. In none of the meetings and presentations by conservation organizations for marine fishers and coastal villagers that I attended were these uncertainties stated. Instead, presenters advanced a clear and simple narrative that marine enclosures are a great fisheries management tool that is guaranteed to improve both the size and the abundance of catch for small-scale resource users. Not mentioned were biodiversity conservation goals and the broader national and international goals of increasing the total marine area under protection. Focusing on the guarantee-to-improve-fishing narrative for MPAs is understandable from a social marketing standpoint, given that some resource users might be unwilling to surrender fishing areas for the establishment of an MPA if the strategy is not guaranteed to improve catch. The foreign scientist quoted above underscores the perceived importance that conservation organizations present a positive, confident narrative about the relation between MPAs and fisheries production. And yet conservation organizations could lose credibility with fishers altogether if a MPA fails to enhance fisheries production or—worse—decreases catch locally. Marine conservation and marine science directors in the national headquarters of international conservation organizations certainly understood this risk. As one director of marine conservation put it, however, "We try and we hope it works."[20]

The strategies that conservation organizations employ to promote the notion that MPAs will improve catch range from strategic frameworks to the use of temporary reserves to demonstrate that fast-growing marine organisms can increase in size.[21] The most common discursive strategy relates to how organizations describe MPAs. For example, in several sites in northeastern Madagascar, conservation organizations call the MPA a *fitarimoan'daoko*, or fish nursery/growing area. At one point in a conversation with a conservation agent working in several communities around a small near-shore MPA, I slipped and called it a reserve. The agent quickly corrected me, saying that they don't use that word.[22] Similarly, some organizations opted for the Malagasy word *banky*, bank. In a long car ride in southwestern Madagascar I took with two international conservation organization agents and three local conservation committee members, one of the conservation agents spent about an hour trying to convince the three fishers to open bank accounts instead of hiding their money at home or spending it quickly. He explained to them that the reason they call the marine reserve a *banky* was because fish grow like money grows in the bank. He then went on to explain interest rates, ultimately returning to the argument that the fishers should keep their money in the bank. That evening, after we arrived in the village, when I asked one of the local conservation committee members from the car ride whether he was going to open a bank account now, he said, "Fish don't stay in the reserve here, maybe my money won't stay in the bank, too," echoing a common feeling of mistrust toward banks because of fear of theft, as well as skepticism about the value of MPAs.[23]

In both northeastern and southwestern Madagascar, international conservation organizations have helped establish temporary as well as permanent reserves. Two marine conservation directors at international conservation organizations and four field-based agents each independently described the establishment of temporary reserves as an educational technique and a strategy to convince (*mandresy lahatra*) fishers that MPAs are good.[24] The two directors and several agents indicated that their end goal was to expand the area within the reserves and to multiply the number of permanent reserves—and eventually to jettison the temporary reserves. Conservation organizations echoed this strategy of persuasion in presentations and meetings with fishers at the village level, talking primarily about a temporary reserve that would open to fishing after several months. The focus in this reserve was on relatively fast-growing, short-ranging marine organisms, chiefly octopus, but also lobster in some areas. Regardless of whether the MPA would produce a net increase in catch, in both casual conversations and community meetings the agencies focused on the direct and ongoing benefits of the temporary reserve. The relative immediacy of benefit—whatever benefit there was to glean from a few months' closure—aided agents' argument that these reserves were by the people for the people. Organizations highlighted the fisheries yields associated with the temporary reserve by having conservation organizations present at each village on opening day of a temporary reserve. The conservation organization agent who observed fishers on opening day of the temporary reserve in southwestern Madagascar, as described at the beginning of this chapter, was there to help document the total kilos of octopus and other organisms caught that day, as well as the single heaviest octopus. The net benefit from the temporary closure, accounting for catch forgone because the area was closed, was not always clearly positive, according to the conservation organizations helping manage the reserves, but as one conservation organization agent pointed out, "It doesn't matter as long as they still believe the reserve helps them."[25]

Understanding the debates and deep uncertainties in the scientific literature concerning the efficacy of marine protected areas as a fisheries management tool is important to unsettle the seemingly solid and singular narrative of fisheries' benefit from marine reserves.

The Contours and Caveats of MPA Science

The science of marine protected areas is fraught with debate. One of the few things that scientists can agree on, however, is that the social and ecological context of an MPA matters. Everything from fishing frequency and fishing targets to the flow of marine currents and reproductive cycles of different marine species affect whether an MPA can benefit biodiversity, fisheries, or both. Although disputes exist, there is some agreement with the assertion that MPAs can help protect marine biodiversity if designed correctly (Di Lorenzo et al. 2020; Topor et al. 2019). There are deeper disagreements, however, about whether MPAs are currently, or can be, an effective fisheries management tool (Hilborn and Kaiser 2022; Lester et al. 2009; Zupan et al. 2018). Several analyses of the MPA literature find that, despite increased interest in understanding how MPAs may benefit fisheries globally, the establishment of MPAs is still based primarily on biodiversity criteria and thus not explicitly designed to benefit fisheries (Baker-Médard et al. 2019; Costello and Ballantine 2015).

The highly contingent nature of MPAs' utility as a fisheries management tool, however, rarely translates to how marine conservation organizations communicate with local fishers. The marine conservation organizations working in the villages included in my research focused their communication, education, and outreach efforts on the idea that MPAs are guaranteed to enhance fisheries production locally. However, an understanding of the precise conditions in which MPAs contribute to stabilizing or enhancing local fisheries is crucial for both more effective MPA management and also clearer communication with and accountability to local resource users.

Outlined here are seven interrelated caveats and contingencies that emerge from the scientific literature regarding if and when MPAs benefit local fisheries. These studies largely focus on marine reserves, the most stringent MPAs in terms of restricting harvest.

The first contingency relates to harvest levels. Models and several global meta-analyses indicate that marine reserves are not likely to benefit adjacent fisheries if harvest levels are low. Instead, reserves are effective at increasing the abundance and diversity of coastal fish populations when harvest levels are high and the fishery is not already well managed (Griffiths et al. 2022; Lester et al. 2009; Micheli et al. 2004; Nillos Kleiven et al. 2019; Vandeperre et al. 2011). These findings indicate that reserves located in highly biodiverse areas with low fishing pressure will come at a net cost to fishers and managers, given the removal of productive areas from fishing. Surveys conducted across northeastern, northwestern, and southwestern Madagascar indicate that the number of fishers per area and how often fishers fish vary widely. Southwestern Madagascar tends to have the highest fishing frequencies per person and number of fishers per capita.[26] This evidence suggests that historical and current harvest levels ultimately determine whether local fishers will benefit from a given marine reserve. In lower-harvest areas, marine reserves are less likely to improve local catch.

The second caveat relates to whether fishers target short-ranging or long-ranging species. A marine organism's range, or the area it travels in for food, shelter, and reproduction, determines how well it will be protected by a marine reserve. Fish respond to protection differentially depending on their size, habitat preferences, and larval dispersal distance; and these characteristics and behaviors in turn interact with such environmental factors as temperature, currents, and rate of primary productivity, resulting in very different species-specific responses to MPAs (Claudet et al. 2010; Ohayon, Granot, and Belmaker 2021). Generally, MPAs have been found to be more effective for medium- to shorter-ranging species than long-ranging species (Claudet et al. 2010; Pilyugin, Medlock, and De Leenheer 2016). For instance, a well-researched MPA at Apo Island in the Philippines shows one of the best examples of an increase in abundance of a short-ranging fish species both within and outside a reserve. The species studied was *Naso vlamingii*, a primarily herbivorous unicorn fish with a relatively small daily range (about 20–30 meters from their starting point) (Abesamis and Russ 2005; Russ, Alcala, and Maypa 2003). Researchers found that *Naso vlamingii* demonstrated density-dependent spillover, meaning that populations of the fish within the reserve were high enough to drive juvenile and adult fish outside the reserve due to space limitation and territorial interactions. Density-dependent spillover is the gold standard in fisheries-focused marine reserve design. This desired goal is elusive, however, for several reasons. If an organism is relatively immobile and a reserve is large, densities of that organism may never become high enough to force emigration outside the reserve, thus not adding to local fisheries production. Alternatively, if a species is very long ranging compared to the size of the reserve, the reserve may minimally benefit the organism through its life cycle (Claudet et al.

2010; Hilborn et al. 2004). Relations between reserve size and species range are being reevaluated through the increased use of acoustic fish telemetry, or "fish with chips" (Pittman et al. 2014).

In Madagascar, fishers harvest both long-ranging and short-ranging species. Because of the gendered division of labor, however, men and women target species with different ranges. The longest-ranging species, including sharks, rays, tuna, and billfish, tend to be caught by men. Women tend to target the shortest-ranging species, including sea cucumbers, bivalves, and gastropods. Medium-range species, such as reef fish, octopus, squid, and eels, tend to be caught by both men and women. These range-based species' responses to MPAs coupled with gendered harvest practices mean that men and women stand to be affected in different ways by the introduction of a marine reserve. Because many of the species women target are relatively sessile, in theory women have the most to gain from a reserve. Yet it may take many years for relatively sessile organisms to display density-dependent spillover; the up-front cost of sacrificing a fishing spot for fisheries management would therefore also fall on women. If women leave the fishery due to this cost, both the fishing practices and ecological dynamics of the area could change in the long run.

The time-specific element of these dynamics brings us to the third caveat: how long a reserve has been in place is a key mediating factor in how both short-ranging and long-ranging species respond to reserves. For ecosystems dynamics to return, trophic structure to recover, and species with long life spans to regenerate, it takes time. Some researchers argue that these processes stabilize only after multiple decades of protection (Edgar et al. 2014; Kaplan et al. 2019; Molloy, McLean, and Côté 2009; Vandeperre et al. 2011); others show that significant recovery can occur in several years (Micheli et al. 2004). The age of a reserve, however, does not function independent of other socioecological dynamics. A meta-analysis by Manfredi Di Lorenzo and colleagues (2020) using data from twenty-three MPAs around the globe finds that MPA age (time since protection) is positively correlated with ecological spillover, although this effect is contingent on whether a species is commercially valuable.

Most of the MPAs in Madagascar have been in place for slightly more than a decade. For those that have existed for more than twenty years (such as Nosy Antafana, Masoala, and Nosy Tanikely), research investigating the impact of reserves on local catch is scant. Some of the strongest evidence of a benefit comes from temporary reserves focused on octopus fisheries in the southwest (Oliver et al. 2015) and lobster fisheries in the southeast (Long 2017).

The fourth contingency relates to the size and spacing of an MPA network. This theme interacts in important ways with the previous two themes concerning MPA age and species range. The relative size and spacing between MPAs matters in terms of marine organisms' mobility and habitat connectivity. Generally, species most targeted by fisheries are from higher trophic levels and tend to have greater dispersal distances in marine systems (Kinlan and Gaines 2003). Thus, either a reserve must be larger than the dispersal distance of species targeted for protection or smaller reserves must be spaced closely enough to ensure connectivity across the dispersal distance and adult home range. However, it is difficult to balance the goal of protecting the dispersal home range requirements of these higher trophic level species with that of enhancing local fisheries (Di Lorenzo et al. 2020; Edgar et al. 2014; Halpern 2003). In essence, sustainability of the fishery requires not only that protected areas be linked by dispersal, so that populations can move among areas and replenish them if needed, but also that reserve density is not so great that fishers lack adequate area to benefit from spillover. Southwestern Madagascar has a relatively high density of small (less than 1 square kilometer) marine reserves spaced at fairly regular intervals for several hundred kilometers. Similarly, in Antongil Bay in the northeast, nearly a dozen small reserves are located near one another. From a design standpoint, this connectivity is well suited to benefit a variety of species and to potentially provision local fisheries. To date, however, there are no studies that show these results. And in most other areas of Madagascar, medium and large reserves tend to be isolated and thus may do little to enhance fisheries locally.

The fifth contingency relates to the static nature of MPA boundaries. Marine protected areas are fixed in space, whereas harvest practices, markets, and ecological processes are spatially dynamic. Numerous studies show that changes in ocean circulation stemming from climate change, including upwelling zones and zones of high primary productivity, directly influence the current and future effectiveness of MPAs (Bruno et al. 2018; Martell et al. 2005). Some scholars analyzing the dynamic nature of both social and environmental boundaries suggest that either MPAs should have flexible boundaries or conservationists should focus on establishing a suite of short-term protected areas that change in location and size as needed over time—deemed a "dynamic MPA" or "mobile MPA" network (Matsuda, Takemoto, and Katsukawa 2016; Soto 2002; Wilson et al. 2020). These researchers assert that there needs to be built-in spatial flexibility with MPAs, especially in relation to climate change. They argue that mobile MPAs might be better suited to protect areas tied to important phases of marine organisms' life cycles that change both spatially and over time, such as the spawning grounds of commercially important species. To date, there are no dynamic MPAs in Madagascar, and other than a few deep-sea dynamic MPA experiments, mobile MPAs remain almost unheard of globally (Maxwell et al. 2020). Although there are temporary reserves to manage lobster (Long 2017) and temporary rotational reserves to manage octopus (Oliver et al. 2015), these reserves are not designed to respond to social and ecological changes across space over short or longer periods of time.

The sixth caveat concerns predator-prey dynamics. Several meta-analyses of MPAs find a lower prevalence of noncommercial fish within reserves due to changes in balance between predators and prey populations and the habitat within marine reserves (Claudet et al. 2010). For example, Aaron Eger and Julia Baum (2020) found a nearly threefold decrease in herbivores (including parrotfish, damselfish, rabbitfish, surgeonfish, and urchins) and a nearly twofold increase in primary producers (such as kelp, seagrass, and macroalgae) within reserves compared to outside reserves. How MPAs influence predatory-prey dynamics remains understudied and is thus a serious shortcoming in the current design and implementation of MPAs globally (Lima et al. 2023).

Herbivorous fish are some of the most important fish for local consumption in Madagascar. Large shifts in the composition of the entire community of marine species, called trophic cascades, can also occur due to predator-prey dynamics in relation to the introduction of MPAs (Baskett 2006; Eger and Baum 2020). As the scientist quoted at the opening of this section indicated, Madagascar has reserves that have experienced a net decrease in reef fish abundance and diversity compared to areas outside them. These findings show that if MPAs are not well calibrated to local conditions and fishing pressures, predator-prey dynamics can negatively affect species important to small-scale fishers.

The final contingency relates to source-sink dynamics. Under the assumption that "not all habitat is of equal quality," Larry Crowder and colleagues (2000, 804) show the importance of siting marine protected areas in sites considered sources, where there is high fish density, biomass, average size, diversity, or other measures of production (overall net growth), which leads to spillover outside the reserve; rather than in sinks, where there is a low measures of production and a net loss of new individuals. Numerous studies show that improper placement of MPAs can harm fish populations and, by extension, local fisheries (Cabral et al. 2016; Crowder et al. 2000). Finding sources and sinks is difficult in the marine environment, given that a source for one species might be a sink for another, and source-sink dynamics interact with harvest pressures, species interactions, and shifts in currents and seasonal weather patterns (Hilborn 2014; Silva et al. 2019; Tuck and Possingham 2000). In Madagascar, a diversity of fisheries coexist. Some fishers are generalists, targeting a variety of species depending on the season, tide, and market prices, while others are specialists, targeting sharks, squid, or seahorses. Some of the best-documented reserves that benefit local fisheries in Madagascar are species-specific, notably those targeting octopus or lobster. For a reserve to be beneficial for the broader fishing community, however, it must accommodate a suite of species-specific movements, migrations, and growth rates. It must have a balanced proportion of protected and open-access areas in order to protect the habitat and life-cycle needs of a suite of species as well as maintain access to these stocks for local fishers. Getting this balance right is extremely difficult (Cabral et al. 2016; Gaines et al. 2010) and again points to the high chance of getting it wrong and decreasing marine populations locally, reducing catch—an outcome diametrically opposed to what conservation organizations want and profess to do.

An MPA meta-analysis aggregating findings from twenty studies of coastal fish populations from thirty-one temperate and tropical locations across the globe found that approximately 20 percent—in some areas, up to 34 percent—of fish species decreased in abundance with the establishment of a no-take MPA (Micheli et al. 2004). Di Lorenzo and colleagues' (2020) study similarly found that noncommercial marine species (a broad metric of biodiversity) did not show a spillover effect, in terms of either abundance or biomass, from MPAs.

These studies highlight the disconnect between the narratives regarding MPAs shared with local fishers in Madagascar and the nuanced conclusions within the marine science literature regarding the efficacy of MPAs in increasing fish abundance locally. The complexity endemic to marine conservation and the variability in how well an MPA performs also contextualizes the embarrassment of that foreign scientist and the conservation organization's desire to hide the results that found decreased fish abundance within the MPAs they worked so hard to establish.

Ultimately, it is important for conservation organizations to find a way to integrate the nuance and contingencies of how and whether MPAs can enhance fisheries production. Doing so not only would be more scientifically accurate but also would accommodate the variety of fish and habitat dynamics that fishers will inevitably observe in the marine environment over time in relation to an MPA.

Beyond the complex array of ecological conditions, many social factors influence the efficacy of MPAs. The primary concern of researchers is the impact of harvest on the marine environment. Other key factors underpinning MPA success are fishers' involvement in the decision-making and management of MPAs and their willingness to follow resource use rules, or buy-in, as some conservation practitioners and researchers term it (Walton, Gomei, and Di Carlo 2013; WCS 2019; Zupan et al. 2018). However, a deeper and more fundamental element of social life is a contingency often ignored in marine conservation projects: worldview or cosmology.

Conflicting Cosmologies

French philosopher and anthropologist Bruno Latour famously argued (2005, 245) that "the world is not a solid continent of facts sprinkled by a few lakes of uncertainties, but a vast ocean of uncertainties speckled by a few islands of calibrated and stabilized forms." The vast ocean of uncertainty is rooted to what feminist philosophers call situated knowledge, or the notion that knowledge about the world and the meaning one ascribes to objects and processes is inextricably linked one's social, cultural, political, geographic, and historical location (Haraway 1988). Situated knowledge is informed by one's cosmology, or the stories one has about the beginning of the Earth, its life-forms, cycles, and seasons, as well as more fundamental ideas of motion, space, time, and causality (Mickey 2018). One's situated knowledge and worldview (cosmology) shapes how one understands human-environment relations and one's ability and desire to change these relations. Establishing protected areas, especially no-take zones, is predicated on a worldview that a land- or seascape without humans is the most ecologically healthy and most biodiverse. This belief is echoed by numerous Western scientists (Costello and Ballantine 2015; Donlan 2005; Noss et al. 2012; Wuerthner, Crist, and Butler 2015), perhaps most visibly by the prominent scholar dubbed the "father of biodiversity," E. O. Wilson, in his book and parallel project *Half-Earth* (2016), which aims to put half of the earth's ecosystems under protection.

Environmental historians and anthropologists have shown in a variety of ways, in a variety of contexts, how the nature-culture divide defines Western ideas and ideologies of nature and therefore nature conservation (Cronon 1996; Descola 2013; LaDuke 1999; Merchant 1980; Neumann 1998). These scholars and others problematize so-called separation thinking, or what Latour (1993) calls the "Great Divide," showing that this dichotomy is not only inaccurate but dangerous because it is ahistorical and depoliticizes environmental and social change (Haraway 2003; Harding 1991; Nightingale 2014; Peluso 2012; White 2006). Concepts such as natureculture or socionature, rooted in Indigenous cosmologies, challenge the worldview that separates humans and nonhumans, unsettling both human-nature hierarchies and the dominant construct of human-as-threat to nature (Cajete 2000; Craft 2016; Deloria 2001; Kimmerer 2013; Simpson 2014). For example, community-based conservation scholar Mehana Blaich Vaughan (2018) describes the interrelated concepts for native Hawaiians of *hō-ihi*, which means "to make sacred," and *kuleana*, meaning "rights as well as responsibilities," as core values that define human-environment relations. Vaughan (2018, 18) explains that, "unlike the word 'management,' which presumes separation and a concept of human power over the environment," the stories she has gathered from elders, fishers, and other community members in Hawaii "illustrate the importance of maintaining mutually respectful and interdependent familial relationships with the natural world." Blackfoot scholar Leroy Little Bear (2000, 77) similarly argues that numerous Indigenous worldviews emphasize how "all things are animate, imbued with spirit, and in constant motion . . . [and] interrelationships between all entities are of paramount importance."

These Indigenous worldviews push against a static, abstracted, and atemporal framework of space and human-environment relations and instead describe a worldview that favors "connections, liquidities, and becomings," or what Philip Steinberg and Kimberley Peters term "wet ontology."[27] Advancing an understanding of the nature and structure of reality based on the fluidity of water, mobility of water-bound organisms, and flow of oceanic materials, wet ontology emphasizes connectivity, interdependence, and ongoing churning and change. Indigenous wet ontologies also align closely with feminist environmental scholar Stacy Alaimo's (2008) notion of transcorporeality, which affirms interconnectivity not only at the scale of society or a given human community but also at the scale of the body. Alaimo (2008, 238) defines transcorporeality as the "time-space where human corporeality, in all its material fleshiness, is inseparable from 'nature' or 'environment.'" Like wet ontology, transcorporeality challenges the human-nature dichotomy, emphasizing bodily inter- and intraconnections and the deeply material entanglements between the human and more-than-human world.

As cultural geographer Elizabeth Johnson and legal scholar Irus Braverman argue in their book Blue Legalities: The Life and Law of the Sea (2020), cosmologies and ontologies that emphasize human-nature interconnection and interdependence, decenter Western environmental frameworks, and recenter postcolonial and decolonial understanding of ocean spaces, aquatic resources, and marine resource governance. Emphasis on interdependence helps work toward a multispecies framework for action and interspecies justice.

Despite conservation organizations' concerted efforts to introduce projects in Madagascar oriented toward educating fishers about a worldview that centers the human-nature divide, Malagasy fishers from different regions of the island whom I interviewed consistently expressed worldviews that countered these Western frameworks. Most fundamentally, they seldom believed the idea that a marine reserve could increase the number of fish locally if all the ecological conditions were met. Numerous fishers also did not accept the idea that fishers' behavior, including the number of fishers or the intensity of harvest in a given area, could substantially alter fish populations. The causal arrows of fish reproduction, the behavior of fish and fishing practices were drawn in different ways by fishers across Madagascar. Many fishers I spoke with emphasized the importance of their knowledge of, respect for, and relationship to the ocean. The ocean, the reef, the seagrass zone, and all the organisms that lived there were active participants in the relationship, not just passive backdrops or objects to be harvested. One village elder in southwestern Madagascar noted that she has seen many changes in her life, but one thing that will never change is the importance of the ocean. She underscored this saying, "The ocean is like God [*sahala dranahary*] because it provides for us."[28]

Fishers emphasized that marine habitats and marine organisms interacted with them on a long timescale, not just at the moment of harvest. Fishers explained that fishing was inextricably tied to one's past, one's ancestors (*raza*), and one's future or destiny (*anjara*). Similarly, places and activities at sea were tied to their counterparts on land: areas on land and in the ocean had connections, and fishers' behavior on land would influence their experience at sea and vice versa. These beliefs largely align with what anthropologist Philippe Descola (2013) describes as totemism, where there is continuity between both interiority (the internal world of subjectivity and intention) and physicality (the substance and physical constitution) across a wide array of human and nonhuman beings.

Given that the number and size of fish, the habitat of fish and other organisms in the sea, and even the sea itself were bound in a reciprocal relationship with fishers over time. The way fishers talked about marine organisms was infused with emotional markers and agency. For example, fishers would explain that fish and other marine organisms would flee (*milefa*) if they did not feel welcome (*tamana*) in an area. Many fishers believed that noise from motorized boats, or the commotion caused by too many nonmotorized boats, would cause the fish to leave an area. In these accounts, the number of fish one catches or sees was tied not to extraction level but rather to the impact of other human activities on fish emotion. When asked where the fish would go, fishers would respond: deeper water (*lalana/laliky*), calmer zones. For example, a net fisher in southwestern Madagascar who was known for going well beyond the reef crest to catch shark and large fish said, "The fishery isn't depleted. I know the fish are still out there, but they go far out in the water, out there where it is very deep."[29]

Many fishers strongly believed that transgressing taboos (*fady*) or not following custom (*fombafomba*) would decrease marine catch. If fishers transgressed a custom or taboo at sea, it could impact them on land. While fombafomba were collectively recognized and tended to be place-specific, fady could work both at the collective level, across a region or within a village, as well as at the individual level (personal taboos are common). As one fisher in southwestern Madagascar explained in a focus group interview: "There are a lot of taboos here. If someone does something bad, all the things [fish and other organisms] in the ocean will flee [*milefa*]." This sentiment was echoed by fishers I interviewed in northeastern Madagascar, where one fisher explained in similar terms, "If you don't follow customs [*manaraka fomba*] here, the fish will flee," and then again in northwestern Madagascar: "Fishers who don't follow customs, don't get any fish."[30]

From these fishers I learned about an array of individually and collectively held fady and fombafoma (some of these are explored in chapter 4). Of the eighty-six taboos and customs I documented across the three regions, examples ranged widely, including restrictions on speech (for example, in the northeast, fishers were required to say *kasaka*, a type of palm [*Ravenala madagascariensis*], instead of rock (*vato*) when describing landmarks or recounting experiences involving rocks from the day); limits on what one can wear (for example, in the northwest, fishers living in one of the region's large bays should not wear black while fishing); limits on when one can fish (for example, in the northeast, fishers expected to fish on Tuesdays and Thursdays because these days were taboo for working in rice fields); controls on what one harvested (for example, in several areas of the southwest, it was forbidden to harvest sea snakes); restricted areas (for example, in all regions fishing right next to certain sacred rock outcrops, small islands, and forested peninsulas was forbidden); and restrictions on bodily functions (for example, in all regions people mentioned taboos against fishing while menstruating).

When asked what would happen if a fisher transgressed a custom or taboo, answers ranged from shifts in the weather to changes in social relations to the transgressor's death. One fisher from southwestern Madagascar explained that fishers follow custom and respect taboos because if they don't, "the sea surges/waves get big, and it becomes very windy [*be riaky misy tsioky*]." He continued, "It's bad, everyone is impacted." Others stated, "You'll be excluded from the community [*tsy ilongoan'ny fokonolo*]." Yet others sketched more severe ramifications, such as "If you go out in a boat [again], it will sink," or simply, "[The] boat will break." Other bleak outcomes included "The ocean will swallow you up and nobody will be able to find you [*atelin'ny riaky iny tsy hita*]" or, "You'll die in the ocean" or "The spirits will kill you."[31]

Notions of fombafomba and fady (called *faly* in southwestern Malagasy dialects) were closely enmeshed with destiny and the will of the ancestors. Ancestors (*razana/raza*) or "great ancestors" (*razambe*) played an important role in rewarding those who followed customs and taboos and punishing those who didn't. Spirits in the ocean or on land could determine where, when, and what fish were in particular places in the ocean. As other authors have noted, ancestors (*raza*), god (*zanahary/andriamanitra*), and such spirits as *vorombe, doany, helo, angatra/y*, or *lolon-drano* were viewed as the true custodians of the sea (Astuti 1995; Lilette 2006; Muttenzer 2020; Nielssen 2011). These spirits can grant a fisher access to marine organisms, and many fishers ascribed their catch to these spirits either acting in favor of or against them at a particular time.

An understanding of the kinds of reciprocal socionatural relations among fishers, the land and ocean, and marine organisms was largely absent from marine management frameworks initiated and led by conservation organizations in Madagascar. Instead, conservation organization workers who were interviewed were not aware of, or in some cases looked down on, traditional knowledge and Malagasy fishing taboos that earlier formed the basis for local fisheries management and customary marine property (Diver et al. 2019). Furthermore, conservation workers broadly subscribed to a contrasting world-view that positions local resource users as threats to the marine environment.

As I have mentioned in relation to highlander-coastal ethnic tensions, most of the Malagasy people working for governmental and nongovernmental marine conservation organizations were not from coastal regions of Madagascar and instead hailed from cities and inland towns that have greater access to educational opportunities that positioned them well for this work. These ethnic, educational, and political-economic differences meant that most Malagasy conservation workers were trained in and aligned their efforts with Western environmental frameworks. In my conversations with international conservation workers as well as Malagasy fishers, I became aware of a fundamental disconnect in the way conservation organizations and many fishers understood the causes of ecological change and what to do about it. Frank Muttenzer, a cultural anthropologist who has studied Vezo people in Madagascar, also explains that foreign marine conservationists and Vezo fishers have different worldviews about the drivers of fisheries decline and marine ecological change. He shows that these two groups differ greatly in terms of what each considers ethical behavior, or what it means to "act rightly" given socioecological change. Muttenzer (2020, 33) argues that for Western-trained marine conservationists, "acting rightly is essentially a matter of persuading local and global audiences that fishery closures and protected areas are an effective means to manage the coral reef ecosystem," whereas for Vezo fishers acting rightly "entails a lifelong socialization in traditional fishing ways seeped in ritual, magic, spirit worlds, and consumption of marine resources." Vezo fishers, Muttenzer (2020, 89) writes, have a deep "confidence in the environment," meaning that they believe the ocean and reefs will provide for them in a way that "is not commensurable with the [Western] ecosystem view of nature."[32] In my research, this confidence in the environment was present not only with Vezo fishers but also with Betsimisaraka, Antakarana, Sakalava, and Tanalana fishers. For many fishers, adhering to customs, complying with taboos, and performing rituals were tied to a sense of responsibility, or acting right, in terms of both one's social relations and one's duty to the more-than-human world.

Understanding Malagasy fishers' conception of socioecological relations, specifically how their threads of causality differed from those relied on by international conservation organizations, provides a deeper context for why some fishers were skeptical of if not wholeheartedly against MPAs as a fisheries enhancement tool.[33] Moreover, by understanding Malagasy fishers' notions of what drives fish behavior and fish catch, we can start to dig into the potential incongruities between Western-based conservation's use of Elinor Ostrom's autonomous commons governance model and the conflicting cosmology and phenomenological baseline on which fishers' decisions are made. Ultimately, although there might be ways in which following local fombafomba or fady may result in biodiversity protection or sustainable use of marine resources, these shared norms and beliefs that govern fishers' behavior do not map well on to management frameworks with a more mechanistic understanding of human-nature relations and Western-derived beliefs concerning the drivers of ecological change. Imposing the commons, an Ostrom-style common pool resource management regime driven by conservation organizations, thus required a change (or, as Muttenzer might argue, at least the performance of change) in resource users' phenomenological perception of fisheries production and environmental change. Conservation organizations seemed to understand this requirement, given that most meetings and community gatherings at the village level were accompanied by environmental education lessons, plays, or videos explaining the utility of marine reserves and such concepts as overfishing, coral regeneration, and fish population growth. These lessons solidified the notion that local people were the cause as well as the solution to marine environmental problems.

Reframing the Problem as a Step toward Self-Determination

By framing marine degradation as a localized problem amenable to localized solutions, conservation organizations have justified intervention measures focused on the local level. Although some organizations have taken steps toward a more integrative multiscalar approach to conservation, much more can be done. A feminist approach to understanding the drivers of change in the marine environment could shift conservation organizations' focus toward the ultimate instead of the proximate drivers of resource use, to uncover the differences between women's and men's fishing practices and instead uncovering new realms of agency and responsibility across entire systems of production and consumption.

Although conservation practitioners acknowledge that many of the marine resources extracted in Madagascar are folded into commodity chains that span the globe, in interviews they tended to echo the statement of a national-level marine conservation director who stated that working with coastal communities was "where we can get things done" and that working with the government or even internationally concerning trade was "much harder and much slower."[34] In the same vein, the regional marine director of another conservation organization noted that saving marine resources was something that was "urgent, and needs action now," so "waiting for the big bosses at higher levels isn't an option."[35] This framing makes clear that conservation organizations are essentially picking the metaphorical low-hanging fruit by focusing their efforts at the local scale. At this scale, conservation organizations can exert the financial and political power to change people's environmental behavior, which disproportionately impacts women and the past.

By criticizing the scalar arguments deployed to justify implementing MPAs in Madagascar, we can more clearly engage the foundational assumptions embedded in this marine fisheries management strategy. By understanding the assumptions concerning MPAs and their ability to improve catch, we are better able to address the debates and caveats in the Western scientific literature as well as Malagasy fishers' worldviews concerning marine production causality. An alternative approach would be for conservation organizations to acknowledge the nuances in the Western scientific literature concerning MPAs and speak to Malagasy fishers with greater transparency and more accountability. Any given MPA may or may not help improve catch in a given area, depending on a complex and interconnected set of ecological and social relations. Malagasy fishers' phenomenological analysis of these socioecological relations, and specifically the disconnect between many Malagasy fishers' understandings and those of international conservation organizations, explains why some fishers remain skeptical of if not wholeheartedly against MPAs as a fisheries enhancement tool. Although the ecological relevance of some fady and fombafomba may not immediately be apparent to a Western-trained scientist, many taboos underscore the interdependence of marine spaces and terrestrial spaces, the marine environment and people, and a single fisher and all the fishers in an area.

Given the disparate understandings of socioecological relations and drivers of fisheries production, as well as fishers' rights to self-governance, Malagasy fishers should be at the helm of decision-making concerning conservation interventions in Madagascar. The multiplicity of fady and fombafomba, as well as the many ways fishers have been connected to each other, the environment, and actors in distant locales through time, underscores the importance of engaging fishers directly.

Ultimately, collective decision-making across multiple scales of social and political organization is necessary to make marine resource management more equitable and reflective of the values and interests of local marine resource users. Figuring out how to structure this inclusive multiscalar process effectively is extremely difficult. Although the work of Elinor Ostrom provides important scaffolding, the framework falls short in crucial ways concerning power differentials across multiple scales. When one focuses on procedural justice in marine conservation decision-making, what are the stakes of not engaging a feminist approach to conservation?

THREE

Self-Determination

What Counts as Community?

Malagasy understand that they can either make the rules for
themselves or here comes the government with its guns and its
top-down rules . . . and if we [conservation organizations] wanted,
we could go to the government and say, "Make this a marine
protected area" and the government would. But they [Malagasy
fishers] don't want that now, do they!

*— International conservation organization field agent, southwestern
Madagascar, August 1, 2009*

Dozens of small islands dot the coastline of northwestern Madagascar. Men in boats with large triangular sails made of canvas or recycled rice sacks catch the strong winds that emerge most afternoons to fish the reefs and deeper waters for tuna, shrimp, shark, sea cucumbers, and shells. Women, wading in shallow intertidal zones and on reef crests during low tides, glean not only sea cucumbers and shells but also octopuses and shoals of small fish.

In 2010, a portion of this region became part of a marine conservation initiative spearheaded by the Wildlife Conservation Society, an international conservation organization headquartered in New York, in conjunction with Madagascar's Ministry for Environment, Ecology, Oceans and Forests (now the Ministry of Fisheries and the Blue Economy).[1] This area was selected because it boasts some of the most diverse coral populations of the planet as well as nesting sites for marine turtles and key habitat for endangered whale species, dugongs, and the critically endangered sawfish. After a five-year process the Malagasy government officially established several large MPAs in the region in 2015. The Wildlife Conservation Society celebrated this success and "commend[ed] the Malagasy Government for creating [the] three newest marine protected areas and for supporting the United Nations Aichi Targets to protect 10 percent of the world's marine habitats" (WCS 2015).

Although the launch of most of the marine conservation projects included in my research preceded my first visit to the sites, I was present for some of the earliest conversations and meetings concerning WCS's marine conservation initiatives in northwestern Madagascar. In 2010, WCS formally launched the project by inviting representatives from several government ministries, regional governmental representatives, regional tour operators, village chiefs, and presidents of local fishing associations for a three-day workshop in one of the largest cities in the region. The workshop started with a presentation by WCS about the importance of establishing marine protected areas in the region. A middle-aged Malagasy man who had worked for WCS for over a decade gave a PowerPoint presentation detailing the benefits of MPAs, which included increased fish populations, the protection of fisheries from climate change, an increase in tourism, and the overall improvement of people's lives both now and in the future. The presentation advanced MPAs as a panacea for the problems and desires of everyone in the room. Colorful photos of vibrant reefs and fishers with their nets full of fish flashed on the screen while workshop attendees sat in the darkened, air-conditioned room sipping beverages and eating refreshments. The starting point of the workshop, introducing the idea of implementing MPAs for the suite of benefits they would bring to the region, was also its ending point: that a network of MPAs would indeed be established and that this room of stakeholders would ensure that it happened. Thus, even though the strategy for marine conservation—the establishment of MPAs in the region—had been predetermined, the people in the room were told that day that community involvement was key to the implementation of this strategy. The fishers and village representatives invited to the presentation were then asked to help decide where the MPAs would be located and how they should be managed. These so-called stakeholders were given the further task of establishing a set of customary rules, in collaboration with the conservation organization, in order to protect these new MPAs and monitor and enforce the rules.

When I was invited by WCS to attend this workshop, I was excited to observe community-based conservation in practice. I wondered how the international conservation organization would respond to local interests and needs and was eager to learn how such collaborations start. I was surprised to learn, therefore, that it was a foregone conclusion that the project would focus almost exclusively on the establishment of MPAs rather than other forms of marine conservation, including those that take their cues from local fombafomba and fady. I was further surprised that many of the rules pertaining to the MPAs were already set in stone. Although I was initially heartened by the prospect of fishers guiding the location of the boundaries of the MPAs, it became clear that even that task was rife with complex power dynamics that ultimately sidelined certain resource users' opinions.

Who holds the power to claim or negotiate access to marine resources, and what are the methods by which they gain and maintain this power? Despite material and discursive commitments to community-based marine conservation in Madagascar, international conservation organizations' values and ideas permeated all aspects of decision-making. Furthermore, although community-based conservation efforts claimed to represent the whole community, few women reported participating in any aspect of management, and even fewer held positions in local management committees. Women's lack of nominal and effective participation in marine resource management both reduced their decision-making power and prevented them from benefiting from paid management opportunities offered by the conservation organizations. In addition to gendered disparities in participation, wealth and education also influenced who participated in marine resource management. Ultimately, an exploration of the micropolitics of community-based conservation helps us understand the drivers as well as the stakes of these inequities. This examination also underscores the importance of proactively addressing potential resistance and backlash to a more feminist, gender-inclusive approach to conservation.

During the second morning of the workshop in northwestern Madagascar, large flip charts were brought into the room and markers were passed around. Attendees were split into the subregions they represented and were asked to draw key marine features in their area and mark where they thought the borders of an MPA should be located. A representative from WCS verbally listed features that each group should consider, such as where fish tend to aggregate, turtles lay eggs, and dugongs have been seen, as well as the location of islands, reefs, and mangroves. This list, focusing on elements key to biodiversity, was one of the many ways the conservation organization shaped what was valuable or important to the seemingly collaborative mapping process. Although the list reflected the core objectives of WCS and other conservation organizations working in Madagascar—preserving biodiversity and fragile ecosystems—it privileged those objectives over other ecological or social elements of the marine environment of value to fishers and other marine resource users.

I sat with one subregion mapping group composed of twelve men and two women, representing a mixture of fishers, local associations, a village president, tour operators, and district and regional government representatives. The two women in the group, one a representative from the regional tourism office and the other an assistant to the district representative, did not speak, nor were they called on to speak during the three-hour discussion and mapping. This gender dynamic was just one element of the power differentials on display during the meeting. I slowly came to understand that there was a careful and calculated dance between the conservation organization running the workshop and the variety of other stakeholders in the room. Stakeholders quickly learned that there were certain steps they were expected to take, gestures they were supposed to make that followed the lead of the conservation organization. Most of the conservation organization agents were based in the capital city and were either white foreigners or Malagasy individuals from the politically and economically dominant highland ethnic groups in Madagascar, the Merina, whereas the various other stakeholders in the room were from the northwestern region and were ethnically either Antakarana or Sakalava, ethnicities that generally are not as politically and economically powerful highlander ethnicities.[2] These ethnic-based hierarchies were heightened by the fact that WCS funded the workshop, provided lodging for all attendees (some of whom came in from neighboring islands and remote coastal villages), and paid local attendees indemnities for the days that they traveled to and attended the workshop (more on this below). There were also great disparities in terms of formal education and Western scientific literacy between small-scale fishers attending the meeting and conservation-oriented governmental and nongovernmental representatives. During the meeting, these disparities resulted in deference to, as one fisher who attended explained, "people who are knowledgeable" (*olo mahay*) or "people who know science" (*olo mahay siansa*). The conservation organization relied on science, specifically the research of marine biologists who had conducted ecological surveys in the region, to convince local stakeholders of the importance of establishing MPAs in the region. Western scientific literacy, as well as racial, ethnic, and gendered hierarchies, tacitly permeated the wide variety of decisions that were made during the workshop.

For example, to start the mapping exercise, the president from a village on an island of great interest to WCS was invited by the WCS marine director running the workshop that day to draw the contours of key marine features in the region. The village president, a slight man dressed in a beige and brown wrap and slacks, was a well-respected elder and a renowned net fisher from one of the larger villages on the island. When I first met him outside the workshop, he was relaxed and confident. He explained that he was born and raised in the region and had sailed with strong winds from his village to the city for the workshop the day before. Inside the workshop, he seemed uneasy as he approached the flip chart to draw the area he knew so well. Using a thick black pen, he slowly outlined the major contours of islands and bays of the region. After the village president sat down, two tall white men, tour operators who represented luxury hotels in the region, stood up unprompted one after the other and used blue pens to add several marks to the map. These marks represented rock outcroppings and dive sites on which their businesses relied. A district government representative, a Malagasy man with a booming deep voice, then asked the group if they had included all the sea turtle egg-laying sites in their region. He glanced sideways at the village president as he asked the question. The village president then added another few marks to the map before sitting down again. Then, before the group started discussing where the MPA boundaries should be, a

Malagasy marine biologist, who had recently conducted dive surveys for WCS in the area, pointed to four spots on the map containing high levels of marine species diversity and intact coral. While the biologist was pointing to the map, one of the tour operators chimed in, saying that these spots would serve the interests of his clients who want to see underwater biodiversity when diving in the area. Then a thick red marker was handed to the village president. The village president slowly got up from his chair again and stood beside the flip chart, waiting for guidance. He twisted the top of the pen, uneasily looking first at the map and then out to the group seated in a semicircle facing the chart and to the marine biologist, who now stood behind the semicircle. The village president tentatively put a red dot on the four locations the marine biologist had touched just moments before. Several people in the group snickered, and one of the regional government representatives laughed and told the village president that the MPA would have to be larger than those small dots. One of the tour operators proposed that the MPA be large enough to encompass all four dots, and several people in the group nodded in agreement. The village president, with the encouragement of the group, then drew a thick red line around a large area encompassing all four dots. Months later, this map would be presented, along with several other maps created during the same workshop, to international funders to demonstrate WCS's community-based approach to establishing these new MPAs. Four years later, this site would be celebrated as one of the "first three marine protected areas in the country that were developed with, and which will be managed in collaboration with, the local community," which "[supports] the United Nations Aichi Targets to protect 10 percent of the world's marine habitats," including "important nesting sites for marine turtles and critical habitats for diverse, abundant, and endangered cetacean populations, including humpback whales, blue whales, sperm whales, and beaked whales" (WCS 2015).

Several months after this meeting, while sitting in the small house of the village president, I learned that the large area he had outlined in red marker would in fact be quadrupled in size, encompassing the entire large island on which he and approximately two thousand others live. Within this large area, some fishing was allowed; however, new restrictions on gear type and harvest method had been introduced, with fines or possible jailtime for in-fractions. I also learned that an area to the east of his village, now considered one of the numerous small no-take zones within the new MPA, included some of the few shallow regions accessible on foot where fishers, mostly women and poorer fishers, harvested marine organisms.

In a conversation with a WCS agent in the capital city shortly after my visit with the village president, I asked why the MPA had expanded so dramatically in size from the maps made at the workshop; he replied that the large area "had been part of the plan for a long time."[3] The agent then explained that the mapping exercise people did at the meeting was really focused on establish-ing the no-take zones. When I explained that during the workshop it wasn't clear that the whole region would become an MPA, he said that he could have emphasized it more but that he didn't think that the limits of the larger MPA were as important as the no-take zones to local fishers. When I asked specifically about the no-take zone in the shallow area where women fish, he said that is where "the community" (*fokonolona*) decided to put the no-take zone so "it should not be a problem" (*tokony tsisy problema*).

The micropolitics on display at the workshop in northwestern Madagas-car illustrate many of the gendered and ethnoracial dynamics at play at mul-tiple levels of social organization—from negotiations at international conservation conferences to debates within households. What I learned while observing community conservation in practice was that fishing com-munities, along with regional governmental representatives and tour opera-tors, were in fact involved in some meaningful ways with the establishment of the new marine conservation project occurring in their region: they were allowed to share their opinions concerning the location of and rules govern-ing the MPAs. However, in the course of the first regional workshop and several other village-level workshops, I observed how, overall, fishing com-munity interests were at times relegated to footnotes in a broader plan. Fur-thermore, decision-making related to the plan involved only a small subset of the community. There were deep gendered disparities in both nominal and effective participation in these workshops. As in the initial workshop, few women were invited to or felt welcomed to attend later meetings where decisions were made concerning where, when, and how marine resources could be used. Thus, even though nearly everyone from a fishing community would show up to initial village-based meetings, those involved with decision-making constituted only a handful of community members and were almost entirely male. These local representatives of coastal villages were invited to provide feedback concerning where the MPAs would be; however, they were not invited to share their ideas about whether the MPA should exist in their area. Similarly, local representatives were invited to add to a list of resource use rules labeled "local customary laws"; however, the list contained many nonnegotiable resource use rules that the Malagasy government required and marine conservation organizations wanted.

One theme that permeates feminist scholarship is the importance of having marginalized identities represented in decision-making in order to shift outcomes for structurally marginalized groups. Ecofeminist scholars such as Silvia Federici, Vandana Shiva, and Carolyn Merchant underscore how the marginalization of women in society was foundational to the rise of capitalism and that ongoing enclosure and degradation of the commons will occur unabated until we restore reciprocity and care across human and nonhuman systems—in other words, re-create the commons. As a corollary, these scholars emphasize that central to the process of restoring the commons is reestablishing agency and self-determination for groups defined and then marginalized by colonial and neocolonial capitalist enclosure, such as women.[4] In *Reenchanting the World: Feminism and the Politics of the Commons* (2018), Federici argues that the chronic underrepresentation of women, poorer communities, and Indigenous and communities of color in environmental and political economic decision-making specifically requires a deep commitment to reparations, coalition building across identity and geographic boundaries, and learning from the communities that have managed to keep their commons intact.

How do gender, race, and class influence participation in community-based conservation projects? What are the stakes of a lack of participation along gendered, raced and classed lines? How are the benefits from these projects understood locally, and who is able to secure these benefits? In this chapter I answer these questions, highlighting both the outcome of class and gender-neutral conservation planning and implementation and what a more feminist approach to conservation might entail. More specifically, I center on two core ethics that underpin feminist conservation: distributive and procedural justice. Focusing on procedural justice, I analyze who had access to decision-making power as well as the frameworks conservation organizations used to legitimize or delegitimize people's participation. With regard to distributive justice, I examine what benefits from the conservation project were deemed valuable to local resource users and who was able to secure these benefits.

The mutually constitutive nature of one's identity and one's struggle over resource use as outlined in chapter 1 helps to de-essentialize and destabilize gender and racial categories. However, all survey analyses displayed in this book, and most interview descriptions provided, illustrate a simple male-female binary. The ethnographic work I conducted in several sites across all three regions showed me that even though no survey respondents selected the "other" category for gender, there were transgender and gender-variant individuals among those surveyed.[5] In both the southwest and the northeast, I cooked, fished, and fetched water with individuals who were labeled by other community members but also labeled themselves *sarin'ampela/sarimbavy* and *sarindahy*. *Sarin'ampela* (southwestern dialect) and *sarimbavy* (used in northwestern and northeastern dialects), meaning "image of a woman," and *sarindahy*, meaning "image of a man," are gender-nonconforming individuals who are either same-sex desiring and/or gender-expansive persons (Palmer 2019). Both sarin'ampela/sarimbavy and sarindahy performed their gender through marine resource use. I went fishing on foot and fried fish frequently with Teliny, a sarin'ampela woman in southwestern Madagascar. I learned that Teliny started fishing on foot as a child and continued even when some of the boys her age (around ten years old) started also fishing from boats. One afternoon while frying fish she explained that "my [male] partner likes when I fish on foot—it's a woman's livelihood here [*fiveloman'po ampela*]. Life is hard and one can fetch a high price for marine products [*letaky vokatry andriake*]."[6] Similarly, Rivike, a sarindahy I interviewed in southwestern Madagascar, was known in his village for being a good fisher because he was able to dive deep into the water to set nets or skin dive for sea cucumbers. Rivike also emphasized fishing as an assertion of his gender identity: "All Vezo dare/struggle with the ocean, but only men dare to dive [*lehilahy avao mahasaky maniriky*]."[7] It was through this daring that Rivike performed masculinity, which in turn afforded him access to a different array of deeper-dwelling marine resources.

Teliny and Rivike's stories underscore how gendered identities are both performed and formed by resource use practices. Gender performance is thus also informed and formed by changes to marine property regimes. The introduction of MPAs into fishing regions across the island, and the maligning of fishing on foot, shaped fishing practices and hence shaped what it means to be female, male, sarin'ampela/sarimbavy, and sarindahy.

A feminist approach to understanding identity as something that both shapes and is shaped by negotiations over natural resource use highlights the importance of new property regimes established through MPAs and marine conservation efforts across Madagascar. It is the complex suite of property relations and access mechanisms that determines who receives the benefits and who receives the burdens of these interventions. This chapter explores how rights and access to marine resources define and are defined by social stratifications and thus shape the distribution of benefits and burdens of conservation decisions.

Gendering Participation

In the early 1990s, multiple high-level international agreements provided both rhetorical and institutional support for integrating social justice and the advancement of the rights of Indigenous people into conservation and resource management. The United Nations declared 1992 as the International Year for the World's Indigenous Peoples and it was the year the Rio Declaration on Environment and Development asserted the importance of granting those who are impacted by environmental issues "the opportunity to participate in decision-making processes" (Rio Declaration, Principle 10). Accompanying this increased recognition of Indigenous rights was a commitment to greater gender equity. Rio's principles 20 and 22 justified the greater participation of both women and Indigenous communities in environmental management with an efficacy rationale: because women and Indigenous people already play a vital role in management, their increased inclusion in decision-making will enhance the efficacy of sustainability programs. Principle 20 states: "Women have a vital role in environmental management and development. Their full participation is therefore essential to achieve sustainable development." Similarly, Principle 22 states: "Indigenous people and their communities and other local communities have a vital role in environmental management and development because of their knowledge and traditional practices. States should recognize and duly support their identity, culture and interests and enable their effective participation in the achievement of sustainable development."

Although these marginalized identities were framed in the United Nations documents as instruments to achieve development outcomes, the recognition that Indigenous people and women have knowledge and deserve a seat at the decision-making table was an achievement. These clauses were hard-won, advanced by women's organizations and Indigenous groups in the twenty years between the United Nations Conference on the Human Environment in 1972 and the United Nations Conference on Environment and Development in 1992 (Clark, Friedman, and Hochstetler 1998; Strydom 2013).

While activists were advocating for resource rights, in the late 1980s and early 1990s scholars started to address the failure of top-down conservation, documenting the variety of problems associated with the colonially rooted approach to conservation while also advocating for greater participation of local resource users, including Indigenous groups and women (Brosius, Tsing, and Zerner 2005; Meinzen-Dick and Zwarteveen 2001). As discussed in chapter 1, Elinor Ostrom's ideas began to shape how conservation practitioners thought about their management practices. In *Governing the Commons* and subsequent work, Ostrom argued that participation is the fulcrum on which collective management of common pool resources pivots. It is represented in both the first and third design principles Ostrom (1990, 90) articulated in her widely cited eight design principles for a successful CPR governance regime: "Individuals or households who have rights to withdraw resource units from the CPR are clearly defined," and "Most individuals affected by the operational rules can participate in modifying the operational rules." These principles of participation stem from an intuitive idea that if most people participate in rule-making, then most people will follow the rules.

The word *most* that Ostrom inserts into her third design principle leaves room for an analysis of power. *Most* could indicate that a majority has been achieved and that this majority either convinces or forces a minority to acquiesce or at least not disrupt the values and management decisions of the majority. However, in practice, *most* is primarily a measure of power, not numbers. Understanding how power works across different scales as well as within a community uncovers a much more complex picture of how natural resource problems are framed and who gets to make decisions concerning these problems. In my research on marine resource management in Madagascar, although women constituted half the individuals in a community, they were seldom represented in decision-making. In my interviews with conservation organization agents as well as with male fishers representing the community on local management committees, they assumed that women's needs and interests were subsumed under general community needs and interests. Similarly, fishers might make up a majority of residents in a coastal area, but governmental and nongovernmental organizations with clear mandates, and a relative abundance of financial and technical resources, carried immense political power.

Given numerous commitments made by Malagasy presidents at international meetings to expand the total marine area under protection and improve resource management (for example, the Durban Vision, the Aichi Commitment), conservation organizations understand that it is a matter of how, not whether, marine conservation projects come to fruition. International conservation organizations thus rhetorically position themselves as advocates for local resource users, using the specter of top-down government-operated conservation projects to compel local resource users to comply with their more community-friendly, decentralized conservation projects.

In interviews with conservation agents, one assumption repeatedly articulated was that conservation organizations know best how to manage marine resources and thus know what management interventions best serve coastal communities. This assumption was accompanied by an incongruous assertion, also articulated in multiple interviews with conservation agents, that conservation organizations were merely on the sidelines of otherwise community-led projects. Common expressions were that conservation organizations were simply "motivators," "scientific advisers," or "technical advisers" to fishing communities.[8]

The conservationists' assumption of knowing best helps to explain the deficit of input from local resource users and women. As other scholars have articulated, community-based conservation following an Ostrom model frequently fails to truly enfranchise local populations or to shift the terms on which power is negotiated among the state, nongovernmental organizations, and resource users and between genders within a community (Borrini-Feyerabend and Tarnowski 2005; Kellert et al. 2000; Meinzen-Dick and Zwarteveen 2001; Ribot 1999; Robbins 2020; Saito-Jensen, Nathan, and Treue 2010; West 2006). This line of argument asserts that while local communities might have de jure control over resources, de facto power remains in the hands of the government and nongovernmental organizations (Campbell 2002).

Since the early 2000s, organizations such as World Wildlife Fund, Wildlife Conservation Society, Conservation International, and Blue Ventures have been at the discursive and organizational helm of marine conservation in Madagascar. These organizations helped to codify and fund the vast majority of marine conservation projects across the country, and they all worked within a community-based conservation model, a model that has a distinct and hard-won history, as described earlier. Across all sites included in my research, these organizations influenced every aspect of marine conservation, including establishing the size and location of each MPA, determining how and whether local representatives were involved with the project, funding educational and organizational meetings, and guiding local representatives to establish the rules and regulations of both temporary and permanent MPAs. Each of the nineteen villages included in my research on marine projects had worked with from one to three international conservation organizations and one governmental organization.

Each village had one or two village-based conservation-oriented associations formed through a mixture of recruitment by the conservation organizations and self-selection. The names of these associations varied from place to place, sometimes simply called the association of the village, sometimes a "fishing association" (*fikambanana panjono/piandriaky*), or else referred to as the conservation organization's (WWF, WCS, CI, or BV) association. Those recruited tended to be elected officials such as village presidents and vice presidents or individuals who had worked with governmental or nongovernmental development projects in the past. Development initiatives focusing on building infrastructure such as wells, schools, and irrigation or new projects related to microfinance or agricultural improvement are common in small villages across Madagascar. These initiatives often operated as the institutional predecessors to conservation projects, influencing who was likely to be involved and which villagers were associated with working with outsiders. Elected officials as well as individuals active in previous governmental and nongovernmental projects tended to be older men and some of the wealthier and more literate individuals of the village.[9]

International conservation organizations asked these initial recruits to get others to join the association. In village-wide meetings, conservation organizations would also encourage people to join. Those who self-selected after the initial stage tended to be either family members or close friends of those initially recruited, individuals interested in building relations with outsiders, or people who thought the project aligned with their interests. Often, once a conservation association filled primarily by men was established, the sponsoring organization would then establish a women's association. Although women's associations were initiated by conservation organizations, in name and mission they were not explicitly conservation oriented. Instead, as elaborated below, the women's associations were most frequently tasked with hosting international conservation agents and other notables (for example, mayors, representatives from environmental ministries of the government); thus women cooked, cleaned, and even danced and sang to entertain conservation agents and governmental representatives involved in conservation projects.

International conservation organization agents then either hand-picked individuals from the local associations or had people self-nominate to serve on village-level and regional-level management committees.

The members these local association were expected to come to all village-wide meetings that the conservation organization held, to participate in environmental education initiatives, and to monitor marine resource use rules. The management committee, however, was the only one tasked specifically with decision-making and enforcement. Most decisions made by the management committee were announced at meetings open to all villagers, and in theory, decisions were contestable. However, I neither witnessed nor heard of any decision made by a management committee that was overturned at a village-level meeting.

How then did the process of recruiting, appointing, and self-selection for village associations and committees influence the gender of representation in these committees? Overall, my research revealed a lack of both nominal (total number) and effective (influence on decision-making) participation of women in all village-based associations and management committees. A clear imbalance in women's participation was shown by both participant observation, such as at the workshop described at the start of this chapter, and a survey conducted across nineteen villages associated with eight marine protected areas. The dearth of women involved in marine resource management was apparent across all aspects of management.

The survey asked if people had worked in any capacity with conservation managers; people were also asked if they had specifically engaged in monitoring, enforcement, or decision-making. Across all research sites, more than 30 percent of men reported that they participated in any aspect of conservation management, as opposed to fewer than 7 percent of women ($p<0.001$). This approximately fourfold difference widens to a nearly seventeenfold difference across all research sites when comparing women's (0.8 percent) and men's (14.8 percent) involvement in decision-making process ($p<0.001$) (Baker-Médard 2017). Thus, although women participated in management at a much lower level than men across all management categories, the disparity was most pronounced in decision-making. This imbalance is particularly significant because, even though all forms of management (notably monitoring, decision-making, and enforcement) are mentioned in Ostrom's eight CPR design principles, decision-making is the foundation on which the others are based.

Women were certainly present at village meetings where decisions were shared; however, few spoke up in these public forums against decisions that had been made. Women were not barred from joining village-based management committees; however, very few joined. Whole communities were invited to help monitor and enforce the rules of the MPAs; however, a miniscule proportion of women surveyed reported participating in these activities.

The survey results on women's participation were comparable to the numbers of women whose names were written down as official participants in local management committees. For example, in the northeast, where I interviewed representatives of six local management committees, among a total of fifty-four members (nine members per committee), just three women held rank in these committees. One was vice president of a committee, and two held the title "second secretary."

Each individual surveyed was also asked an open-ended question about why they did or did not participate (table 2). These responses varied by gender. Women's most commonly stated reason for not participating, comprising a quarter of the responses, was that they, as women, were not wanted (*tsy mila ampela/viavy*) or allowed (*tsy mahazo ty ampela/viavy*) by the managers to participate. About 15 percent of women said they did not know how, or did not know enough, to be involved. This second most common response for women was the top reason (22 percent) men provided for why they did not participate. In fact the third, fourth, and fifth categories for why women did not participate in the marine conservation project were the second, third and fourth categories, respectively, for men. Yet of all the men surveyed, not one replied that they did not participate because of their gender.

Illiteracy (*tsy mahay taratasy*) was a subset of the responses within the broader category of "I don't know how / don't know enough." Both women and men reported illiteracy as a rationale for not participating; of all individuals reporting illiteracy as their rationale, however, a larger percentage of this group was men (58.3 percent) versus women (41.6 percent). This result stands in contrast to a national average of more women (32 percent) than men (25 percent) being illiterate (UN Women Count 2019). The national trend parallels survey results showing that across all research sites men had more years of formal education than women (5.8 versus 4.2 years, respectively).

***Table* 2.** Top Five responses from self-identified women concerning why they do or do not participate in marine conservation projects

---

Panel A. Why I do not participate in marine conservation projects (*n*=320)

They [conservation organizations] do not want women to participate	26.5%
I don't know enough / I don't know how to be a manager	15.3%
The MPA is bad/doesn't work	9.4%
I wasn't selected/chosen	8.4%
I don't care about the project	5.0%

Panel B. Why I participate in marine conservation projects (*n*=24)

I am involved in the Women's Association	37.5%
My husband/family member participates in management	20.8%
I am part of the community	8.3%
The MPA is good/I like the project	8.3%
I feel obliged/forced	4.2%

Notes: Respondents' answers sometimes applied to more than one category; participants who were *sarindahy* or *sarimbavy* chose to identify along the gender binary.

People's explanations of why they did or did not participate in the marine conservation project elucidate the difference between rights and ability, as well as why this distinction matters in terms of community involvement in common pool resource management. Although technically everyone in each village where a marine conservation project occurred had the right to participate, potentially fulfilling Ostrom's principle (1990, 90) that "most individuals affected by the operational rules can participate in modifying the operational rules," many women did not believe that they had the *ability* to participate because they felt that their presence would not be welcome.[10] Women thus understood not only that they should follow the rules established by the conservation committees but also that they themselves would not be making the rules. This point illustrates the importance of qualifying the words *most* and *can* in Ostrom's principle in terms of intracommunity power dynamics.

Intersecting Inequities: Hierarchies of Class and Education in Local Participation

In a statistical analysis of participation rates across multiple social stratifications, gender was the strongest determinant of whether an individual participated in marine resource management across all participation types (table 3). Each individual was asked who the MPA managers were, whether they work/ed with or help/helped (*miaramiasa na manampy*) these managers, and if they worked or helped at any point in any capacity in the marine conservation project. Next, regardless of the answer to the first question, individuals were asked three questions concerning whether they had ever monitored, made decisions regarding, or enforced rules related to the marine conservation project in their area. If the individual replied yes to any of these four questions, the individual was counted as a participant.

Intersecting and often overlapping factors, including an individual's wealth, educational status, and age, also influenced participation across certain categories. The analysis of intracommunity differences helps us to dig below the surface of idealized CPR regimes. How and why these factors influenced participation enriches our understanding of the differences that exist within seemingly cohesive and homogenous communities.

The more politically weighty participation categories such as decision-making and enforcement were primarily filled by older, more educated, and wealthier men. These findings show that not only was sexism was operating within conservation planning and implementation but so was classism, educational elitism, and ageism. Analyzing various aspects of social stratification separately is important; however, it is perhaps even more important to understand how these factors overlap and intersect. Gender does not operate independently from class, education, and age categories. As with formal educational attainment and wealth, numerous studies show that women, especially widowed or single women, are overrepresented in low socioeconomic categories (Bradshaw, Chant, and Linneker 2017; Filmer 2020). In general, extreme poverty across Madagascar is higher among female-headed households in which women are either widowed (40 percent) or separated (34 percent) and has worsened in the past decade (World Bank

Table 3. Multivariate analysis looking at the effect of wealth, gender, education, and age on four conservation participation categories

	Dependent Variables			
	Involvement	Monitoring	Decision-making	Enforcement
Wealth	0.426**	0.078	0.342	0.411*
	(0.249, 0.603)	(−0.122, 0.277)	(0.130, 0.555)	(0.179, 0.643)
Gender	1.942***	2.357***	1.417***	1.641***
	(1.735, 2.150)	(2.093, 2.621)	(1.153, 1.682)	(1.334, 1.947)
Education	0.084**	0.043	0.072*	0.082*
	(0.051, 0.118)	(0.005, 0.081)	(0.032, 0.111)	(0.039, 0.124)
Age	−0.003	−0.011	0.032***	0.027***
	(−0.011, 0.005)	(−0.021, −0.002)	(0.022, 0.041)	(0.017, 0.037)

Notes: Statistical significance: *$p<0.1$, **$p<0.05$, ***$p<0.01$. Best fitting model uses a GLM framework with a Gaussian error structure. Independent variables directions: wealth (higher scores on the wealth index), gender (male), education (higher number of years of formal education), and age (higher age). Dependent variables include (a) involvement in any capacity with the conservation project, (b) involvement specifically in monitoring fisher behavior, (c) involvement specifically in decision-making regarding marine resource management, and (d) involvement in enforcing rules. The higher the factor loading (number above each parentheses), the stronger the effect on participation.

2014). Women's earnings are consistently lower than those of men across all classes, educational levels, and ages. Additionally, as noted above, literacy rates are significantly lower for women than men, as is the total years of formal education.

In my survey, the lowest-wealth category intersected with gender in important ways, given that women were some of the poorest in the community. Informants' wealth was scored based on the assets they possessed.[11] The phrase "I wasn't chosen to participate" (*tsy voatingy/voafidy*) was one of the most common responses in the lowest-wealth quintile to this open-ended survey question, along with variations on "I am not knowledgeable" or "I am not literate" (*tsy mahay taratasy*). Literacy was not explicitly stated as a prerequisite for MPA involvement. As marine conservation organization agents emphasized in semistructured interviews, local people could get involved in a variety of ways that did not require the ability to read or write, such as helping to decide marine resource use rules, weighing in on the location and size of no-take zones, monitoring resource use, or helping to determine possible punishments for transgressors.[12] That said, responses related to lack of literacy reflected what individuals with the lowest wealth scores perceived as the skills valued or required by the organizations helping to implement marine conservation projects. This finding aligned with trends that emerged from the survey analysis in relation to educational attainment and participation rates. Those who achieved higher levels of formal education participated in marine resource management at higher rates than those with lower levels of formal education.[13]

Last, individuals with the lowest wealth scores also emphasized the importance of their relative poverty in shaping why they did not participate in marine resource management. Identity-related responses from people with the lowest wealth scores included such phrases as "I am not wealthy" (*tsy manandraha*), "I'm insignificant" (*madiniky zaho*), and "They only want important people" (*mila olobe na olo mahay avao*). These responses align with other studies showing a strong relation between personal wealth and social status or political standing (Berg-Schlosser and Kersting 2003; Narayan and Pritchett 1999), and they mirrored women's dominant response for why they did not participate in the conservation project.

Rights versus Abilities: Examining the Underlying Drivers of Disparities

What are the causes of this classed and gendered hierarchy of participation in resource management across all research sites? And what did conservation agents think of these trends? Although women and poorer individuals had the right to participate in any and all aspects of conservation management, including in decision-making, their gender, age or lack of wealth—or all—hindered their participation. The line between "not supposed to" and "not allowed to" was blurred for most of these individuals.

When conservation organization agents who worked at the village level were asked about gender-, educational age and class-based imbalances in MPA management, they often replied that the disparity wasn't intentional, instead emphasizing that they worked primarily with established village leaders. Interestingly, the conservation organization representatives working directly with the communities included in this research showed a similar gender imbalance: nearly all the field-based agents (total of thirty-one of thirty-two agents across the nineteen villages) were Malagasy men, with the exception of one Malagasy woman who worked in southwestern Madagascar. When asked specifically about the lack of women's participation in community-management committees, a common response was that they were careful to work within "local norms." When asked why they didn't push back against local norms, the agents provided a variety of answers ranging from gendered stereotypes to assertions such as "women work less in the ocean than men," and the idea that it is easier to work with men than women because "men are more direct and can make decisions quickly."[4]

An exploration of some of these responses by agents reveals underlying drivers of the disparity in participation. The assertion that women work less in the ocean can be assessed in two ways: how many women fish and how often they fish. Roughly 40 percent (39.5 percent across all research sites, $n=489$) of women reported that they fished, compared to 79 percent of men ($n=461$). An additional 8 percent of the women who said they didn't fish reported that they had fished in the past. Thus, one confounding factor in these data is that conservation intervention itself, as described in earlier chapters, contributed to women exiting the fishery; if a woman is no longer able to fish because her fishing habitat is located in a no-take zone, it is reasonable to assume that she will be less likely to participate in marine resource management.

As for fishing frequency, the vast majority of women living in the coastal areas included in this research fished during spring low tides, which average twelve days per month. Some women, however, fished every day. Men by contrast tended to fish either daily or seasonally (several months a year). Ultimately, there was a small but statistically significant difference between how often women (2.97 on a 6-point scale) versus men (3.43) fished across all research sites (see accompanying illustration). Thus, although fewer women fished and fished on average less often than men, women's work in the ocean was significant.

Regarding agents' claims that they worked with established leaders, both women and men have leadership roles in village affairs. Key elders interviewed asserted that men traditionally facilitate village meetings. However, they also stressed that traditionally both men and women had the authority to decide whether a meeting was needed, to call the meeting, and to make decisions during the meeting. Beyond public forums, both historically and currently women undertake village-level leadership. In many cases, though, their leadership is less visible or legible to conservation organizations because it occurs around village wells, in the thatched shade of fish-collecting stations, on woven mats where people braid hair or repair sails, and within every household. The argument that conservation organizations want to work within existing leadership structures reflects a particular leadership ideal, public facing and individually executed, that is legible to these organizations. It also relies on the notions of tradition and custom to shirk responsibility for deeper community engagement.

Working with other forms of leadership would require conservation organizations to have a different way of operating, to find new forms of engagement. This kind of engagement is potentially more time consuming because it necessitates deeper observation and a savviness about the local context. It is necessarily less top-down, instead engaging people in the forums and milieus where a wider range of people express themselves. This was perhaps understood by some conservation agents and expressed through their assertion that men were easier and quicker to work with, illustrating a disturbing form of social path–dependence. Couched in terms of efficiency and tradition, conservation organizations reinforced a patriarchal hierarchy of power in marine resource management. Again, a paradox emerged: the collaborative and community-based conservation paradigm with which

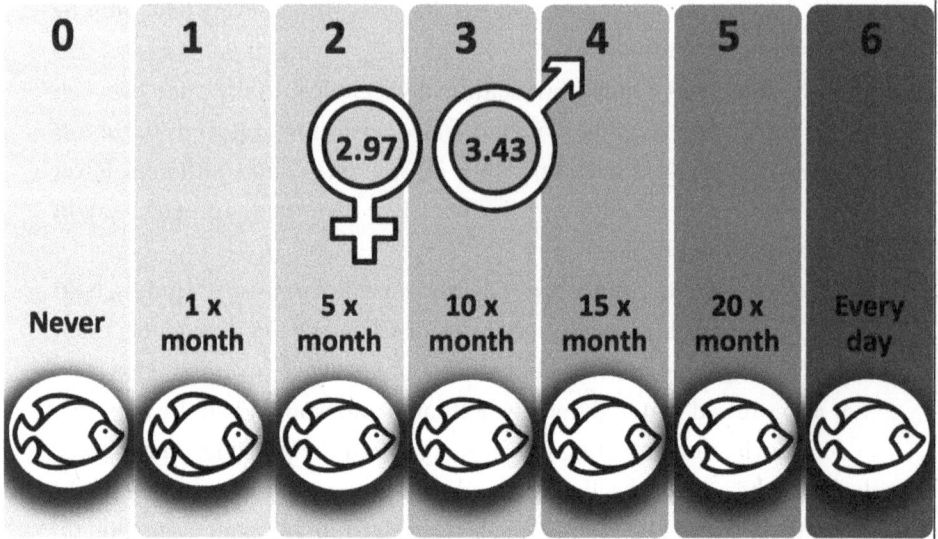

0	1	2	3	4	5	6
Never	1 x month	5 x month	10 x month	15 x month	20 x month	Every day

The average frequency of fishing by men and women across all regions, ranging from never (rank of 0, or "never fish") to every day (rank of 6, or "fish one or more times a day"). The average score for men was 3.43 and for women 2.97.

conservation organizations approached the pursuit of marine management reified gender education and wealth disparities in coastal communities.

What are the stakes of this gender imbalance in marine resource management? In what ways does bias in participation in conservation matter? Although the arguments about why women, the less educated, and the poor were not involved in management of marine resources are important in their own right, the cost of exclusion and nonparticipation raises several broader issues.

First, men and women—and to some degree individuals with varying levels of wealth—use marine resources differently. Gender helps to determine not only *what* is fished but also *where* in the marine system and in particular *how*. The poorest in a community tended either not to own boats or to own very small boats that are not used in deeper waters and to have simpler and cheaper gear (such as a spear instead of a speargun). These gendered and class-based marine resource use practices mean that restrictions concerning what resources are targeted and where restricted zones are placed will affect some fishers more than others. As the quoted vignettes demonstrate, placing no-take zones in an area where primarily women fished hampered women's ability to access marine resources; in extreme cases, placing a no-take zone in women's primary fishing ground forced most women to stop fishing altogether.

Second, due to gendered and classed divisions of labor, there are important differences in individuals' knowledge of the marine environment. Based on how fishers harvest, what they harvest, and where they harvest, they will learn different things about marine organisms' characteristics and behavior as well as seasonal and other temporal changes in the environment. Women described in vivid detail the signs that an octopus was protecting eggs. Because women fish primarily on foot they have deep familiarity with foot-based injuries, most notably potentially lethal wounds from the poisonous stonefish (*Synanceia verrucose*). Women herbalists in coastal villages tend to be the primary healers of this kind of wound. Generally, there are one or two women in each village who specialize in removing the venom from this fish to prevent neuropathy in the foot and leg and even death.

Drawing on a different array of experiences, men described in great detail the difference between how a coral-dominated reef sounds when they press their ear against their oar versus the sounds of a more mixed environment with seagrass, macroalgae, and coral. Male line fishers knew the exact depths at which grouper tended to hang out and which kind of moon would make squid more active. Female net fishers knew the best weather (in terms of rain and wind) and stage of the moon that would bring schooling herring into the shallows near shore. This intimate environmental knowledge is invaluable to strategies and choices in resource management.

To exclude the full range of this knowledge is thus not only unethical but irresponsible and counterproductive. The importance of local knowledge, as nuanced and holistic as possible, is a key rationale underpinning Elinor Ostrom's twin principles of rule-making and representation. The rule-making principle states that there must be "congruence between appropriation and provision rules and local conditions," whereas the representation or "collective choice" principle states that "most individuals affected by the operational rules can participate in modifying the operational rules" (Ostrom 1990, 90). As Ostrom (1990, 90) argues, if rules "restricting time, place, technology, and/or quantity of resource units" are congruous with "local conditions," and if "most" individuals affected by the operational rules can participate in modifying the operational rules, then collectively the rules will be robust enough to serve the collective.[15] A similar argument is advanced by Bina Agarwal, a feminist political economist who has conducted extensive research at the intersection of gender and natural resource governance. Agarwal (2010) found, through several decades of research on women's participation in community forest governance in South and Southeast Asia, that efficiency and effectiveness of forest management generally improved with increased participation of women. Agarwal asserts (2010, 13) that although "women's presence in decision-making may not guarantee outcomes in their favour but it could guarantee them representative voice, and this has both intrinsic worth and instrumental value."

Third, gender, age, and class invariably inform a fisher's values concerning both the marine and social environment. The lack of representation in decision-making of women, young people, and the poorest in a community means that their priorities and interests are not adequately considered when deciding marine resource rules. Thus, representation at its core is a matter not only of whose livelihoods are protected but also of whose values are upheld and whose are devalued or suppressed. These values relate not only to the marine world but also to life on land. As shown in the previous chapter, women bring more of their catch home for consumption. A lack of representation in marine resource management may reduce marine resource access, ultimately affecting how much there is to eat at home.

Following the Rio Declaration on Environment and Development and the trend of gender mainstreaming in conservation in the early 2000s, international conservation organizations worldwide have committed to advancing social justice through their institutions and programming. These social justice commitments, generally codified in policy statements published on their websites, have specific sections on gender equity. For example, WWF's gender policy "ensure[s] that WWF's conservation policies, programmes and activities benefit women and men equally and contribute to gender equity" (WWF 2011, 1). Similarly, Conservation International's gender policy document, created in 2012, states that CI will "actively work to incorporate gender issues and anticipate gender-related outcomes in design and implementation phases [of their programs]" (CI 2019, 4). For its part, WCS put out a report on gender dynamics in marine fisheries, focusing on "fish-dependent coastal communities" to "identify opportunities to improve fisheries management through the engagement, empowerment, and leadership of women in fisheries around the globe" (Matthews et al. 2012, 4). All three organizations are also part of a larger initiative launched in 2009 called the Conservation Initiative on Human Rights, or CIHR, which comprises seven of the largest international conservation organizations in the world.[16] According to the initiative's website, these organizations believed that "by working collectively, [they] could better advance [their] work to promote the positive links between conservation and rights of people to secure their livelihoods, enjoy healthy and productive environments and live with dignity" (CIHR 2020). The CIHR published multiple statements and best practices worksheets in the early 2010s dedicated specifically to gender equity. Within these policy statements, worksheets, and reports reference is frequently made to the importance of socioeconomic status intersecting with gender and also as an "important social and cultural characteristic" in and of itself (CI 2019, 5). These organizations clearly recognize the moral and ethical importance of equity along gendered and, to some extent, classed lines. Unfortunately these organizations inadvertently continue to perpetuate the very problem they have so clearly identified.[17]

Although many women and some of the poorest in a community were very upset by shifts in access to marine resources, one complaint I commonly heard centered on something I had initially dismissed: per diems, daily allowances or indemnities one receives for both traveling and participating in workshops, meetings, and conferences organized by conservation organizations. Over several years of observation and conversations with those who did and didn't receive per diems, I came to understand why per diems were so salient: they were immediate, tangible, and conferred on an individual. Whereas many of the negative outcomes described in these pages occurred slowly with planning and codification over months or years and were collectively experienced (by women or by the poorest in a community), failure to receive per diems was immediate and obvious to people. How did the fraught deployment of per diems in marine conservation efforts perpetuate gendered and classed inequality?

Why Participate: Benefits and Patronage Politics

The success of community-based conservation—and, many scholars argue, any conservation—requires interest in and participation from local resource–dependent communities (Andrade and Rhodes 2012; Cetas and Yasué 2017; Soliku and Schraml 2018). Here I explore what people shared with me in casual conservations about why they chose to participate in marine resource management.

In conservation literature, the term *buy-in* most commonly means commitment to a project based on a belief in the rationale and/or moral grounds of that project (Agardy 1994; Ban et al. 2009; Berkes 2007; Buchan 2003; Cooper et al. 2007; Lele et al. 2010). In interviews with directors of three of the four key marine conservation organizations included in my research, interviewees discussed the importance of buy-in in relation to the start of each conservation project.[18] The French word *l'adhésion* was used frequently in reference to the notion of local buy-in, along with such Malagasy phrases as "mandresy lahatra" (to convince or win over) and "mba manaiky" or "mba hifanaraka" (to make agree). As one director put it, "If local people aren't convinced [*resy lahatra*] [about the merits of the project], then the project will not work." Following a similar line, another director said that marine fishers should realize that they have a "moral obligation" (*obligation morale*) to participate in marine conservation for future generations (*amin'ny taranaka ho avy*). The rationales these directors advanced assumed that community members would make ethical judgments about the common or "greater" good.[19]

Political ecologist Paige West's foundational book *Conservation Is Our Government Now* (2006), underscores the fundamental flaw in Western conservation logic that assumes local people will naturally make pro-conservation decisions if they are simply taught the value of biodiversity as an economic resource. Through her deep ethnographic exploration of the relations between an international conservation organization and the Gimi of Papua New Guinea who lived next to a new conservation area, West reveals that Gimi assumed that by sharing their food, labor, land, and friendship with conservation organization agents, they would reciprocally be provided medicine, new technology, school funding, and other materials associated with Western development, hence the title of West's book. West (2006, 44) notes that many Gimi viewed attending conservation project meetings "as forming the basis for what they expected to be long-term social relations with outsiders who would help them access goods and services in exchange for what was being called conservation."

This fundamental disconnect regarding motivation, trust, and reciprocity between the conservation organization and local resource users is an important element of the fraught understanding of participation in marine conservation in Madagascar.

At the outset of my research, I imagined that those who agreed to participate in marine conservation perceived the merit of the overall project and had a strong sense of obligation to their community and future generations. Through observation, interviews, and analysis of survey responses, however, I learned a different story. In particular, semistructured interviews illuminated the benefits people obtained from the marine conservation project. In initial interviews with individuals living next to an MPA, if I came across someone who participated in any aspect of the MPA project and asked why, their response often sounded as if it was being read off a PowerPoint slide: "To protect marine resources for our future generations," or "We depend on the ocean for our livelihoods, so we must take responsibility and sustainably manage it," or even "To increase the diversity and abundance of marine animals in the ocean."[20] At first, I was awed by these concisely packaged responses, thinking that the local environmental education had been really effective or that these folks just happened to have an ideology that aligned with the conservation project objectives. Then, after observing NGOs administer village-based training sessions, I realized that local representatives of the conservation project often have the task of transmitting these specific messages to other community members, on occasion having folks repeat, word for word, phrases such as the ones cited above. As the years passed, these canned answers wound up in booklets, pamphlets, and comics given to villagers, on T-shirts distributed free at soccer tournaments hosted by the conservation organizations, in films shown on large white sheets at dusk in fishing villages, and via a host of other activities aiming to help fishers understand their impact on the marine environment and their potential to make things better via marine conservation and MPAs in particular.

Going beyond canned answers to understand the motivation and perceived benefits of those who participated in MPA management took time. In interviews with both men and women, most responses about the benefits individuals or the community received were vague, such as "development" or the village will be more "welcoming." Rarely were marine benefits, such as improved marine habitat or increased number and diversity of fish mentioned. Sometimes informants provided hopes or future-oriented examples such as "A school will be built" or "A health clinic will be established." On occasion, informants provided concrete examples of things that had already occurred, such as "A deep well was dug" or "We received a water pump." In one area where an MPA had existed for six years, a village president expressed the hope that "some financial help will certainly come here at some point," although he wasn't sure when.[21]

Across almost all answers, no sense of duty or moral obligation was expressed. Instead, most people gave transactional reasons related to either collective benefit (such as a well or a health clinic), or personal benefit, specifically indemnities (per diems). Looking not to the conservation literature but to business and management writings, *buy-in* is defined as a transaction, or the "sale of . . . services, typically involving a commitment to a vision" (McSween, Myers, and Kuchler 1990). In relation to this literature, then, participation in conservation would indicate a willingness to invest (time, energy, money) in a conservation project, to provide a service for something in return. In stark contrast with the moral rationale that the conservation organization agents assumed that buy-in depended on, the business literature's notion of buy-in aligned much more closely with how fishers understood their participation in the marine conservation project.

Discussions around indemnities were often very heated, and individuals who normally remained fairly quiet in groups would chime in with their opinion. These conversations would often arise as local MPA management committee members gathered and waited for conservation organization workers to arrive. I was privy to the chat among the almost always all-male MPA committee members as we sat under the shade of a tin roof awning of a local committee member's house or sometimes ate calamari at a roadside bar after a series of meetings in the big city. It was in these casual forums that local MPA management committee members would talk about indemnities. During one conversation I witnessed, a committee member said that he would not go to the next event planned by the conservation organization because the per diems were too low. Another committee member agreed and lamented the fact that, compared to the previous NGO working in the region, the new organization had gotten stingy and offered less than half of what committee members used to be paid.[22]

In several interviews with conservation organization workers, I learned just how differently they perceived the benefit to villagers from indemnities. In one focus group interview, they explained that per diems were to help "compensate villagers for travel and time spent at meetings, or trainings" with the conservation organization and away from villagers' regular "livelihood activities."[23] "Minimal compensation for time not fishing" was another phrase commonly repeated by conservation organization representatives. Per diems were most frequently disbursed to individuals when conservation organizations held meetings, workshops, and conferences to launch new initiatives or to bring committee members together to share best management practices. These meetings were held usually in a regional city and occasionally in the capital city.

In conversations among village MPA management committee members and nonmembers, I heard the word *indemnité* often replaced by the words *karama* and *asa* ("salary" and "work" in Malagasy). As one young man explained, he helped the conservation organization because he would "probably get a good salary from it soon."[24] He was an avid fisher who did not have a formal role in the community management committee, but he helped the conservation organization agents every time they came to the village because he wanted to get a job and receive pay. When I asked him to clarify what he meant by job (*asa*) and pay (*karama*), he explained that he wanted to become a committee member and get hired to work part-time for the conservation organization. The use of the words *karama*, and *asa* highlight the perception of village-based participants that they were working for the conservation organization. Indemnities were not perceived the way conservation organizations hoped—as minimal compensation to cover expenses and make up for missed work—but instead were seen as negotiated payment for a villager's labor for the conservation organization.

Indemnities were a key source of tension between conservation NGOs and village-based community members. Just like salaries, per diems were often negotiated. Several NGO workers complained to me in the privacy of their offices that some local participants wouldn't show up for meetings or trainings (even if done in the partner's hometown or village) if they were not given an indemnity. Many of the field-based NGO workers I spoke with lamented that often indemnities were the first order of business when they talked about scheduling a meeting, workshop, or training. How much each person was going to be paid, and for how many days, would have to be negotiated before the conservation organization workers could talk about other activities.

In one conversation I overheard in southwestern Madagascar concerning indemnities between the president of the local MPA management committee and a field-based conservation agent from an international conservation organization, things got so heated that people in adjacent thatches stopped what they were doing to listen to the loud argument. I was in the kitchen of the committee president, an elder Vezo man, helping his wife prepare lunch. The conservation agent, a young Merina woman who had driven up in a four-wheel-drive truck, came into the committee president's house to drop off papers and other material to distribute before an upcoming workshop. Given the labor required to distribute the material to other villagers, the committee president asked about his and other committee members' indemnities and when they would be picked up to get a ride to the workshop (in a neighboring village). The conservation agent responded that there were not going to be any indemnities for this workshop, nor was anybody going to be picked up, implying that the president and others would be expected to walk two hours to the neighboring village. The agent continued in a frustrated and loud tone, bellowing that in another area where the NGO worked, one woman walked two days to attend a meeting and asked nothing in return. That woman, the agent said, is intelligent/understands things (*mahay raha*) and is kind/has a good soul (*tsara fanahy*), unlike the committee president. The committee president, unwilling to stand down as he was confronted with criticism that clearly his neighbors could hear, yelled back that he and the other committee members would not attend, adding that the conservation agent was conniving (*fetsy be*) and probably crazy (*vasa gegy*). He then loudly described how, the month before, all the committee members from his village were supposed to be paid their salary (*karama*) of 10,000 Ariary (US$3) per day to attend a meeting in the regional city, but the conservation agent gave them only 3,000 Ariary, and only after negotiation that involved the field agent's superior did they receive 6,000 Ariary per day. The committee president said that he wouldn't let the conservation agent take advantage of them anymore (*tsy manararotra eky*), whereupon the conservation agent headed back up the sand dune to the idling truck, loudly proclaiming that maybe there would be no project in the future because of the committee president's terrible personality (*toetra ratsy*).[25]

Although this conversation happened in the president's house, many other people overheard it. This degree of semipublic denigration is rare, especially toward an elderly man (the committee president) or someone who is politically powerful (conservation agent), which speaks to the strong emotions attached to the conversation. The conflict between this young highlander female conservation agent and an elderly Vezo (*coastal*) male around per diem payments sheds light on the politics and power dynamics within conservation projects. The committee president's age and maleness, both of which would situate him in a higher social status than a young woman in his region, were superseded by the ethnic, educational, and financial privilege of the young female highlander. The interplay of ethnicity, gender, education, and financial privilege in this scenario underscores the importance of engaging an intersectional analysis to unpack power and politics in conservation projects. The scenario also highlights a significant thread regarding the gendered distribution of benefits and burdens of conservation projects. The sacrifice of the kind or good souled woman in the agent's example broadly illustrates the disconnect between the way international conservation organizations understand participation in a project and how local actors understand it; however, it matters that the kind or good souled person was a woman. It allows us to see the deeply gendered patterns informing whom conservation organizations expect to bear the burden or gain the benefits of conservation interventions.

One section of the survey conducted across all regions showed a clear gender difference in perception of benefits from marine conservation projects. Individuals were asked if they personally benefited from the MPA project. On average more men than women responded yes. Although both groups indicated that overall, they did not benefit much (falling between "none" and "a little" on a Likert scale, or 1.69 for women and 1.80 for men), the differences in responses were statistically significant ($p<0.01$). Yet when individuals were asked whether they thought the broader community benefited from the MPA, on average more women than men thought the community as a whole benefited (2.30 for women and 1.98 for men). Women's responses thus illustrated their sense of sacrifice: few women reported personally benefiting from the MPA, but many more women reported that others were benefiting. The gendered differences in these responses were also statistically significant ($p<0.01$).

Not only did a higher proportion of men perceive personal benefit from marine conservation projects than women, but a much higher number of men than women received indemnity payments. Despite the fraught and contentious conditions under which indemnities were provided, they were an important element of community participation in conservation projects, and one where women's presence was sorely lacking. One's ability to receive an indemnity was tied primarily to whether one represented a local management committee. Women made up less than 5 percent of all local management committees. The underrepresentation, and sometimes complete absence, of women at meetings where per diems were granted meant that they missed out on one of the most concrete and coveted benefits conservation projects offered local people.

In one focus group interview with women about the costs and benefits of the MPA project, a woman's response was telling: "Received benefits? Nothing. We always give, but we never receive benefits from the project." Another woman agreed, commenting that compensation was often a plate of food that the women themselves fixed for the guests that they served. When I asked the group what changes they would like to see, one lively woman shouted, "We want to be on the committee, they get salaries!" The group laughed, and then someone added that the committee "sometimes gets 10,000 Ariary per day." Several women shook their head, a gesture that demonstrated simultaneously awe and discontent.[26]

Expecting and Addressing Backlash to Feminist Approaches

The men in the conservation committee like the idea of talking about equality between men and women but say that there remain differences and that men must remain in charge.

—*Middle-aged female fisher, southwestern Madagascar,*
October 16, 2020

In this chapter thus far I have argued the case for Malagasy fishers, and especially women younger and poorer fishers, having greater control over conservation programming and processes. Any movement toward decolonial and feminist processes and practices of conservation, however, means shifting the status quo and thereby disrupting power hierarchies. Although women resist the enclosure of their favorite fishing spots by fishing at night (as I experienced with Maman'Gary), women who want to serve, and the few who end up serving, on conservation committees have faced pushback (Baker-Médard et al. 2023).

Numerous women interviewed explicitly stated that many women are interested in participating more and taking on leadership roles in conservation committees; however, as one woman from northwestern Madagascar stated, men are "overprotective of women" and as a result, "There are women who don't really dare express themselves [*tsy mahasaky mistanga, tsy mahasaky mivola*]."[27] One women fisher from southwestern Madagascar said that it took her a while to realize that fishing could be a way of life for her because "some men tell women it's forbidden to go fish in the danger- ous ocean, so women don't go. They [some women] simply agree to it [*ekenan-zareo*]." She emphasized the importance of women training women to fish to help surmount the fear men sometimes instill. She said, "Women sometimes need to be convinced [*mandresy lahatra*] that they have rights [*fa manana zo*] to marine resources, too."[28]

One man from northwestern Madagascar stated that he was surprised that some of his male counterparts were against women fishing, despite women's long history of fishing in the region, and that some of them were vehemently opposed to women taking on leadership roles within conservation commit- tees. He said, "Some men are brutal [*mahery setra*] toward fisherwomen. They are shameless [*tsy mataho toly*] with how they treat fisherwomen."[29]

Resistance to women's leadership within and beyond marine conserva- tion goes beyond verbal admonition. For example, a woman from north- western Madagascar said that when women take a stand and make decisions on their own it can be dangerous. She described what happened to a woman in her village who decided to buy furniture with money she earned fishing. When her husband found out what she did, "he violently threw and broke apart the furniture [*nirobata par morceau*]. He told her that she needs to wait for him to say 'yes, go buy it' before she purchases anything in the fu- ture ['*ia vangà' zay vo tokony hivanga*]."[30]

Such resistance is not isolated to Madagascar; rather, resistance—sometimes violent—is common globally. In "Backlash: Or How to Snatch Failure from the Jaws of Success in Gender and Development" (2001), Janet Momsen carefully traces several poignant case studies of women participating in development pro- grams who experienced violent outcomes. Momsen stresses that gender-based programming needs to give careful attention to the social, economic, and po- litical contexts and create a support system to address the contextual needs of the women participants.

Even though procedural justice—redressing a lack of representation in decision-making—is a core ethic of a feminist approach to conservation, re- search shows that improving women's political representation alone does not often lead to the structural change required for a more equitable society. For example, in *No Shortcut to Change* (2017), Kara Ellerby illustrates how legislative quotas for women in political positions across the globe did little to shift outcomes such as violence against women and predatory political economic structures that disproportionately burden women. Neither Momsen nor Ellerby advocates for eliminating programming or policies that try to create greater gender equity, specifically representation in decision-making bodies, yet both assert that women's representation in local, regional, and national economic structures and politics is but a small part of the change needed to address broader institutional and political economic drivers of gendered inequality.[31]

A more equitable spread of decision-making across multiple axes of difference, whether of gender, class, race, ethnicity, or other trait, thus should reflect broader political, social, and cultural shifts that enable and support a more equitable spread of decision-making power. Finding ways to preemptively address resistance to and backlash from greater participation and leadership of women, poorer individuals, and those ethnically marginalized within a community requires community groups and organizations to address the underlying beliefs, assumptions, and structures that prevent greater participation and leadership from these groups.

Numerous scholars provide specific organizational and framing recommendations for how proactively to address resistance to programming and policy that aims to equalize power within a society. For example, research commissioned by the Victorian Health Commission in Australia found that organizational strategies such as securing support from key actors already in positions of power, forming strategic partnerships with groups who are most likely resistant to the programming or proposed policy, framing programming and policies in terms of fairness and justice, and developing clear narratives concerning the collective benefits that will likely accrue can all help to reduce resistance and diminish backlash (Flood, Dragiewicz, and Pease 2018). These recommendations echo some of the strategies a community-based small-scale fisher network used in a novel program they launched in 2020 called the Fisherwomen Leadership Program (FWLP). I describe the FWLP in greater detail in chapter 6; here I briefly outline a few ways the FWLP worked to prevent resistance and backlash to its female-focused programming.

One strategy the Fisherwomen Leadership Program used was to invite supportive men from the villages and regions from which women fisher attendees came. Husbands, male village leaders, and male governmental representatives, as one of the FWLP organizers put it, "learned alongside women about the benefits of including women in fisheries planning and marine conservation."[32] Inviting male allies was part of FWLP's carefully calculated strategy to counter gender-based backlash as well as to promote the development of regional- and national-level multigender fisheries management networks. Some of the men invited were recognized in their regions as key stakeholders in fisheries processing, trade, and marine resource management. Their attendance bolstered the legitimacy of the FWLP initiative and protected women participants politically in part because of the respect these men and the institutions they represented held within their respective villages and regions.

This strategy also aligns with what Jacqui True, a feminist political economist whose research focuses on understanding and preventing violence against women, identifies (2012, 188) as the need for "men to change men" so that men are held accountable to address their own and other men's problematic behavior toward women and thereby shape a new understanding of masculine identity. True and other feminist scholars emphasize the need for those working to end violence against women to invite men to join the struggle, working in solidarity to raise awareness of violence and gender inequality.

Last, the Fisherwomen Leadership Program training and information-sharing used a framing strategy that emphasized both the utilitarian and ethical benefits of including women's knowledge and perspective in organizational planning. This two-pronged framing strategy, as one FWLP leader asserted, was important because it helped people see that when the "whole community works together towards their own conservation goals, the work is easier and women are finally seen for all that they already contribute to marine conservation and fisheries."[33] Two FWLP attendees echoed the importance of the two-pronged rationale for the program. An older fisherwoman from western Madagascar emphasized, "We [men and women] need to come together as one [*hikambana, hiray*], deliberate together so our communities can thrive [*hampandroso*]." A young woman fisher from southwestern Madagascar shared a similar sentiment: "Back home where I am from women are put in their place [*ampela aloha hoe apetraky*], they are told that they aren't capable of doing anything [*tsy mahavita*]. But the way I see it is that men and women must work together and to help each other to protect the ocean because it's the basis of all our livelihoods, especially for communities on the coast there is nothing else but the ocean to sustain us."[34]

Who Loses?

Root causes of the postmodern conservation paradox are clear: even though many conservation institutions have moved in the direction of more collaborative and community-based orientations, their projects reify gendered and classed divisions of labor and access to natural resources and to money in the form of indemnities. In the past two decades, despite a discursive and legal shift toward enabling resource users to participate in decision-making concerning their marine environment, few fishers in the sites included in this research participated in management decision-making. International conservation organizations' claims of being mere technical advisers to an otherwise community-driven enterprise belie their deep influence on all key decisions concerning where, how, and when marine conservation occurs. When local resource users were involved in decision-making, primarily men, more educated and wealthier individuals in a community participated.

As the opening vignette of the planning meeting vividly shows, international conservation interests wielded far more power than Malagasy resource user interests in driving the decisions about how to conserve Madagascar's marine resources. The ethnic, class, gender, and educational hierarchies on display in regional-level marine conservation planning were echoed in intracommunity hierarchies relating to gender, class, and educational status. Specifically, the lack of women's representation in decision-making regarding MPAs precluded pushback against the enclosure of spaces or restriction of fishing methods used primarily by women. Similarly, women's lack of participation in local conservation committees prevented them from obtaining indemnities from the conservation organizations, considered by many fishers to be the most direct benefit from the establishment of marine conservation projects in their region. And last, the experience in and knowledge of the marine environment that women and the least wealthy in each village held was not represented in decision-making, thus affecting the efficacy of the conservation intervention and its value to all local marine resource users.

Framed in terms of Ostrom's design principles, women and the poorest in a community were expected by conservation organizations to acquiesce to the interests of those who represented the "community." This expectation relates to the notion of "most" in Ostrom's third principle: "Most individuals affected by the operational rules can participate in modifying the operational rules." In practice, "most" was tied to power rather than numbers. Similarly, the word *can* (as in "individuals *can* participate") speaks to one's rights rather than actual ability to participate. Thus, although theoretically everyone had a right to participate in these marine resource management committees, gender, wealth, age and educational status prevented people from participating. Furthermore, when women participated in meetings, their labor was expected to be free. Examples such as the one the conservation agent provided in the heated debate with the committee president illustrate how women sacrificing their time and energy epitomized community engagement in the eyes of the conservation organization.

These findings highlight the importance of privileging both procedural and distributive justice to ultimately transform conservation planning and implementation. From the examples outlined in this chapter, achieving the fair share ethic of distributive justice—in other words, securing direct benefit from the marine conservation project—was predicated on procedural justice. Thus, working toward more equal nominal and effective participation in decision-making by women and the poorest in the community provides an important foundation of a feminist approach to conservation, which seeks to transform systems that confer benefits and burdens from conservation projects.

Moving toward decolonial and feminist processes and practices of conservation is not easy and will likely lead to resistance and backlash. However, there are multiple strategies that community groups and organizations can use. Programming such as the FWLP addresses some of the structural barriers women face participating in marine conservation and fisheries management and reframes how people see the importance of women's agency and self-determination.

This path toward greater equity at the local level, however, does not address the deeply unequal power dynamic between coastal communities and international conservation organizations initiating and funding these conservation projects, which requires a wider lens to examine underlying drivers as well as the responsibility of people and communities at multiple nodes of the commodity chain. Furthermore, procedural justice requires more than just getting a seat at the table. It requires a reexamination and thus rebuilding of the table itself. Why is having a seat at the table simply not enough?

FOUR

Customary Law and Imposed Tradition

Dina is a great and visible local governance mechanism. It is
something that is unique here in Madagascar and something
we can capitalize on for conservation.

—*director of marine conservation, international NGO,*
November 16, 2011

Dina did not exist here before. . . . The NGOs want to use it.

—*President of fishing association, southwestern Madagascar,*
August 4, 2009

In 2010, in a village located twelve hours via bush taxi north from Toliara
in southwestern Madagascar, ten women sat under the shade of a tama-
rind tree, engrossed in conversation. Their village was nestled between sand
dunes and spiny forest, next to a marine conservation project led by two international conservation organizations. On this hot, sunny day, the women
were angry because one of their most frequented fishing spots would be
closed for four months due to newly established dina, or customary law,
and nobody had bothered to see if they cared. Two of the older women led
the discussion. They were sisters, both widowed, and were recognized locally as avid fishers. They regularly took boats out to the reef, a little over a
kilometer from shore, to fish on foot with their daughters, granddaughters,
and grandsons. Earlier that day the older of the two, approximately sixty-
five years of age, went to the reef to fish despite fairly heavy onshore winds.
Before she left, she stood on the beach with her daughter and daughter-in-
law and looked around for a fourth person to help row her heavy boat out
to the reef on a less than ideal fishing day. She spotted a young boatless
man holding a fishing spear, hollered a quick hello, and invited him to join

Heading home with a morning's worth of octopus catch, northeastern
Madagascar. Photograph by author.

them. He looked up and shook his head, waving her on with his hand. She
then shouted, "Women can get things done, too!" (*ampela mahavita raha
koa*) and signaled to the two other women that they would go anyway. Sure
enough, the trio returned after three hours with four large octopus, an eel,
twelve sea cucumbers, and several edible conch shells. They had fished
in an area familiar to the women, a part of the fringing reef. It was known
locally for being very shallow during low tide, with lots of hiding spots for
octopus and fish amid flat top coral, sponges, and algae. In two weeks, however, this area was slated to be closed for three months, a temporary marine
reserve enabled by marine conservation–oriented dina.

The two sisters advanced the idea that the whole group should talk to the
president of the local conservation committee the following day. The others

agreed and said that he should know that they were upset about the closure of their best fishing spot. One of the younger women explained that if that area were closed, she probably wouldn't fish at all during the three months because she didn't know the other spots on the reef as well and they were more exposed to the wind at that time of year. A few others in the group hummed in agreement.

The two international conservation organizations had scheduled a meeting the next day with the fishing association and local conservation committee. These two international NGOs were supposed to arrive in the early afternoon but did not show up until early evening. Sandy and pitted rock roads make travel difficult, even in four-wheel-drive vehicles. As evening approached, men started gathering around the town hall, a small tin building built adjacent to one of the four major wells in the village. The group of men sitting in the shady sand next to the building slowly grew from three individuals to more than thirty. As the group increased, four women led by the two sisters approached a man sitting near the entrance of the tin building. He was the president of the local conservation committee. The women sat down next to him and traced their fingers in the sand as they spoke. They quietly explained how they thought the area slated for closure was too large and took away an important fishing spot, one they relied on every day during low tides. The man nodded and said that the local conservation committee, which had met the day before, also opposed the location of the new temporary reserve because the village just to the north, which also worked with the same two international conservation organizations, had selected a temporary reserve directly next to theirs. Representatives of the fishing association and local conservation committee from the village to the north were also upset that the two temporary reserves locations were too close (*tery be*) to each other. Leaders of both local conservation committees agreed that the southern village should move their reserve to avoid having such a large contiguous area closed to fishing. Several of the men sitting nearby were from the village to the north. They wanted to join the meeting to make sure the conservation organizations knew that representatives from both villages hoped to change the temporary reserve location. The women smiled as he finished speaking; it was clear that their interests aligned with those of the two conservation committees. Pleased with this news, the women thanked the conservation committee president, retreated to an area twenty feet behind the all-male group, and sat in the sand. I asked one of the sisters where the other women were, and she replied, "They don't dare [*tsy mahasaky*] come here."

At dusk an agent from one of the international NGOs arrived with a driver. As he exited the truck, representatives from the local conservation committee stood up to greet him. The conservation agent shook the hands of several men and then sat on the small cement porch of the tin house. He apologized for being late, thanked everyone for being there, and said they should address the business at hand—getting signatures from the local conservation committee members to make official the closure of the new temporary reserve. As he reached for his bag to retrieve the papers, the president of one of the fishing associations requested permission to speak. The international NGO agent nodded, and the fishing association president proceeded. He started by thanking the international NGO agent for all his guidance, help, and interest in managing the fish in the ocean. He then went on to thank the ancestors for their guidance and protection. As the sun started to set, he repeated an account similar to the one told to the four women just twenty minutes earlier. The conclusion of the fishing association president's speech was that the reserve location should change. Across the crowd of people sitting around the tin building, heads were nodding in agreement, accompanied by "yeses" and many hummed approvals. As the president of the local conservation committee listened to the fishing association president's speech, he initially nodded his head in approval. However, when the fishing association president made the case for changing the location of the reserve, the conservation committee president surprisingly stopped nodding his head, then started shaking his head "no"—he was looking at the international NGO agent, who was vigorously shaking his head. The international NGO agent was silent after the fishing association president spoke and looked at the conservation committee president to speak. Then, awkwardly the local conservation committee president said to the crowd, "It won't work [*tsy mety*], it won't work." He then signaled to the international NGO agent to explain why.

After thanking the conservation committee president, the international NGO agent slowly, in a scolding tone, explained that dina didn't work this way. He said that moving the reserve was not logistically possible (using the French word *logistiquement*). He then explained that dina concerning the timing and location of the reserve had been signed by governmental officials at the district and regional offices earlier that day, in the presence of his superior at his organization. He said it took him days to coordinate with the governmental offices for the signatures. He went on to explain that changing anything would be too hard to do before the scheduled opening day of the reserve: it would require him to return to Toliara, reprint written dina documents, set up meetings with both district and regional representatives, explain to his boss why things had to change, and then return again to the village. As the international conservation organization agent spoke, the conservation committee president began to nod his head in agreement and then reiterated the same sentiments to the entire group, repeating the words, "It can't work, we are too late" (*tara mare tsika*).

At this moment a young and bold fisher, eschewing public oratory practices of thanking people and contextualizing one's speech, yelled out, "Change the date" (*afindrao le daty*) of closure as a solution to buy time for the signatures. The international NGO agent again paused, looked at the president of the local conservation committee, looked out to the crowd, and then repeated in a solemn tone that dina didn't work that way. He then clarified that the dates of closure were not decided at the local level; rather, all date-specific dina were decided at the regional level. He said the goal was to coordinate closures and openings across all temporary reserves to decrease the impetus for migrant fishers to travel opportunistically from opening day to opening day of reserves across the region. He then added that this approach is best for regional sustainable management (*fitananana regionaly maharitra*).

Shortly after the meeting, the local conservation committee members, including the fishing association president of who had stated his opposition to the location of the reserve, signed the documents. Before the meeting ended, the international NGO agent reminded people that he and the conservation committee would anchor a white flag on the southern- and

Flag marking the edge of a marine reserve in southwestern Madagascar. Photograph by author.

northernmost boundaries of the new temporary reserve the following week, and that according to article 8 of the dina established in this area, everyone was in charge of monitoring the reserve once it was closed.

The four women I was sitting with were visibly dismayed. One of them stood up, brushed the sand off her wrap, and in an exasperated tone, looking out at the horizon, said, "Alright, man" (*eka lahy*) then left. The others stayed for a few minutes longer before returning home to light fires for dinner.

The fishers' frustration concerning the timing and location of the temporary marine reserve demonstrates how the process of cross-scalar governance can undermine local control, especially with tight budgets and timelines determined by international conservation organizations. The process of decision-making in the community-based conservation project was deeply shaped by the technical support of nongovernmental organizations. When it came down to it, decisions of both the local conservation committee and the broader community of fishers were confined to the boundaries previously established by the international NGO working with the coastal community. Although the local conservation committee was able to weigh in on the part of the reef to close temporarily to fishing, they deferred to the international NGO even when they received information about the location of other reserves in the area and about the particular interests of women fishers challenging the suitability of this reserve placement. The local conservation committee lacked the administrative or technical ability to make changes to such key elements of their marine conservation dina as the time and location of their reserve.

It would have been easy to criticize the administrative roadblocks to more meaningful participation in conservation decision-making; however, I understood the international conservation agent's response during the meeting. In a conversation with him several weeks later, he said that the small change mattered primarily to the fishers in the area, which did not warrant upsetting people and processes at district and regional governmental offices, given the cost in time, gas, and revising paperwork. He said that the issues raised by the village fishers were neither something he could directly address nor something he had the authority to change. He emphasized that reallocating funds for additional gas was difficult, given his carefully calculated operations budget. He added that changing his travel schedule was not something he could do without the approval of his supervisors. In other words, his hands were tied. Thus, local autonomy over resource use rules was circumscribed by nonlocal logistics such as the price of gas, the need to obtain signatures at several levels of political organization, and administrative procedures.

The result of these administrative roadblocks was that fishers in the area had to adapt to closure of a large contiguous area. Although this meeting was only one in a string of dozens in this village over the year, it weakened local buy-in to the temporary reserve. Through interviews with local committee and association members, I learned that this meeting was a turning point for some. They felt disenfranchised by the process and more clearly understood the limits of their decision-making power. Some went as far to say that they had no power and that the white foreigners (*vazaha*) and highlanders had ultimate power, which they fully exercised.

The iterative process necessary for ongoing and dynamic participation across spatial scales (village, district, region) takes time, money, and a willingness to adapt midstream. How marine conservation rules were concretized, or rendered static, stemmed in part from the fixed values of conservation organizations regarding how to manage marine environments in Madagascar and in part from logistical hurdles that emerged due to working with multiple decision-makers across space. Figuring out how to enable greater input from local resource users by improving institutional flexibility over time and space is a key challenge in the pursuit of a more feminist and postcolonial approach to conservation. Finding avenues for resource users to have greater autonomy in the decision-making process would also help address the neocolonial dynamics and persistent racial and ethnic hierarchies at work. Representation, to return to a core component of a feminist approach to conservation, is essential in robust and accountable decision-making frameworks. Rules concerning access to and control over resources are simultaneously both the most in need of flexibility over time as ecological and social conditions change, *and* they are the most prone to becoming entrenched.

In a focus group gathered several weeks after the temporary reserve closed, eight of the ten original women were present. I asked what they thought of the conservation project now. Several said that they didn't trust the project or the conservation committee president. One of the sisters said, "Yep, I'm not going to get involved with politics anymore. They don't want women [*tsy mila ampela rozy*]."

How natural resource use decisions are made and who makes them matter. Women fishers were at the bottom of a power structure determining who, how, and when fishers have access to marine resources. And disparities in decision-making power were present not just between men and women but also in ethnic and racial divisions among local fishers, regional authorities, and regionally based international NGO agents. This disparity extended through the chain of command within international conservation organizations, where the insight and agency of local conservation agents was undermined by organizational restrictions determined by people working at the national or international level.

How did these disparities in participation become codified in natural re-source use rules, or dina? How and in what ways is Malagasy customary law used to legitimize access to and control of marine resources, who mobilizes its use, and why? Conservation organizations believe that by using the structure and names of "traditional institutions" they will obtain local interest in and adherence to biodiversity conservation goals. In Madagascar, dina has become an important avenue through which international NGOs assert control over marine spaces, limiting fisher access to as well as control over these spaces.

After examining archival documents on the history of dina, I argue that conservation organizations' current use of dina parallels colonial efforts to "civilize" and organize a population seen by the colonial government as eco-logically destructive and in need of administrative modernization (Baker-Médard 2020; Petit 1925). This finding aligns with what historian and political economist Sara Berry (1992, 338) argues was common across colonial Africa: "After World War I, colonial regimes across Africa moved to codify custom-ary law and formalize the structures of indirect rule, in keeping with the general trend toward rationalization and professionalization of the colonial service." Understanding how this history is tied to current conservation efforts is an essential step toward feminist conservation.

An important principle of feminist conservation is a deeply participatory and context-driven approach to resource management decision-making. Ultimately, conservation strategies must move away from cooptation of the so-called traditional or customary law, which in the case of marine conservation in Madagascar has supplanted local interests and leadership in favor of foreign and male-centered conservation strategies. Instead, conservation organizations should allow local cosmologies and ontologies to guide conservation goals and strategies.

Customs, Shared Norms, and Resource Access

Custom and tradition are concepts that occupy a large space in postcolonial legal studies. Scholars deeply debate the meaning and application of customary law in both historic and current contexts. Some scholars define customary law simply as "a body of rules governing personal status, communal resources, and local organization" (Joireman 2008, 1235), while others view customary law as the invention of colonial powers, a way to embed authoritarian rule into particular locales (Chanock 1991; Ranger 1997). Still others view customary law as a hybrid of previously existing social processes redefined and manipulated by colonial and neocolonial institutions (Berry 1993; Lund 2008; Moore 1986). In this last camp, scholars highlight how institutions and processes established in the pursuit of codifying customary laws are particularly important sites of struggles over natural resources.

Celestine Itumbi Nyamu (1998), a Kenyan legal scholar, argues for a "critical pragmatic" approach to understanding specifically how struggles over women's self-determination and access to resources function in a postcolonial context. Nyamu's approach emerges from her critique of both the "women in development" school of thought—which blames culture, not law, for the discrimination against women and advocates to abolish customary rules—and the "legal imposition" school of thought—which blames Euro-centric ideals and hegemonic aspirations for the discrimination against women and argues for a return to egalitarian customary rules. Like other scholars in the "hybrid" camp of postcolonial law, Nyamu shows that custom is not a static category and that it interacts with formal law in important ways. Nyamu underscores that both formal and customary law shape how and through what means women's rights to resources change. Her critical pragmatic approach does not attempt to create a totalizing theory of customary law but rather emphasizes the importance of specificity regarding how legal structures work in practice and in place. She argues that specificity is needed to devise strategies to change gendered hierarchies and other forms of oppression.

I engage with Nyamu's "critical pragmatic" approach in considering the relation between customary law and conservation practice in Madagascar. I am not interested in either condemning or extolling the legal categories I analyze here but rather in understanding how they influence access to and control over marine resources in the locales I observed. The dozens of interviews I held with conservation organization agents representing both international conservation organizations and Malagasy government conservation institutions make it clear that conservation organizations see customary law as the key mechanism through which the Ostrom-style common pool resource management principles of collective choice, self-monitoring, and establishing rules to match local conditions can occur. Seduced by the common misconception of customary law as an immutable social contract, many conservation organizations believe that if they can just orient or shape customary law to Western scientific conservation principles, the imagined preexisting and harmonious social order will ensure that these rules are upheld. According to the Ostrom model, if resource users are the rule makers, they will police themselves. For conservation organizations, therefore, customary law potentially encompasses free self-monitoring and enforcement due to its embedded local legitimacy. In this logic, customary institutions, and dina specifically in Madagascar, are a way to address shortcomings of top-down resource governance, including a dependence on governmental policing and a lack of legitimacy in the eyes of local resource users.

Legitimacy, considered buy-in or stakeholder acceptance in the realm of conservation practice, is the aim of all conservation projects. The power of a given politico-legal institution to uphold its claims is contingent on the institution's ability to be recognized as an authority by those whom it aims to govern (Lund 2002; Sikor and Lund 2009; Verdery 2003). In other words, the authority of a resource-governing institution is predicated on the ability of the institution to gain and sustain legitimacy in the eyes of the resource users (Fortmann 1995, Lund and Boone 2013, Moore 1988; Sikor and Lund 2009). Gaining and sustaining legitimacy, however, is also predicated on the governing body's ability to persuade or subordinate defiant individuals or resistant factions of a community (Blomley 2003; Peluso and Watts 2001; Rose 1994).

The Malagasy government and international NGOs are of course not monolithic authoritative entities, yet their authority is exercised through displays of programmatic spending and individual payments, as well as through the mobility of conservation agents who represent their interests across multiple locales. They gain and maintain their institutional legitimacy through presentations, environmental education campaigns, workshops, and training sessions at multiple scales of social and political organization. Nongovernmental organizations derive some of their authority over natural resource policies and practices through their interaction with governmental

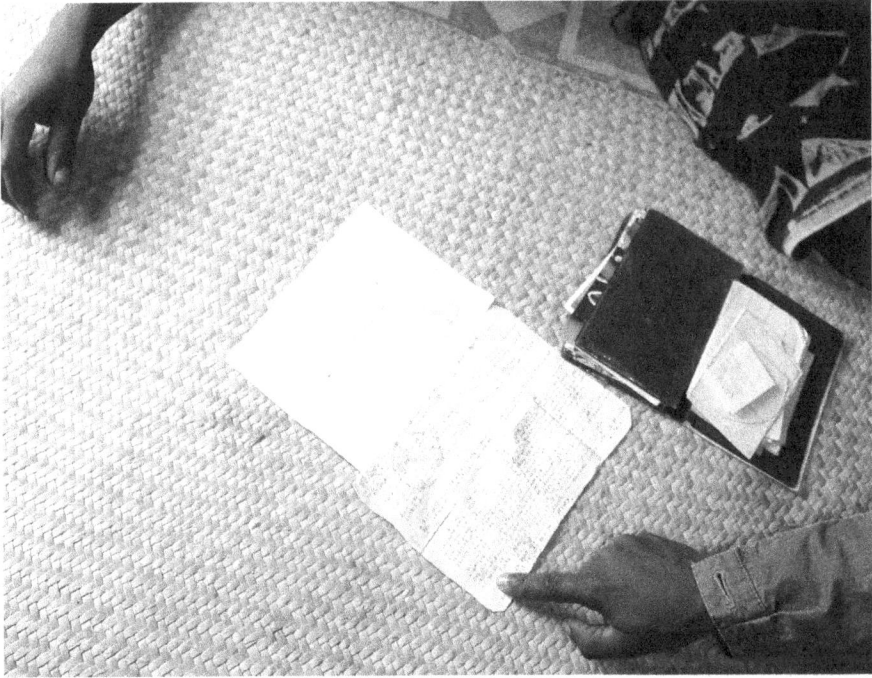

Fine and court citation documents issued from Madagascar National Parks to a
fisher in northeastern Madagascar who took fish from within the boundaries of
a marine protected area. Photograph by author.

institutions; however, they also function independently of the state, leaning
on their role as outside advisers and technicians in both government- and
community-managed conservation projects (Corson 2011a; Haley and Clayton 2003). Moreover, because NGOs exist in the liminal space between the
state and the society as well as between the public and the private (Duffy
2005; Lund 2006), they are able to navigate across different scales of social
and political organization with ease. Drawing on an international network
of scientists and financial backers, most environmental NGOs are able to
maintain and, in some cases, increase funding for their conservation projects
despite political change or upheaval (Baker-Médard 2019).

As described above, the interests of a group of ten women and other
Vezo (*côtier*) fishers were subordinated by the interests of the conservation

organization and the logistical chain of command it created in order to legit-imize dina at the local, regional, and national level. The fishing association president who spoke on behalf of numerous villagers, including the ten women, was persuaded that his request wasn't as important as the rollout of the MPA closure as planned, a fact the international NGO agent bolstered by emphasizing the importance of "regional sustainable management." This small moment in the longer trajectory of marine conservation initiatives in this village underscores how dina, and more broadly the notion of local norms and local institutions, were created by and primarily for international NGO objectives. How and why the interests of the ten women were dis-missed related not only to the political and economic primacy of the interna-tional NGO, but also to the deference of local committee members to the NGO. The reason for this deference is likely rooted in patronage politics and the specific benefits these local actors accrue from powerful international conservation organization, but intracommunity hierarchies also play a part.

Nyamu argues that the common fallacy of egalitarianism in customary institutions precludes deeper analysis of intracommunity hierarchies and the constant renegotiation of roles and entitlements. During the meeting described earlier, the conservation committee president and the fishing as-sociation president operated as stand-ins for the whole community in the marine conservation project. Their decisions theoretically reflected the will and the interests of the whole village. However, important intracommunity stratifications also existed, underscoring the challenges associated with true collective choice arrangements.

Elinor Ostrom's work relies heavily on the notion of shared norms, sum-moning the specter of customary law, in relation to decision-making over common pool resources.[1] Ostrom (1990, 50, 198, 204) argues that shared norms are essential not only for facilitating collective choice but also for suc-cessfully matching rules to local conditions, reducing the cost of monitoring and sanctioning, and resolving conflicts that arise. Rather than critically in-terrogating this notion of shared norms, however, Ostrom (1990, 184) instead naturalizes them as something that emerges organically "when individuals interact with one another in a localized physical setting," "have lived in such situations for a substantial time" and through "patterns of reciprocity . . . possess social capital with which they can build institutional arrangements for resolving CPR dilemmas." This conception of shared norms is problematic in practice for two reasons. The first concerns Ostrom's use of bounded localism, or the notion that the local somehow operates independently of regional or global forces. The second relates to Ostrom's apolitical framing of reciprocity and social capital, factors that lead to shared norms and facilitate collective decision-making. The notion of shared norms thus resembles the false notion of a harmonious and homogeneous community. However, norms—like rules—are actively established by individuals and groups of people within a larger community and are actively maintained (Comaroff and Roberts 1986; Lund 2008; Moore 1988).

As Ann Whitehead and Dzodzi Tsikata (2003) show, an emphasis on engaging "local" and, in particular, "customary" governance systems is in and of itself a political act that values particular ideologies and undoubtedly favors some people over others within a given community. Whitehead and Tsikata (2003, 101) argue that the "the language of chieftaincy and tradition may mask many different kinds of economic and political processes" that underlie social and institutional hierarchies. Thus, if one sees customary law as a debate over access to and control of resources, then gender, customs, and the scale of administrative organization become highly relevant. As John Comaroff and Simon Roberts argue in their influential book *Rules and Processes* (1986), when we focus on problems or disputes related to rules, we can better understand their influence on the sociocultural hierarchy and vice versa. The group of ten women who wanted to change the location of a temporary MPA appealed to the legal process tied to conservation dina. Their desire to maintain access to marine resources was mediated by an institutional arrangement theoretically based in collective choice. However, given the requirements of regional coordination across multiple MPA sites and the interests of the NGO facilitating the conservation dina, the women's subordinate position in the hierarchy of decision-making was laid bare through the process of contesting a proposed constraint on their resource access.

Appreciating dina as a key site of deliberation and debate concerning claims over marine resources made at multiple scales of social and political organization sets the stage for better understanding how community-based institutions such as dina and fokonolona emerged and were used in Madagascar's history. This history contextualizes why a feminist approach to conservation must move beyond archaic notions and invocations of "customary" and "tradition" to engage the complex and dynamic beliefs, values, and goals of small-scale producers and resource users.

An Abbreviated History of Fokonolona and Dina

The history of how customary law was conceived in Madagascar is critical to understanding how customary law became the central focus of most marine conservation efforts. The terms *fokonolona* and *dina* were malleable and were employed by different political actors to introduce particular forms of social organization however, the use of fokonolona and dina to serve top-down or outsiders' interests is not new.

The administrative history of fokonolona, which means community or collective of people in a village or small neighboring villages, dates back to the time of King Andrianampoinimerina (r. 1787–1810).[2] Scholars credit Andrianampoinimerina with advancing this form of social organization as a way to ensure that services for the king were carried out, rules envisioned by the king were followed, and small grievances could be resolved locally (Arbousset 1950; Delteil 1931; Julien 1931). Although some decision-making autonomy was granted to this new administrative unit, rules made by the fokonolona were subject to the king's approval (Julien 1931, ix). While the words *dina* and *fokonolona* are commonly used together in conservation and development circles today, the word *dina* is scarce in documents published shortly before or during the colonial period in Madagascar. Instead the word *fanemkem-pokon'olona*, or "agreement/covenant of the community," appears more frequently. In *Tantara Ny Andriana Eto Madagascar: Documents historiques d'après les manuscrits malgaches* (Callet 1908), a twelve-hundred-page book regarded as one of the definitive historical texts of early Malagasy history, only one passage refers to dina. The context concerns the loyalty of a particular clan (the Zanakandrianato) to King Andrianampoinimerina; the passage focuses on the Zanakandrianato's efforts to provide the king with weapons and to fight in his name against threats to his kingdom. To support such efforts, the Zanakandrianato instituted a family-level tax called *dina*:

> Then Zanakandrianato came up with dina and strategies to provide bullets and guns for Andrianampoinimerina: "Come listen" [Raini-betrano] said, "Those who have a slave buy an *angalisa* [flint-lock musket], those who have eight zebu [type of cattle] buy a *marovy* [type of gun], and those who have seven zebu buy a *tsifidianana* [type of gun]"—which are different names of guns. Then the Zana-kandrianato agreed and said: "Even if we have to worship people who are of similar status, we will make sure this comes to fruition." So, this dina and agreement were reported to Andrianampoinimerina.[3]

In this passage dina is a class-scaled family-based levy collected to help the Zanakandrianato stockpile weapons. Although how the dina was decided on is not specified, it is clear that dina was created to serve the king and necessitated reporting to him.

During colonization, the French used the administrative unit of the fokonolona to organize, discipline, and extract taxes and labor from Malagasy people (Arbousset 1950; Delteil 1931; Imbiki 2011). Although the administrative unit was initially confined primarily to the highlands during Andrianampoinimerina's reign, the French introduced the term *fokonolona* and the expectation of place-based social organization across the whole Island.

The French generally engaged in direct rule in their colonies, a system of governance that usually replaced prior governance structures, ensured that colonizers held positions of power and authority, and focused on sociocultural and political assimilation to the new order (Deschamps 1971; Wallerstein 1961; Whittlesey 1937). In Madagascar, however, the French took a different approach in certain domains. The colonial government's use of the fokonolona was more akin to indirect rule, preserving local governance structures and leadership. In 1931, French colonial jurist Pierre Delteil published *Le Fokon'olona (commune malagache) et les Conventions de Fokon'olona*. Delteil (1931, 93) applauded efforts to codify the fokonolona as an administrative unit of the new colonial order.[4] The fokonolona, he reasoned, would help pacify the Malagasy people, extend the reach of the French colonial government, and simplify governance:

> Nothing reassures the natives better than to place them again in the frame where their fathers lived. Reinstituting [the fokonolona] also had a considerable advantage. It relieves the French administration from a lot of cumbersome business. The European official must not be bothered and paralyzed by the minutiae of the native administration. He must only lead it from above in order to be clearly aware of the questions which, by their importance, require his intervention. . . . These are the advantages we should recognize in what is called "indirect rule."

Elsewhere Delteil (1931, 79) frames local rules made by the fokonolona as an ideal way to fight against the inertia or apathy (*l'inertie*) of the Malagasy people. He points specifically to how sanctions applied at the local level (fokonolona) will help "force the lazy [*paresseux*] to work" (92). As a corollary, he advances the logic that the fokonolona is in fact the perfect vehicle through which to modernize and civilize the Malagasy. He argues, "Without doubt, the native's world is evolving more rapidly with our contact, it cannot remain frozen in its archaic life. The role of the civilizing State is precisely to preside over this evolution, to direct it" (94). For Delteil, local rules and the village as an administrative unit were critical institutions through which the colonial government could modernize a primitive people and their antiquated ways of operating. These institutions were seen as the ideal decentralized strategy to extend the reach of the colonial government—a dynamic paralleling the current decentralized conservation paradigm.

Even during the height of colonial rule, some were well aware of the paradox of co-opting precolonial administrative units, the fokonolona, as conduits through which colonial powers would assert their interests. The honorary governor of Madagascar M. G. Julien, in the foreword to Delteil's book, underscores this contradiction, exclaiming: "In truth, powerful foreign influences all too often exert their interests on the activity of the fokonolona, especially in matters of religion and education, a pressure which often leads to deplorable results [*résultats deplorables*]. Old traditions then break, or get distorted [*heurtées, parfois faussées*], and hierarchies are overturned" (Delteil 1931, x). Julien saw the exertion of colonial interests on fokonolona as "deplorable" but necessary to advance the French colonial interests on the island. One can see this paradoxical tension between preserving Malagasy traditions and modernizing or developing the Malagasy people emerge in every period of Malagasy history since the colonial period.

Although Madagascar was granted independence in 1960, some scholars mark the early 1970s, with the rise of nationalist pride and protests against the dominance of French nationals in Madagascar's political economy, as the point at which Madagascar took key steps to decolonize (Brown 2002; Rakotondrabe 1993; Sharp 2002). Not until the country's turn toward socialism did fokonolona and dina shift in meaning. These institutions changed from being entirely imposed and controlled from above to institutions where local taboos were considered a key facet of dina and the fokonolona was considered a site of shared power (Leymarie 1975). As one Malagasy scholar explains in the manifesto *Fokonolona: Fotory ny Firenena* (Fokonolona: The foundation of the country), "Dina says what is required (kinship and custom) and dina says what is forbidden (taboo), which is the foundation of the Malagasy society" (Ramasindraibe 1975, 86). Although this era of fokonolona and dina marked an important discursive shift of authority, where groupings of people were invited to advance rules that served their community, in practice the Malagasy government still oversaw the orientation and goals of these institutions. At the time, the pursuit of improved economic development and agricultural production were particularly high priorities for the Malagasy government. Consistent with socialist ideals of communal rural life, ordinances passed in 1973 (Laws 73-009, 73-010, 73-073) implored place-based groups of people, titled *fokonolona*, to establish dina in order to "take responsibility [*mandray an-tanana*] for development and to ensure the collectivization of work [*fiarahamiasa*]" for the benefit of the country (Malagasy Government 1973a–c). By the mid-1970s, communities, primarily in the highlands, started publishing their *dinam-pokon'olona*, or community customary law, focused on rules pertaining to activities such as husbandry, farming, building schools, repairing roads, owning a dog, and taking care of the deceased (Fokontany Akany Sambatra 1973).

Although dinam-pokon'olona documents published in the 1970s applied to many practices and processes of rural life, the use of forest, freshwater, and marine resources was scarcely mentioned. Not until the mid-1990s, with the nation's turn toward decentralized conservation and the passage of new legislation to enable this decentralization, did dina start to include explicit language regarding the protection, or sustainable use, of natural resources. In searching for a method to accomplish their aims, and the increasing global popularity of an Ostrom model of resource management, international NGOs turned to an old playbook dating back to both the colonial era and the socialist government of the 1960s and 1970s.

Imposing Conservation Dina

Dina is a great and visible local governance mechanism. It is
something that is unique here in Madagascar and something we can
capitalize on for conservation.

—*director of an international conservation organization,
Antananarivo, November 16, 2011*

In the mid-1990s, in line with the global shift recognizing the importance of affected citizens and communities' participation in decision-making on environmental issues, the Malagasy government put into law a type of resource governance that involved a three-way contract among the state, the rural commune, and a "local community group" (*communauté locale de base*) (Law 96-25). The linchpin of this contract was dina (Henkels 1999; Imbiki 2011; Kull 2004; Pollini and Lassoie 2011; Rakotoson and Tanner 2006). Dina was elevated as a socially compatible rule-making strategy through which conservation ideals and strategies would be legitimized into the traditional rule-making process (Henkels 1999). With this legislation, community-based conservation projects would function with a set of locally specific resource-use dina that would be upheld by the fokonolona.

Since the mid-1990s, there has been a steady proliferation of dina documents produced by governmental (Madagascar National Parks, ministries of the environment) and nongovernmental organizations (WCS, WWF, CI, BV and SAGE—Service d'Appui à la Gestion de l'Environnement) in collaboration with communities living in sites selected for conservation intervention. Establishing resource-use dina has been a primary focus of most conservation institutions when working with communities. Conservation organizations believe that by using the structure and names of these so-called traditional institutions they will obtain local interest in and adherence to biodiversity conservation goals (Grandcourt et al. 1999; CI 2017; Langley 2006; MEF 2010; WCS 2012; Westerman and Benbow 2014; WWF 2017).

In 2009 WWF, in collaboration with other international conservation organizations, national government agencies, and NGOs, held a conference about the use of customary law in conservation. The purpose of the three-day event, held in Toliara, the largest city in southwestern Madagascar, was how to develop laws governing the use of marine resources that could be upheld by local as well as state institutions. It focused on the two social institutions of the fokonolona and dina.

Conservation organization personnel made up the bulk of attendance; however, each day there were also representatives from various branches of the government, a handful of students and researchers, and a few village presidents and fishing association representatives from villages in the southwest region. A little under a quarter of the attendees were women, only two of whom came from fishing villages. The remaining women either worked for conservation organizations or, like myself at the time, were students.

As an international NGO agent facilitating the conference explained at the outset of the three-day series of presentations, workshops, and discussion, the aim of developing marine conservation-oriented dina was to "develop" and "professionalize" small-scale fisheries. He continued that by working with fishing communities to develop dina, conservation organizations would be able to "professionalize fishers [*mpiandriaka matihanina*], improve their lives and livelihoods [*tsara fari-piainana*], make sure they are well equipped with appropriate gear, and ensure that fishers are responsible for the sustainable management of marine and coastal fisheries."

On the first day of the conference, an older Merina (*haut-plateau*) man who worked for WWF introduced the word *dina* as an acronym: "*Didy*

Ifampifehezana Natao Ampiharina, or the application of self-directed laws."
Standing on stage, he flipped through several PowerPoint slides of fishers in
boats or mending nets on shore as he advanced a core tenet of the conference: coastal communities were best positioned to make and monitor rules
about the marine environment, so conservation organizations should help
them do so. Also that day, a young white man representing Blue Ventures,
another international marine conservation organization working in the region, stood up and explained how dina have helped fishers. Blue Ventures
prided itself on its community-based approach to marine conservation
and in the decade after this conference won several international awards
celebrating its work with communities to establish locally managed marine
areas. The Blue Ventures representative at the workshop explained that his
organization helped fishing communities in the southwest come up with
dina in order to protect temporary rotational octopus reserves, noting that
thus far the "application of dina has been successful at protecting marine
resources."[5]

During the second day of the conference, the conversation pivoted from
why dina was important to how to implement dina, specifically as it related
to the community, or fokonolona. Up until this point, it was not clear to participants how the fokonolona would create dina. After a presentation by a
young Malagasy man working with Blue Ventures of an example of dina,
specifically the dates and duration of temporary octopus reserves, a middle-
aged fisher from a village just north of Toliara stood up to ask, "Who was on
the committee that created [*mpamolavola*] [those] dina?" Instead of going
to the front of the room and taking the microphone to speak, he spoke
loudly from where he stood, in the middle of a cluster of men who were also
village presidents and representatives of local fishing organizations. As the
middle-aged man spoke, the men around him nodded their heads, silently
seconding the man's question. The man elaborated, "For example, is it the
whole community? It's difficult to communicate with the whole community. Is it district representatives? Is it village elders? Is it children and
women?" The young man working with Blue Ventures who had just presented examples of specific dina still had the microphone and laughed for
a minute, and then replied, "Yeah right, dude, women [*aia koa koahy,*

ampela]? Children and women formulating dina [*aja aman'ampela koa moa hamolavola dina*]?" He paused again to chuckle, and then added, "That's not possible [*tsy mety*]. A committee of fishers alone will formulate [the dina] [*komity mpiandriaky avao mpamolavola*]."[6] At that point, the conversation pivoted toward lunch and what time we needed to return for afternoon sessions.

Nobody addressed the implication that women were not considered fishers and therefore would not be part of a committee of fishers, let alone the broader disparaging of women's potential role as decision-makers and formulators of dina. The implicit exclusion of women from an otherwise exciting opportunity to legally codify community-based natural resource management rules was left unaddressed, not only then, but also for the remainder of the conference. This was a clear moment in which the women in the audience were reminded that, despite the framing of dina as an opportunity for the whole community to participate in shaping marine resource rules, the central players in determining the rules would be men. Narratives play a large role in the process of defining and defending rules over who can access and control resources (Rose 1994). Gendered narratives around women's illiteracy, men's natural ability to lead, what kind of fishing counts as real fishing—all legitimize who will be invited to the table to decide. Placing women in the same category as children is an effective rhetorical maneuver to sanction their relative absence at a regional conference and their lack of representation in local conservation committees and participation in decision-making.

Despite clear gender bias in who contributes to the creation of dina, numerous researchers studying natural resource governance in Madagascar reference dina as proof of community acceptance and approval of conservation and development projects (Barnes and Rawlinson 2009; Bruggemann et al. 2012; Chaboud and Galletti 2007; Cinner 2007; Cripps 2009; Dhital, Vololomboahangy, and Khasa 2015; Lilette 2006; Mayol 2013; Oliver et al. 2015; Raik 2007; Rocliffe et al. 2014). Similarly, the World Bank uses dina as a box to check to ensure that a development project has touched the local level. The term *dina* appears in the bank's results and monitoring framework as an "intermediate results indicator." Those filling out World Bank forms to be eligible for additional loans or grants must answer a simple question: "Has Dina been activated? Yes or No" (World Bank 2011). The passive voice "has been activated" is telling, abstracting the deeply power-laden political process of rule-making.

Large companies extracting resources, including QMM (QIT Madagascar Minerals), which mines ilmenite in southeastern Madagascar, also use dina to demonstrate that they have taken the necessary steps to obtain permission for their work from local communities. Unsurprisingly, research shows that QMM has used dina to legitimize coercive community displacement as well as less-than-optimal compensation for communities' lost access to land and other resources (Seagle 2012).

In these examples, dina is conceived as a lever an organization can pull to access local legitimacy, purportedly embedded in a traditional institution that automatically aligns with local wants and needs. These uncritical references to leveraging or activating dina fail to look at how dina are produced, by whom, and in accordance with whose interests, thus making dina a site rife with neocolonial dynamics. The use of dina by conservation and development organizations illustrates how customary law is a power-laden site of struggle over access to and control over resources.

The unquestioned nature of dina allows it to be cordoned off in the seemingly timeless realm of the traditional, tied to a spatially bound notion of the local, echoing the use of dina and fokonolona during colonial times. These ideas of traditional and local serve parallel notions of what conservation and development organizations consider authentic and therefore legitimate. Several authors argue that dina provides a mechanism to unite what is considered legitimate locally and what is deemed legal by the state (Andriamalala and Gardner 2010; Rakotoson and Tanner 2006). In these instances, fokonolona is conceived as an intrinsically legitimate authority, and it is precisely this notion of legitimacy that is problematic—born from the same notion as the idealized cohesive and harmonious community and spatially bound localism. However, when dina fails to work as a conservation measure, conservation organizations or researchers advancing the use of dina, tend to blame outsiders (migrant fishers, traveling traders, adjacent communities), which simply ends up entrenching the notion of an untouched and pure local (Andriamalala and Gardner 2010; Dhital, Vololomboahangy, and Khasa 2015; Rakotoson and Tanner 2006). The deep history of trade, migration, and travel all around Madagascar, especially in coastal regions, is omitted from these authors' framing of how fokonolona and dina *should* work.

Nearly twenty years after the boom in community-based conservation efforts in the terrestrial realm, conservation work in the late 2000s marked a concerted effort to revive the use of fokonolona and dina to protect biodiversity and manage resources in the marine realm. Although the push to leverage dina for marine conservation was predicated on an interest in legitimizing local authority over marine resources, the practice of institutionalizing dina in most ways worked to buttress the ideas and ideals of international NGOs. An illustration of this can be found in a report from Mananara-Nord Biosphere Reserve, a combined terrestrial and marine protected area on the eastern coast of Madagascar. The report states that development assistance for the villages next to the protected area is contingent on community members signing dina that "respect the protected area and biodiversity conservation" (Jürg and Willy 2009). In places where the use of dina predated the more recent push to introduce new conservation-focused dina, people distinguish between dina *fototra* (literally, dina of the base or source, implying derived locally) and dina *kaominaly* (commune-level dina) (Kull 2002).

Similarly, as Gildas Andriamalala and Charlie Gardner (2010) explain, adherence to local dina often required "priming" through social marketing and environmental education campaigns. The region that Andriamalala and Gardner reference is where the well-known conservation organization Blue Ventures is based. Andriamalala and Gardner's description of Blue Venture's social marketing and environmental education campaigns illustrates that even when conservation planners were careful to involve as many local people as possible in the establishment of dina, it still had to be marketed, sold, and taught to the population; in other words, these dina were not intrinsically legitimate, and expecting the community to follow dina was something that required intense campaigning.

In all the coastal research sites I visited in the southwest, northeast, and northwest of Madagascar, no dina regarding marine resource use existed before the recent establishment of a marine protected area. The establishment of dina, and in some cases (notably in the southwestern part of the island) the introduction of the term *dina*, came from either governmental or nongovernmental conservation organizations. The vast majority of people interviewed for this research knew the word *dina* but defined it primarily as another word for a financial punishment. *Vono dina*, people explained to me, means one must pay a fine. As one participant in a women's focus group in southwestern Madagascar explained, "Dina is when one is punished [*voan'sazy*] or fined [*lamandy*] . . . it means money [*jala*]." In a few large coastal cities in Madagascar, dina is written on the walls of houses, fences, and buildings threatening passers-by that if they pee in that area, they will be fined. Some writings on walls also use cultural insults in an effort to embarrass the potential peeing public, declaring, "He/she who pees here is a dog, and in accordance with dina will be fined 5,000 Ariary" (about $US1.25).[7]

The colonial roots of the entrenchment of the word *dina* around the island and the highlander origin of the word is not lost on some coastal leaders. The president of a regional fishing association in southwestern Madagascar explained during an interview, "Dina did not exist here before. Dina is *not* Vezo, it's Merina [the dominant ethnicity in the capital city]." He said that they use the word because the "NGOs want to use it."[8]

Ultimately, dina governing marine resource use is embedded in a top-down management regime operating under the pretense of a grassroots strategy. The operationalization of dina by conservation organizations echoes the conservation-driven mandate of 1996 from the Ministry of Interior to all rural communes to establish dina that restrict the use of fire for agriculture (Kull 2002), which again is rooted in colonial strategies of indirect rule.

Spirits, Taboos, and Dina

A harmonious social order with clear rules pertaining to marine resources did not exist in any of the areas investigated in my research; yet a number of individuals I interviewed articulated rules about marine harvesting that were followed by many in the community—upheld primarily by a fear of retribution from the sea, spirits, and ancestors. These rules were almost completely ignored by conservation organizations working in the area because most of them did not align with a Western conservation ethic. For example, in one coastal area in northeastern Madagascar, a widely acknowledged local resource use rule is that people with Merina ancestry are not allowed to fish there. This anti-Merina rule was rooted in the history of the region where, under King Radama I (r. 1810–1828), Merina led internal colonization efforts that resulted in the forceful, and sometimes violent, subordination of the locally dominant Betsimisaraka people in order to extract resources and slaves from the region (Campbell 2005). Then, shortly after European colonization, the French used Merina to collect taxes, oversee corvée labor (unpaid unfree labor for the state), and remove people forcibly from the area to be trafficked in the slave trade (Brown 2002; Campbell 2005; Sodikoff 2012). Although a marine conservation organization worked with local people to write dina for the area, this rule was not included. A disproportionate number of governmental and nongovernmental conservation agents are Merina (relative to the total proportion of Merina in Madagascar), including some of the field-based agents working at the regional and local level. Adopting a marine resource rule against Merina was inconceivable, according to several Merina conservation agents who worked in northeastern Madagascar for over a decade. One explained that anti-Merina sentiment is "something of the past" and isn't an "appropriate conservation rule because it's prejudiced against Merina."[9]

This small example of a rule that some Betsimisaraka fishers in the region knew and followed underscores how ethnic constructions and marine resource use rules and practices were and continue to be deeply entwined. This particular rule also illuminates how collective memory, or collective trauma, shaped and continues to shape fishing practices and access along ethnic differences. The anti-Merina rule, with a history perhaps more easily traceable than others, was not deemed acceptable and therefore not institutionally validated by either conservation organizations or the Malagasy government.

Through hundreds of interviews, I came to learn of the existence of an enormous number of other local and regional marine resource use rules or norms, many of which were more opaque in origin than the anti-Merina rule. Each has a history, often told in lore, and reflects changing values and beliefs across time and space. A wide variety of rules existed across southwestern, northeastern, and northwestern Madagascar. Some of these rules applied to a large region, while others were particular to a single village. To provide context for the spread and variability of the rules, here is a sampling of the rules people mentioned (some of these were listed in chapter 2):

No killing whales
No killing of dolphins
No killing sea snakes
No killing sawfish (*vavana*) (*Pristis*)
No killing guitarfish (*soroba*) (*Rhinobatidae*)
No killing a particular family of fish (e.g., *Siganidae,*
    Antennariidae)
Forbidden to pull dugongs onto the beach
Forbidden to fish around certain islands, atolls, or rocks
Forbidden to use traps
Forbidden to fish while menstruating
No killing, eating, cleaning, or transporting pigs at sea or on the
    beach
You must perform an offering to the spirits (*manao voady*) if you
    have a problem at sea
You must pour red rum and coins into the ocean if you use a
    large-meshed gill net (*jarifa*)
Forbidden to tell people you are going to the reef
Forbidden to tell people you are going fishing
Forbidden to say "cow" or "pig" while at sea
Tuna harvested, if dead once ashore, must be cooked; if while
    cooking it a child cries, it is a sign of danger (*fambara loza*), so
    one must burn a piece of the child's clothes
Forbidden to bring military personnel in your fishing boat
Forbidden to bring Merina or Betsileo (highlander ethnic
    groups) into your fishing boat
Forbidden to bring Antambahoaka (southeastern coastal ethnic
    group) in certain areas of the ocean
Forbidden to bring foreigners (*vazaha*) in certain areas of the ocean
Forbidden to speak Merina at sea

Forbidden to excrete in the sea

Forbidden to carry a cat while fishing

Forbidden to open an umbrella while fishing

Forbidden to wear red clothing while fishing

Forbidden to wear black clothing at sea

Forbidden to wear a grass hat at sea

Forbidden to bring a torch while at sea

Forbidden to throw fire into the ocean

Forbidden to smoke when in a boat

One must call a rock (*vato*) "palm" (*kasaka*) when in the sacred
    peninsula's waters

Forbidden to say the name of sea spirits while at sea

Forbidden to use a shovel as an oar

Forbidden to scream or make loud noises while at sea

If you see a fish in the sea, it's forbidden to yell while seeing it

Forbidden to get naked in the water

Forbidden to bring food into the water

Forbidden to throw salt into the sea

Forbidden to bring gold into the sea

Forbidden to bring silver into the sea

In all regions there were also rules around how to keep the ancestors and spirits happy because they were the real managers and custodians of the ocean. For example, in southwestern Madagascar the *vorombe* or *doany* spirits determined where, when, and what fish were accessible to fishers. Cultural anthropologist Frank Muttenzer vividly describes rituals fishers performed in southwestern Madagascar related to these spirits. Muttenzer observed fishers invoking taboos and performing sacrifices to sea spirits in order to resist MPA enclosure of their fishing spots.

Helo, angatraly, or *lolon-drano* were respected sea managers or custodians in other areas of the island. As mentioned in chapter 2, these spirits granted a fisher access to marine organisms and were instrumental in punishing fishers who transgressed customs and taboos. Many fishers ascribed their catch to these spirits, acting either in favor or against the fisher at a particular time. In villages in both the southwest and northwest, I observed numerous sacrifices (sea turtles, goats, and zebu) and hundreds of ritual offerings from fishers to appease, entreat protection from, or request wealth from spirits of the land and sea in relation to fishing.[10]

In all the marine conservation dina documents I analyzed, few coastal taboos and rules were included. Most were not included because they were seen, as one Merina conservation agent explained to me, as "crazy beliefs [finonom-poana adala] from long ago."[11] One of the few rules that emerged in two dina documents that did not obviously align with a Western conservation framework but reflected a local taboo was "One is not allowed to strike the water in the ocean" (tsy azo atao mively rano). In the northeast and other coastal regions across the island, striking the water demonstrated an oath of loyalty but was also deemed disrespectful to the ancestors, some of whose spirits reside in the ocean. The appearance of this rule demonstrated that either the conservation organization workers helping to constructing the document had enough local knowledge to include this rule or the local fishers were given some agency over the rules that would be listed in their local dina document.

Even when rules seemingly aligned with conservation interests (such as banning the harvest of a particular shark species or fish), they were not often present in dina documents. This surprised me at first; I thought conservation organizations would seize the opportunity to embed these so-called locally established rules into their conservation framework. However, on further inspection of dina documents and after observing how dina was established, I was no longer surprised. Establishing dina occurred in a tightly controlled process, where the formulation and orientation of what becomes customary law was largely predetermined. Governmental and nongovernmental conservation organizations working with fishing communities would come with sample dina documents that they had formulated elsewhere. Ultimately, the narrow focus of governmental and nongovernmental organizations left out a vast realm of meaning that the marine world holds for coastal residents.

Conservation Dina on Women's Access to Marine Resources

How, then, do dina influence resource access across gender and class? The rules constructed in conservation-focused dina disadvantage women's and the least resourced (e.g. boatless) fishers' fishing practices, often restricting methods of fishing such as fishing on foot, turning over dead coral, or using small-meshed nets. In some cases, dina do not explicitly restrict women and the poorest individuals from participating in a community's fishing methods but indirectly deter them from using marine resources.

The processes through which dina were established, as well as the content advanced as dina, both undermined local ownership and exacerbated gendered and class-based access to marine resources. I analyzed fourteen dina contracts that were ostensibly generated at the village level and theoretically represented the interests and values of the communities that generated them. All fourteen documents focused on the protection of a village-level marine reserve. For example, in the southwestern region of Madagascar, four village-level dina contracts were titled "Community Dina concerning Marine Reserves." The title alone illustrates how no-take zones (reserves) were equated with marine conservation. In northeastern Madagascar, the first article of six dina contracts focused on the total size and location of the marine reserve. Marine reserves were the unquestioned starting point of these dina documents. Whether marine reserves aligned with local interests and values was not up for discussion. Community representatives were invited to devise what punishment a fisher would face if caught fishing in the reserve, not whether the reserve should exist in the first place.

Other than the focus on marine reserves, the dina documents demonstrated how existing national laws were infused into local level governance. Dina in six villages in the northeast restricted the size or weight of targeted organisms and established fishing gear rules aligned with national policy, and in some cases colonial marine resource use rules. For example, all six documents established to the same restriction that octopus must be over 350 grams, lobster must be over 18 centimeters (including tail), and crabs must have a carapace over 8 centimeters. A minimum mesh size of nets in these documents was set at 2.5 centimeters, and the use of poison to fish was banned. All of these rules reflect national-level laws, some of them established during the

Shell harvest, southwestern Madagascar. Photograph by author.

colonial period. Rules concerning lobster and crabs match word for word a de-
cree established in 1922 by the French colonial government titled "Regulating
Marine and Coastal Fishing in the Colony of Madagascar and Dependencies"
(Petit 1930).[12]

Furthermore, close look at the fourteen dina contracts generated by conservation organizations in collaboration with regional authorities and community representatives in the early 2010s clearly shows that the ideas and
ideologies of conservation organizations inscribed there are implicitly gendered. In numerous cases, dina restricted methods of fishing primarily used
by women, and in some cases dina indirectly deterred women from using
marine resources. One rule found in more than half of the dina contracts
was one that all fishers in the area must have (*tsy maintsy manana*) a fishing
card. Because few women had fishing cards, this rule implicitly restricted
women from fishing (see chapter 5).

Three rules that most commonly appear in the contracts include: it is
prohibited to walk on the reef; it is prohibited to turn over, break, or move

coral; and it is prohibited to use fishing nets with a mesh size under 2.5 centimeters (for example, mosquito nets).[13] These rules are logical from the perspective of a Western-trained conservation biologist, given that coral reefs are key habitat for many marine organisms and are fragile; thus fishers should not walk on them or disturb them (move or turn pieces over) when fishing. In a similar vein, tiny mesh nets capture juvenile fish and other marine organisms, preventing them from reaching reproductive maturity and therefore potentially threatening the stability of marine populations. If, however, one looks at these management strategies in context, it is clear that they are not necessarily the only or best way to protect marine fisheries and biodiversity.

First, as detailed in chapter 3, fishing on foot is not necessarily damaging to the marine environment, specifically coral, but instead is contingent on the frequency and specific practices of fishing on foot. Second, fishing harvest techniques using small-mesh nets (seine nets) vary widely. Beach seines have been fairly well documented as key factors contributing to a decrease in fish abundance, fish diversity, and ultimately fisher income.[14] They are large nets that are taken out from shore by one or several boats, then gradually and arduously pulled in by a group of people (anywhere from five to twenty individuals, including men, women and children). However, beach seines are but one kind of seine with a mesh smaller than 2.5 centimeters. For example, although some women participate in beach seining, the majority of women who net fish do so in small groups (two to four people), wading into the shallow zone next to the beach. These women (and sometimes children) use sheets of cloth (*lambahoany*) or small-mesh nets such as mosquito nets (*mostikera*, well under the 2.5 centimeter rule). While some women do this activity year-round (19 percent), most women use this harvest technique seasonally (81 percent), targeting schools of fish that have reached sexual maturity but run during a certain time of year, such as round herring or anchovies. Although I cannot point to a study attesting to the relative ecological impact of large beach seines compared to much smaller seines commonly used by two to three women at a time, the scale and scope alone of these two practices on a given day indicates that these techniques likely differ substantially in their ecological impact. In other words, a blanket rule such as the

2.5 centimeter minimum net mesh size does not adequately account for the scale, season, and specific practices associated with different seine fishing techniques. These nuances matter to women: without adequate consideration of these factors, women's work in the ocean will be rendered illegal.

Last, the codification of specific conservation objectives identified by international NGOs into resource use dina at the local level ultimately operates as a messaging tool that conservation organizations employ to extinguish practices they deem antithetical to conservation. Conservation organization messaging, beyond working to change behavior, also seeks to change fishers' ontological beliefs around what drives marine resource change. This theme, also explored in chapter 2, underscores the importance of feminist conservation moving beyond instrumentalist invocations of customary law, and instead enable local cosmologies and ontologies to guide conservation intervention.

Beyond the Instrumentalization of Customary Law

As the opening vignette illustrates, dina has been a key site of struggle over access to and control over marine resources in Madagascar in relation to community-based MPA management. The vignette also highlights how women have been agents in this struggle, albeit disempowered in important ways, and underscores the tensions around the role of conservation agents in the process of community-based conservation. The invocation of dina in marine conservation in Madagascar exposes the power differences among international NGOs, governmental organizations, and different marine resource users within a village. Dina classifies the rights of individuals and organizations to access and control both marine spaces and marine resources. Understanding who is activating dina, and to what end, thus helps us identify who benefits the most from dina.

Conservation organizations were one clear beneficiary of dina. Leveraging what they consider local customary law, organizations used dina to legitimize enclosing marine spaces and restricting different kinds of fishing. A disproportionate burden of these rules fell on women and the poorest fishers, given the focus of dina contracts on activities like fishing on foot.

In theory, the formalization of fokonolona and dina at the local level should help ensure that the values and interests of local people are privileged in decision-making. In practice, however, the interests and values of officials and organizations at the regional and national level often superseded local interests and reifyed racial and ethnic hierarchies. Local values and interests were upheld when they aligned with the interests of higher levels of social and administrative organization and were made legible to decision-makers at these levels.

Ultimately, a feminist approach to conservation that grants communities the power to devise, implement, and enforce their own resource use rules would require existing organizations at the district, commune, regional, and national level to give up their decision-making power to the resource users themselves. Not only does this go against the administrative mandates of these organizations (Fritz-Vietta, Rottger, and Stoll-Kleemann 2009), but it also means that what conservation organizations or governmental offices believe should happen to protect, conserve, develop, and professionalize Malagasy fishers may not come to fruition. It is therefore not surprising that dina has been a key conduit in the co-optation of community-based conservation, allowing nonlocal actors to shape, if not determine, the rules of resource use access and control.

The leveraging of customary law parallels colonial efforts to extract and render static natural resource use processes and practices that are deeply dynamic and do not always align with Western conservation ideology. Fishing on foot, maligned by most marine conservation organizations in the regions included in my research, thus became a common item for conservation organizations to include in dina. In so doing, conservation organizations established a hierarchy of what is considered ecologically good and worthy of professionalizing and what is deemed bad and important to curtail. How, then, did the idea of professionalization end up shaping fisher identity—and what (or whose) fishing practices were uplifted or disparaged in the process?

FIVE

Professionalization, Identity, and Persuasion

> Normally, all fishers must have a card. Because the philosophy
> is to professionalize fishers. We want to make it mundane, like
> a driver's license and all that.
>
> —*Conservation NGO agent, southwestern Madagascar,*
> *June 30, 2018*

> I'd like a fishing card, I've been waiting for a long time. Some of my
> family members have a card, but only men.
>
> —*Fisherwoman, southwestern Madagascar, July 3, 2018*

On an afternoon like most afternoons in Bemena, a small village in southwestern Madagascar, I sat with fishers as they warmed themselves in the last rays of sunshine. Propped up on elbows and leaning back on boats that had earlier been lifted above the high-water line by family members and fish traders, a group of women talked about how they hunt for octopus on the reef. Tomely, an elderly woman known for her hunting skills, said that she intuitively knows which holes in the reef they like. Mamisoa, a middle-aged woman, said that she looks for the eye of an octopus: the dark slit of the octopus's eye is unlike the rest of its body because it can't be camouflaged. Two others agreed with Mamisoa, and one added that her spear guides her: it can feel into spaces that she can't see.

Mamisoa, a stout woman with soft eyes and weathered hands, got up and nodded to me "let's go." I had requested the day before to ask her a few questions about being appointed to Bemena's local conservation committee. We had talked many times while out on the reef or fetching water from the well in the early morning or playing cards in the afternoon shade. But today was the day I could dig into some unanswered questions. Mamisoa is the president of Bemena's women's association. She is esteemed by other women for being smart and direct as well as for marrying into a large politically and financially powerful fishing family in the village. Her husband asked her to join the local conservation committee two years ago and she became the first woman on the committee. She is one of ten local committee members, all of whom represent the village in the larger regional fishing association. When we arrived at her home, she opened a small blue notebook that was tattered on the edges and slowly counted as she whispered names to herself. She moved aside a small vase with plastic flowers in it and opened the book on the small table between us. She smiled: "Look, there are now six women." She read me their names and the villages they represented. There were more than 150 people involved in local conservation committees across the region. Mamisoa explained, "When the committees first formed, there was only one woman [she pointed the pen toward herself], so things have improved." In the crease of her book was a small white card with her picture on it. When I asked her what it was, she lifted it out and stated, in the Malagasy dialect used in the nation's capital, that it was her fisher identity card (*karatra mpanjono*). I nodded, impressed, and asked her if everyone had to get one. "Yes," she said. "Everyone who fishes is required to have one if they want to continue to fish, but only people part of a fishing association can get one."

I asked Mamisoa if Tomely and the other women we were sitting with earlier also had cards. She replied no, and then added, "Mostly men have cards, only a few women." When I asked why these women who fish regularly don't have cards, she paused for a moment and then explained to me in a tone that emphasized how obvious it was, "Women have the same rights [*mira zo*], but do not carry the same weight/are not at the same level [*tsy mira lenta*] as men. That is what makes women, women [*izay maha ampela ty ampela*]."[1]

We have now seen how many Malagasy fishers, especially those who are women and the poorest in a community, lack agency in determining the present and future configuration of human-nature relations. Now I show how programs advanced by international conservation organizations, the

Net fisher pulling up a net in southwestern Madagascar. Photograph by author.

World Bank, and the Malagasy Ministry of Marine Resources and Fishing (now the Ministry of Fisheries and the Blue Economy) to professionalize and modernize small-scale fishing in Madagascar were in fact some of the more insidious forces in shaping small-scale fishers' access to and control over marine resources: they intensified gendered and wealth-based divisions of labor and in so doing reshaped and redefined categories of gender and poverty. More broadly, the sociocultural and political economic processes of fisheries management deepened social stratifications regarding race, gender, and class. Mamisoa's prescient remark regarding the disproportionately low number of women who had fisher identity cards as something that "makes women, women" underscores the power of conservation programming in shaping definitions and meanings of gender.

The widening of social stratifications in access to and control over marine resources, framed in the tidy narrative of so-called professionalization of small-scale marine fisheries, emerged from governmental and non-governmental interests in formalizing and modernizing fishing. A feminist approach to conservation should resist mandates that require formalization and modernization of resource-based livelihoods, which deepen social stratification. Fisher identity cards were a core feature of the formalization and modernization programs advanced by nongovernmental and governmental conservation organizations. Beyond codifying who was deemed a legal and thus a legitimate fisher, several organizations also used fisher identity cards to confine to one area previously itinerant small-scale fishers.

Ultimately, efforts to professionalize and modernize small-scale fishing in Madagascar infused greater parastatal surveillance over new watery places and marine-based people and reshaped gender and class categories. The notion that conservation and development programming concerning fisheries professionalization and modernization in Madagascar were rolled out, as governmental and nongovernmental organizations assured me, in an unbiased way "open to all" and thus blind to race, class, and gender, paradoxically perpetuated racialized, gendered, and classed disparities in the outcomes of these programs. By showing how fishing identity became redefined and spatially bound through fisher identity card programs, I denaturalize the seemingly normal and necessary process of modernizing small-scale fishing in Madagascar and highlight the importance of feminist conservation in interrogating "modernization" and "professionalization" projects.

The Professionalization of Fisheries and Its Colonial Roots

To understand the drivers of current racial relations between small-scale fishers and national and international organizations pushing to modernize Malagasy fishers we must look at the deeper history of Westernizing efforts in the fishing sector.

Foreign interests in modernizing and professionalizing fisheries in Madagascar date back to the colonial period. A major proponent of this modernization, as discussed in chapter 1, was Georges Petit. Petit conducted research on Malagasy fisheries in the early 1900s. He was one of the key architects of marine fisheries law during colonial rule in Madagascar, which left an indelible mark on the legal landscape of postcolonial marine conservation.[2] Like other colonial conservationists of the time, Petit promoted the idea that the colonial state had a duty to conserve marine species both for rational economic exploitation, or "wealth from which European industry could certainly make a successful profit," and for the protection of hapless unique species from "Indigenous vandalism"(Petit 1930, 318).[3] This racialized anxiety concerning natural resource use legitimized colonial policies that restricted fishing practices and fishing areas, an earlier version of conservation as development. Petit and other Western conservationists at the time linked conservation to development as a way to ensure economic growth and capital accumulation but also to advance a modern and civilized society, one with the philosophically and theologically informed attribute of preserving exotic species in the lost Edens of the colonies. France's National Society for the Protection of Nature, similar to Britain's Society for the Preservation of the Wild Fauna of the Empire, was instrumental to the advancement of conservation ethics and legislation in France and French colonies such as Madagascar in the early twentieth century.[4]

These framings of conservation as development during the colonial period were important antecedents to the post–World War II international conservation movement in Europe and the United States, which similarly extended its reach into biodiverse countries in the Global South. In Madagascar, the colonial state saw conservation intervention as a means to discipline so-called ignorant and backward Malagasy resource users and their barbarous practices, such as fishing for sea turtles and dugongs, while advancing technocratic modernism and scientific resource management (Baker-Médard 2020). These frameworks constructed Malagasy fishers as morally and technically inferior to their white European counterparts. For example, Petit wrote that Malagasy fishers in eastern Madagascar used "lazy techniques" (*technique paresseuse*), which treated fishing more as a hobby (*passe-temps*) than as a profession. "Professionalization" was promoted as the remedy (Petit 1930, 337). Racial differences, and to a lesser degree gender differences, in fishing methods were the focus of colonial anxieties and interest in professionalizing Malagasy fishers.

Conservation policy and practice became an important facet of colonial racialization, guided by a white European moral and economic imperative. Petit encouraged the colonial state to implement a two-pronged plan that would educate fishers to use different gear and new techniques and establish state-trained Malagasy monitors to enforce colonial conservation rules at dozens of areas around the island. Petit thought that, through education and monitoring, Malagasy fishers would be less destructive to the marine environment and that their labor would reduce malnutrition and improve fertility across the island (Petit 1930, 342–349). Marine conservation policy that emerged during the colonial period included a suite of strategies such as restrictions on fishing seasons, organism-specific harvest size, and gear, as well as small no-take zones and a permitting system that limited the numbers of harvesters of particular organisms.

Colonial marine conservation, both as a conduit for ongoing capital accumulation and as a means to modernize and civilize Malagasy fishers, hinged on establishing clear resource use rules and a robust political economy linking the colonizer and the colonized. Early marine conservation as development established the discursive and material foundation for the emergence of neoliberal marine conservation strategies, which dominate marine conservation policy and practice in Madagascar today.

In the twenty-first century, the push for sustainable management of Madagascar's marine and coastal environments is enmeshed in global and regional politics of economic development, evidenced by the rollout in 2017 of a US$83 million World Bank project called the Second South West Indian Ocean Fisheries Governance and Shared Growth Project (SWIOFish2 for short). SWIOFish2, which closed in 2023, was part of a broader regional effort to grow, sustainably and economically, the so-called blue economy across many Indian Ocean nations (Andriamahefazafy et al. 2020; World Bank 2017c, 2020). A World Bank press release (2017b) articulated this mandate, stating that the SWIOFish2 project "will substantially improve Madagascar's ability to reverse the decline of marine fisheries, improve local livelihoods of fishing communities, and enhance fisheries management along the supply chain in cooperation with the private sector." Parts of this agenda coincided and aligned with the efforts of international NGOs to protect marine resources. As one conservation organization agent who worked with the World Bank to roll out SWIOFish2 in Madagascar stated, the program was the perfect confluence of shared goals because "they [the World Bank and Malagasy government] want to develop the island and we [conservation organizations] want to professionalize fishers to try to conserve resources."[5]

The "professionalization of fishers" seemed to be one goal people at all levels of governmental and nongovernmental conservation organizations agreed on. It was seen as a panacea for conservation and development problems facing coastal areas and the nation at large, including fisheries decline, lack of small-scale fisheries data, regional and national poverty, and threats to coastal and marine biodiversity. As one conservation organization agent put it, "The professionalization of local fishers supports all fishing industries, which is an important part of the Malagasy economy. . . . When fishers register [for ID cards] they can be more closely monitored." An agent at another conservation organization stated that "biodiversity conservation wasn't possible without fisher professionalization," given the importance of moving fishers "further out [to sea, and away] from reefs, but also ensuring they are not using illegal fishing gear." Yet another agent from a third conservation organization said that "professionalization and the process of fisher identification would help improve coastal development because it has been very difficult to come up with statistics on the number of fishers, especially traditional fishers," and that conservation organizations "benefit in the form of grants if they can provide program statistics to funders."[6]

A core component of the SWIOFish2 program was registering fishers and providing them with fisher ID cards and boat number plates. The SWIOFish2 fisher ID cards program built directly on two prior programs initiated by the Malagasy government and international conservation organizations. The first started in 2008, when the Malagasy government implemented a fisher and boat registration program in order to meet "minimum data requirements" needed for "effective fisheries management in three artisanal fishery types: tuna, shark and small pelagic fisheries" (FAO 2008, iv). According to a Ministry of Marine Resources and Fishing (MRHP, now MPEB) agent in-

Truck with ice coolers transporting catch from the village to the processing facility, southwestern Madagascar. Photograph by author.

terviewed, the registration program was devised in 2004 by the FAO, World Bank, and European Union to "modernize all fishing across Madagascar, work against illegal fishing and bring us up to European standards. [The European Union] is interested in the traceability of the [marine] products." However, the program did not roll out until 2008. The MRHP agent clarified, "From 2008 until now we just encouraged fishers to get cards; now we mandate that all fishers have cards."[7] The second program, initiated primarily by several international conservation organizations working in nearly every region of Madagascar, started in 2011 and created site-specific fisher ID cards. One agent working for one of the international conservation organizations that used site-specific IDs explained that, by limiting the area fishers use, both biodiversity protection and total catch per fisher will improve.[8]

The rollout of the SWIOFish2 fisher ID program made evident the influence of the previous fisher ID programs. According to a MRHP agent, the program expanded databases created by the MRHP, updating and merely administering new cards in some regions.[9] SWIOFish2 fisher ID cards also required a regional designation; these designations, however, were much broader (on the order of several hundred kilometers) than the site-specific ID cards associated with the international NGOs, which constrained fishers to several dozen kilometers. The spatial restrictions tied to SWIOFish2 fisher IDs were hotly debated and the source of political protest in several areas. Numerous international NGOs were heavily in favor of having named and highly geographically specific, village-level site designations on each fisher ID, and the MRHP initially favored this approach. During a visit to several towns on the western coast of Madagascar in 2018, however, the MRHP minister was confronted with "protests from fishers" who demanded that they "maintain the freedom to fish in any region of the ocean."[10] After this, the MRHP decided to allow international conservation organizations to maintain their site-specific fisher ID cards in the villages and regions in which they work but would not include site-specificity in the SWIOFish2-supported national fisher registration program.

The compromise meant that some fishers had greater spatial constraints on where they were allowed to fish than others (discussed below). Yet the underlying goal of both the SWIOFish2 and international NGOs' fisher ID cards, similar to colonial antecedents, was to track and better manage Malagasy unprofessional (read unruly, backward) small-scale fishers. The racial hierarchies and colonial undertones of this venture were hard to miss. Another feature of both fisher ID programs was the disproportionally low enrollment of women and the poorest in coastal communities. The overarching goals as well as the logistical rollout of these programs deepened social stratifications within coastal communities, shaping both legal categories and normative understandings of race, gender, and class. Fishing efforts, especially those of women and the poorest in a given community, were rendered illegal if they did not comply with the new fisher ID system. Normative values relating to what constituted legal fishing, and also what was deemed professional, infiltrated fishers' understanding of their ocean-based activities.

Gendering Fisher Identification

In a project appraisal report released in conjunction with the launch of SWIOFish2, the World Bank (2017d, 18) acknowledged that "women represent 21 percent of the fishers and [that the percentage] is higher in coastal areas"; that women represent "13 percent of [fishing vessel] crews"; and that women represent "half of the fishers who do not use vessels." And yet the report also affirms that there are no "project-relevant gaps between males and females" to address in the rollout of SWIOFish2 (2).

A World Bank report (2017d, 54) stated that specific actions oriented to "improve women's empowerment" would be taken, which the report later related specifically to ensuring that women's groups would be invited to develop "alternative activities . . . and business opportunities along the entire value [fisheries] chain." The alternative livelihoods listed were broad and included such activities as "vocational training or job placement in seafood handling, processing, and marketing, aquaculture, non-seafood sector-related activities, provision of small equipment, and community work such as mangrove plantation" (54).

Thus, despite recognition of women's role as fishers and the potential for SWIOFish2 programs to exacerbate gender inequalities in marine fisheries, the World Bank played into a pattern of programming with clear historical antecedents, which focuses on developing alternative livelihoods for women fishers while expanding and developing additional fishing opportunities for men. For example, since the early 2010s in several regions of Madagascar, conservation organizations offered numerous alternative livelihood trainings to coastal fishers. The workshops and training sessions they organized were clearly gendered: several conservation organizations, for instance, offered land-based alternative livelihood training for women fishers, including basket weaving and handicraft production. Meanwhile, these same organizations offered marine-based livelihood training for men, including fiberglass boat building to enable men to venture into deeper waters further offshore.

Additionally, the World Bank report missed an important gendered and classed element of the SWIOFish2 program. The fisher ID program required individuals either to have listed themselves as fishers (*panjono*) on their gov-

ernment-issued identity card or to be an enrolled member of a fishing association. Both prerequisites heavily favored men. For example, in the southwest
region of Madagascar, based on a database from Toliara that the MRHP
combined with databases from two marine conservation organizations working in the region, fisher ID cardholders were 84.8 percent men and 15.2 percent women. In surveys conducted in coastal villages in the same region,
approximately 89 percent of all men and 57 percent of all women reported
regularly fishing. Based on these ratios, the number of women who should
have IDs, based purely on whether they regularly fish, should have been dou-
ble what they were, closer to 36 percent of all ID holders.

The disparity in ID card holders by gender led to a disparity in whose
ocean-based activities were deemed legal versus illegal, and this reshaping
categories of gender. Professionalism and maleness were paired through the
legal frameworks associated with the fisher ID program, whereas being an
amateur and incompetence were associated with femaleness.

The outcomes of lacking a fisher ID are not yet fully understood, as
SWIOFish2 just ended. However, a new US$42 million project, funded by
the Global Environmental Facility (GEF), cosponsored by six other international conservation organizations, and called Expanding and Consolidating Madagascar's Marine Protected Areas Network, has taken over some
components of the Fisher ID program. In some areas of the island, local
governmental officials are already monitoring and enforcing the fisher ID
card system (WWF 2018, MEDD 2019). Numerous fishers reported that
they were told by government officials that they cannot fish without one.
Some fishers were more hesitant to fish without an ID, while others reported no change. Beyond changes to fishing practices, the fisher ID system
affected how people understood their identity as a fisher. By emphasizing
that the fisher ID program was just for fishers (the noun *mpanjono*), instead
of anyone who fishes (the action *manjonnao/miandriaky*), the approach to
building the ID database and distributing cards did not align with how
women identified themselves, drastically reducing the number of women
who enrolled to obtain a fisher ID.

While men as a proportion of the fishing population and the frequency
with which men fished were indeed higher, the difference was not large and

certainly did not justify the disproportionately low number of fisher IDs distributed to women. Instead, the significant underrepresentation of women in the fisher ID database was likely due to the way conservation organizations operated in each village and to how distributing organizations framed the IDs.

Understanding this gender disparity more deeply requires us to look at several underlying processes. Through interviews I learned that few women identified primarily or professionally as fishers. Instead, women identified with a suite of activities and were reluctant to choose a single livelihood identity, which governmental officials required for obtaining a national ID card. Therefore, women who fished regularly did not attend meetings where ID photos were taken and cards were distributed. As one woman in a woman's focus group plainly stated with reference to the fisher ID program, "It's not for us, it's not for women." Another chimed in, "They don't want women. They don't distribute fishing cards to women."[11] A second important driver of the disparity was that men's modes of fishing in the ocean were seen as legitimate and thus worthy of professionalization, whereas women's modes of fishing were largely maligned and not deemed worthy of professional development.

Making the Common Strange and the Strange Common

Reducing the pressure [on the reef] is also regulating fishers that use the area. So that is why we have the specific fishery licenses just to alleviate pressure on the reef and fish catch.

—*Conservation organization marine director,*
Antananarivo, July 18, 2018

To facilitate the neoliberal turn in marine conservation as economic development, conservation organizations working in the coastal villages spent a great deal of time and energy to instill new norms concerning fishing practices for local people. Promoting a new sense of right versus wrong conduct lays the psychological foundation on which restrictions, codified in legal regimes, work to eventually extinguish the maligned activity (Foucault 2003; Gramsci 1971). The establishment of a large MPA network across the island, along with significant changes in how, where, and who fishes, required a massive transformation of fishing practices. In order to accomplish this change, governmental and nongovernmental organizations had to make strange what was once common and to make common what was once strange.

The norms governmental and nongovernmental conservation organizations focused on ranged from disfavoring the previously common practice of fishing on foot to favoring the previously uncommon practice of small-scale fishing in deeper waters away from coral reefs. Furthermore, the common practice of small-scale fishers traveling seasonally to fish along the coast and adjacent to islands far from their home region was disfavored in order to narrow the spatial focus of fishing efforts closer to home.

Conservation organizations worked hard to educate local fishers via meetings, workshops, conferences, brochures, illustrated signs erected near the ocean, and one-on-one conversations. One director of a conservation organization working in southwestern Madagascar explained that their organization's environmental education strategy sought to induce a psychological change concerning what is right or wrong and that "they [fishers] need to come to their own understanding of [for example] the problem of fishing on foot, see what we already know as true."[12] Similarly, a director of marine conservation at one of the largest international environmental NGOs in Madagascar, when asked what he thought could help marine conservation in Madagascar, replied, "Professionalization of fishing." He explained, "I mean real fishing; we need to modernize fishing across Madagascar. There are many unprofessional fishers here." When probed to explain what he meant, he answered, "Fishing on foot—women turn over pieces of coral, walk on the reef, this needs to stop. We will make it stop."[13] The marine conservation director emphasized women's place in relation to Madagascar's pursuit of modernity. In other words, in order to professionalize and modernize fishing, women's mode of fishing would need to be extinguished.

The gendered stakes of these efforts to change the perceived common sense of fishing practices are particularly important to examine in pursuit of a more feminist approach to marine conservation. Without deeper examination, it might seem obvious why conservation organizations would want to decrease fishing on foot. As one international conservation organization agent in northeastern Madagascar argued, "Coral reefs are sensitive; they are the most important piece of the ecosystem. So it's only normal that we want to stop all forms of fishing that ruin the reef."[14] In several reports and documents published by governmental and nongovernmental marine conservation organizations, sections titled "Solutions" or "Suggestions" concerning the problem of fishing on foot emphasized the need to "improve fishing techniques by introducing new technologies," "professionalize," or "modernize fishing," to replace fishing on foot. In the process of rendering fishing on foot "unprofessional," even though that kind of fishing was identified as done more by women, these reports ignored the implications this had for men versus women.

Ultimately, as conversations concerning the solutions to the problem of fishing on foot revolve around the words *professional, rational,* and *modern, the* broader history and wider social, political, and economic context is wiped away. As we have seen, only in the context of the long history of fishing on foot in coastal regions of Madagascar can the professed unsustainability of a particular fishing practice be called into question.

Only in recent decades, with expanding global markets and an increasing demand for such products as sea cucumber, opercula, and octopus, has fishing on foot quickly become viewed as unsustainable. When we examine resource use, specifically fishing on foot, from a historical perspective, it is clear that women's fishing techniques per se are not the primary source of degradation. Framing ecological destruction as a problem that stems from local fishers' backward ways or lack of knowledge makes invisible the underlying historical and political-economic processes that are driving the increase in marine resource extraction.

The rise and subsequent dominance of commercial export-oriented fishing in numerous regions of the island persists today. This context is important when trying to understand drivers of ecological change in the marine realm. The decline and collapse of fisheries are the discursive foundation on which marine conservation organizations and development agencies communicate why small-scale marine resource users need their aid and assistance. Conservation organizations' efforts to malign fishing on foot work to make this common fishing practice seemingly strange. Simultaneously, conservation organizations, in creating a fisher ID database, worked to make this new form of fisher identity commonplace.

Inscribing Identity

If you are a true fisher, you must have a card.

— *Male fisher, southwestern Madagascar, June 23, 2018*

Fisher ID cards have been used elsewhere globally to achieve a variety of conservation and development objectives. For example, in Somalia a fisher registration program cosponsored by the FAO registered artisanal fishers to help develop fisheries programming in the region and to combat piracy off the Somali coast (Gilmer 2016). The rollout of the program, however, heavily favored some regions over others and marginalized individuals who engaged in pastoral as well as fishing activities. These incongruencies were important in the daily lives of fishers because any non-ID-carrying fisher could then be suspected of illicit activities and subject to arrest. Similarly, in Madagascar, although fisher ID cards create an avenue to legitimize the practices of the fishers who carry them, beneath this validation lies the opposing truth: if fishers with ID cards are legitimate, those who fish without them become illegitimate. Therefore, whereas noble goals might underpin fisher identification programs, their impact is highly uneven and can exacerbate existing inequalities.

In SWIOFish2 program literature, the registration of fishers and fishing vessels was identified as crucial to "proper" fisheries management and "optimization" of revenue generation:

In the absence of a proper management system fisheries stocks are exploited beyond optimal biological, social and economic limits. Less than 10 percent of the canoes are registered and catches are being largely unreported, stock assessments are rare, economic data are limited and widely dispersed among agencies. The limited data undermines the policy decision-making process for development and management. The result is that Madagascar is exploiting its fisheries stocks without knowledge of maximum sustainable yields and—as has recently been evidenced in the shrimp industry where the causes of massive declines are still being debated—incurring direct social and economic losses or failure to optimize revenue generation. (World Bank 2016, 10)

This sentiment was echoed by a MRHP worker in Antananarivo: "We have also thought about how to best track the fisherman in Madagascar, so it is about the professionalization of fishermen." He added, "We need to register and track fishers so we can improve fishing, just like people operating rickshaws/tuk-tuks, they have licenses and are registered."[15] Similarly, an international conservation organization worker in Antananarivo said that the ID card system is "focused on fisheries, but it's promoting the professionalization of local fishers, supporting fishery industries."[16] Although education and training were also part of the SWIOFish2 program, these officials emphasized the importance of data collection and fisher registration in achieving conservation and development outcomes.

Reports and documents published by governmental and nongovernmental marine conservation organizations emphasized the need to professionalize or modernize fishing by implementing a fisher ID card system. Embedded within these conversations concerning fisher IDs as a solution to a conservation and fisheries production problem were implications that Malagasy fishers were unprofessional, primitive, and backward, in other words, in need of governmental or nongovernmental help.

Ultimately, fisher IDs were seen both as a metric through which the Malagasy government and World Bank could measure progress toward implementing SWIOFish2and as a point of leverage to optimize fisheries production through the calculation of approximate total small-scale fisheries yield. Metrics captured on this first kind of ID included fishers' name, national ID card number, address, fishing association affiliation, region in which they fish, the number, size, length, and depth of each boat they owned, and the type of fishing gear (including size of each net) they used. Although capture metrics were absent from the card, multiple governmental and nongovernmental officials emphasized the potential to model or approximate yield once the number, location, and gear of fishers were documented. Furthermore, fisher ID cards were, as one worker at a regional MRHP office explained, a way to reduce the total number of fishers, or as he put it, establish "a barrier to entry [*barrière à l'entrée*] into the fishing sector and each region to ensure the professionalization of fishing."[17]

The focus on identity cards as an avenue to professionalize and modernize marine fishing in Madagascar resonates with French philosopher and historian Michel Foucault's concept of biopolitics. Biopolitics refers to knowledge and power undertaken by the state to manage, regulate, and optimize the economic potential of a population by "classify[ing] and inscrib[ing] identities as legal and bureaucratic categories" (Ruppert 2011, 219). Through biopolitics, the state and statelike actors such as international conservation and development organizations can create a "legible people" by means of such population metrics as surveys, censuses, and birth registration (Ruppert 2011, 219). Institutionally, biopolitics seeks to "normalize, structure, optimize, and subordinate the forces of individuals to enter them into the machine of the economic system, to make them *productive members of society*" (Cisney and Morar 2015, 6, emphasis in original).

Foucault's emphasis on classifying and inscribing identities into legal and bureaucratic categories in order for society to be more "productive" is foundational to understanding the rise of fisher IDs in Madagascar. In her article "Measuring the World," anthropologist Sally Engle Merry (2011, 10) examines the rise of what she terms "indicator culture," which places an immense amount of "trust in technical rationality, in the legibility of the social world through measurement and statistics, and in the capacity of numbers to render different social worlds commensurable." Indicator culture's seemingly benign emphasis on evidence-based decision-making and results-based management requires "knowledge that is classified, categorized, and arranged into hierarchies," thus shaping normative understandings of what, and therefore who, is valuable (Merry 2016, 4). Building on Merry's central thesis, anthropologists Cris Shore and Susan Wright (2015, 422) argue specifically that "auditing has become a central organizing principle of society," where individuals and organizations arrange their livelihoods and operations around evaluations of how "creditworthy" they are for future investments.

Merry as well as Shore and Wright warn that although indicator (or audit) culture is ostensibly universal—relying on the universal language of numbers—the metrics, classifications, and hierarchies created to evaluate programs or individuals stem almost exclusively from the Global North, where banks, international organizations, and aid institutions promote, devise, and disseminate indicator requirements southward. Furthermore, they warn that indicators are too often presented as clear-cut and objective, erasing the deeply power-laden process of research design, implementation, and analysis.

The process of normalizing and structuring fishers in Madagascar through the fisher ID program allowed fisher activity to became legible to the state, international conservation organizations, and bilateral and multilateral aid networks. The metrics captured on the card reflect what the state deemed important or worth optimizing. The metrics on the ID card also signaled the overarching objective of the ID program: increasing economic output of the fisheries sector while controlling fisher behavior to ensure sustainability. Productivity was linked to the number and size of boats, the type of gear used, and the region in which the fisher resided. For fishers, the ID itself structured what it meant to be a real or professional fisher, shaped by what was or was not captured on the ID card itself.

The distribution of ID cards and boat numbers was haphazard as of 2018, operating primarily through conservation NGOs working in coastal areas. One international conservation organization agent reported that a large pile of boat placards was dropped off at their office with no explanation or direction of what the NGO was to do with them: "The Ministry's been on a mad distribution spree of these cards. They came by our field office and nobody was there; it was a Saturday or a Sunday. They dropped off hundreds of cards, nothing else. They were these sort of fishing licenses, licenses for the boats, so they came with screws to put on people's boats and then blank ID cards for the fishers. So maybe in [the Ministry's] books they checked off our region. But they literally just dropped off the things and didn't give us an explanation."[18]

However, despite potential difficulties in enforcing this strategy to manage and optimize fisheries across the island, even with a partial rollout as of 2023, the fisher ID card system had already shifted fishers' notions of who was a legitimate or real fisher and who was not. One fisher in southwestern Madagascar who obtained but then lost a fisher ID reported having "problems in another location because I didn't have my ID card with me."[19] A village president in one village in southwestern Madagascar said that because it is difficult for the CSP (fishing surveillance organization) to monitor the entire coastline, he and the village vice president helped monitor and enforce fishing IDs. He said that migrants from inland should not be allowed to fish because they aren't as skilled at fishing, and he saw the new card system as helping to stop inland migrants from fishing in the ocean around his village.[20] Many fishers expressed the belief that the card served to legitimize their occupation. For example, a group of eight fishers in a focus group interview in southwestern Madagascar agreed that "men that are truly fishers need to have a card."[21] This sentiment illustrated how conservation organizations intended the ID cards to function. The analogy of a driver's license appeared frequently in conversations with MRHP as well as conservation organization agents. Although no test was required to obtain a fisher ID, this metaphor bolstered the notion that one must be a competent fisher to merit an ID card and that not everyone was competent just because they fished.

It was clear that the process of creating the fisher ID cards was not simply a process of identifying gendered, classed, and racialized subjects of the state but one of producing them. This is aptly described by Evelyn Ruppert (2011, 220), who asserts that the practices of identification "do not simply reveal subjects as already formed and unchanging but produce them."

Ultimately, not only were some fishers and village-level governmental representatives enforcing the law by checking for IDs, but they were individually and communally defining themselves in terms of a category created by the bureaucratic institution. Through the introduction of the fisher ID card system, racial and ethnic divisions were reified, gender binaries solidi-

Fisher pointing to his favorite fishing spot. Photograph by author.

fied, and class stratifications naturalized. The ideals and ideologies held by the World Bank in conjunction with the Malagasy government and international conservation organizations reified these stratifications through their access to formal legal institutions such as courts, policy-making institutions, and law enforcement.

Before the introduction of fisher IDs, fisher identity had often been as fluid as the medium in which fishers work. How, where, and when a fisher worked was highly seasonal, based on tides and weather, and changed with age or due to relationships with family members and neighbors who might take a fisher to a special fishing spot or teach them to fish in a new way. Although the fisher identification process rendered individuals more legible to governmental and nongovernmental organizations tasked with managing coastal people and marine resources, the process flattened, and in many cases erased, relationships fishers had with each other or with fishing spots and marine organisms that inhabited these areas. The privileging of certain modes of fishing over others was a step toward shifting norms as well as structuring and optimizing fishing activities for the interests and needs of the nation and international conservation and development actors, too. As organizations worked to collect fisher information and disseminate ID cards, fishing methods were placed in a hierarchy. Some configurations in which people fished, such as fishing on foot or fishing primarily during spring tides (typically for several days at a time twice in a month), were deemed less professional or real than other fishing practices such as fishing from a boat or fishing daily. Many women I interviewed didn't even consider themselves to be fishers (*piandriake, panjono*), even though most of them fished. They thought about fishing as something they did, not something that was attached to their identity. Living with and from the ocean was woven into everyday practices, along with fetching water, tending to gardens, collecting firewood, caring for children, washing, cooking, weaving, and a multitude of other activities.

In addition, even though the fisher ID system theoretically aimed to register all marine fishers in Madagascar, systemic bias left out a subset of fishing communities. Previously existing class and gender inequalities were exacerbated by the seemingly benign requirement that people who register for a fisher ID card must first have a government-issued ID card. Although everyone in Madagascar was in theory eligible to have a government-issued identity card, not everyone interviewed had one. This was true in several remote coastal villages and was especially true among the poorest of each community. One of the key documents required to obtain a government-issued identity card is a birth certificate. However, of eight people interviewed in one village who lacked a national identity card, five were women, and all of them cited the lack of money to travel to district and regional governmental offices as obstacles to obtaining an ID. This trend aligned with findings from a UNICEF (2020) report in which "distance" was cited as the primary factor preventing people in Madagascar from being listed in the national register and from a World Bank (2017a) report that cited a slightly lower birth certificate possession rate for women than men (61.3 percent versus 62.4 percent, respectively). According to the World Bank (2017a), in some rural areas only 46 percent of children from the poorest socioeconomic quintile had birth certificates. These numbers highlight the gaps and uneven national registry terrain in which fisher IDs operated, revealing systemic bias embedded in this marine conservation and resource management strategy.

Ultimately, the bias in who tended to obtain fisher IDs—primarily men and wealthier individuals—skewed who could secure rights to benefit from marine resources. National registry dynamics combined with a delegitimization of certain fishing practices contributed to an insidious imposition of gendered and classed hierarchies on marine resource access.

Imposing the Commons: Sedenterizing as Territorialization

As mentioned, several years before and during the rollout of the SWIOFish2 fisher ID system, international NGOs created their own fisher ID card system. These cards were issued solely to fishers living in or near MPAs. The ID cards granted fishers usufructuary rights, or rights to harvest resources, in the multiuse zone of a particular MPA. In return for these special use rights, fishers in the area were tasked with patrolling the area to prevent fishing there by those who did not live next to the MPA. Fishers without cards were forbidden to fish in the multiuse zone of the MPA.

According to my survey results, although fishers in every part of the island reported traveling to fish, fishers in southwestern Madagascar had the highest rates of migration for fishing. Of all informants surveyed who said they migrated to fish, 70 percent ($n=90$) were from southwestern Madagascar.[22] Of those who migrated to fish, 70 percent ($n=63$) were men and 30 percent ($n=27$) were women. In coastal southwestern Madagascar villages, it was common for individuals aged eighteen to forty-five migrate up to hundreds of kilometers away to fish for two to six months. Other research from this region finds that on average, fishers spend at least eighty-six days a year fishing for sharks and sea cucumbers in remote and seasonal fishing areas (Cripps and Gardner 2016; Iida 2005).

The geographic specificity of MPA-associated fisher IDs was the key element in conservation organizations' strategy to reduce outmigration by incentivizing fishers to stay at home and prohibiting them from fishing elsewhere. The strategy was predicated on the idea that spillover of marine life from well-protected MPAs into the fishable zones would allow fishers to concentrate their efforts in a more geographically constrained area close to home. Fisher IDs provided the foundation for this sedentarization process. The fisher ID cards reconfigured and narrowed fishers' socioecological relations into a space that could be monitored and managed. This spatial and identity-based narrowing was necessary in order to align with metrics and objectives promulgated at the national and international level: again to develop Madagascar's blue economy in order to expand the marine fisheries sector's contribution to the nation's gross domestic product and to decrease marine biodiversity loss and habitat destruction (World Bank 2016).

Fisher IDs tied to MPAs attempted to create the commons, imposing an Ostrom-style common resource management regime on fishing communities that were otherwise migratory. A World Bank report outlined the logic of this approach:

> As small-scale fisheries modernize or the number of fishers increases, the limited potential of many coastal fisheries will require that the fishing effort be reduced to adjust to optimal resource regeneration capacity. . . . Reduction or elimination of destructive fishing is also a significant governance and social challenge, as communities are dependent on the declining catches from this spiraling environmental and economic depletion—typical of the tragedy of the commons. Co-management approaches can serve as important pathways out of overexploitation and poverty—particularly for the poorest—through providing communities with the mandate and skills to manage and benefit from fishery resources. (World Bank 2017d, 13)

Here, the World Bank sees "co-management" as a way to prevent the tragedy of the commons and cure poverty. The use of the word *mandate* in this report underscores that marine conservation and fisheries management is in fact a directive from the World Bank, international conservation organizations, and the Malagasy government to coastal marine resource–reliant communities to create community-based resource management regimes.

Ostrom's work detailing the ability of communities to govern their own common pool natural resources is predicated on the assumption that the collective interest, instead of individual interests, will guide communities to establish rules and practices that conserve the resources on which they rely. Although some CPR management regimes function well and help protect resources and the livelihoods of resource users, the MPA-ID regime introduced in Madagascar was significantly different both ideologically and institutionally from those regimes outlined by Ostrom. First, in Ostrom's work (1990, 92), the rules of conduct and use were created from those most intimately familiar with the resources, ostensibly fashioned from the values and worldview of the people vested in preserving the reciprocal socionatural relationship on which their sustenance or livelihoods rely. In the MPA-ID system, by contrast, fishers were expected to participate in protecting no-take zones, the goals, size and location of which were established with the strong guidance, or in some cases blatant coercion, of international conservation organizations. Second, Ostrom's (1990, 101) "rights to organize" principle indicates that "external governmental authorities" should not challenge the rights of resource users to devise their own rules and processes for managing natural resources. However, with the MPA-ID program, fishers were held responsible for performing to organizational and resource use standards set forth by governmental and nongovernmental organizations. Thus, fisher IDs were the avenue through which funding organizations such as the World Bank, the Malagasy government, and international conservation groups were able to control who used marine resources and where and how they did so.

As a conservation organization agent working in the southwestern region explained, fisher ID cards allowed the conservation organization to limit, and eventually freeze, the total number of fishers permitted to fish in an area. He said, "What logically follows is a reduction in resource use, improved biodiversity protection and better catch for those who are allowed to still fish; here we are trying to limit the number of fishers to fifty."[23]

In interviews, conservation workers identified fishing pressure as a significant threat to reef ecosystems; successful conservation therefore required controlling the number of fishers in these spaces. As the director of one international conservation organization asserted, "We have to manage fishers in addition to fisheries. Managing fishery activities means managing fisher activities."[24] A field agent outlined even more directly that his conservation organization's objectives were twofold: "to professionalize fishers and conserve resources, we have to change where they fish to conserve the ocean."[25] The spatial limitations of both MPAs and fisher IDs aligned with the broader project of territorialization.

Territorialization is a process in which individuals or groups in power delineate boundaries of exclusion by allocating resource use (and other) rights to individuals within a particular geographic space (Vandergeest and Peluso 1995).[26] Territoriality focuses on allowing or restricting specific activities within particular spaces. Regulation, legitimation, force, and market incentives are all used in the boundary-making process to exclude some, to include others, and to shape and then reinforce the boundaries (Hall, Hirsch, and Li 2011). The demarcations of spaces, and the regulatory frameworks constructed to give meaning to the demarcations, are how the modern state classifies, organizes, and simplifies socionatural complexity, thus making people and territory intelligible to government (Scott 1998). The demarcations and regulations tend to create territories that are seemingly linear and homogeneous (Vandergeest and Peluso 1995). Protected areas are particularly useful in the territorial process, given that they are "discrete, measured and eminently countable" (Igoe, Neves, and Brockington 2010, 495). While making spaces easier to conceptualize, simplified or abstract space neglects heterogeneity, change over time, and the lived sociospatial relationships of humans to place (Vandergeest and Peluso 1995). On maps of coastal Madagascar, the MPAs appear as blue blocks of color with small variations based on the type of fishing allowed within certain areas. These maps provided the Malagasy state and international NGOs a method to categorize otherwise politically, ecologically, socially, and culturally complex places and mark them as protected. Dynamic processes such as fish migration patterns, human migration, economic changes, and cultural and spiritual practices were flattened in the process of abstracting place into territory.

The enclosure of these marine spaces required the creation of social boundaries layered onto spatial boundaries. Although it was advanced by international NGOs in conjunction with the Malagasy government, the process of establishing social boundaries, determining who was allowed to access marine resources, was led by regional and local actors. Therein lays a paradox: even though territorialization resulted from foreign and national interests in obtaining greater control over people and resources in marine areas and concentrated power in the hands of key national and international conservation organizations, this approach relied on a decentralized governance strategy. Decentralization was necessary both to legitimize international NGO intervention in small coastal villages next to marine biodiversity hotspots and to decrease the financial costs of establishing this new marine resource management strategy.

Beyond giving warnings and seizing illegal gear, international conservation organizations lacked the legal standing to enforce marine resource use rules. Instead they delegated monitoring and enforcement to resource users themselves and worked to embed local laws or dina into the state's judicial system. International conservation organizations through SWIOFish2 emphasized educating fishers and working with the Malagasy government to improve the performance of local, regional, and national monitoring, control, and surveillance of fishing (World Bank 2016). As one marine director explained, "Within our seascapes we have our community control surveillance committee, CCS. The CCS runs patrols within the MPAs. Their role covers also checking on fisher licenses, if one has one or not, if one is allowed or not. This is the way we have law enforcement on the ground."[27] In a village where ID cards had been distributed several years earlier, a member of the local surveillance committee confirmed the role of fisher IDs in monitoring: "The fisher cards are very useful for us for the regulation of our zone [discipline de zone], to protect our zone [protéger notre zone], and to respect the regulations. If there are people from other villages who are not from our zone, who don't have a fisher card, who bring illegal fishing materials, we will send them to the authorities."[28]

Which fishers were included as insiders was determined by local management committees in conjunction with the international conservation organizations working in each village. As one international conservation organization field agent explained, "Decisions are made by both the local fishing association and us [the conservation organization], and then once the list is finalized the request goes to the Ministry of Fishing to decide."[29] The director of another international conservation organization emphasized the role of local fishing associations organized by the NGOs, asserting that fishers who want IDs "have to pass through the local association so [the international conservation organization] can approve the request. They have to be a member of a local association to get a fisher license."[30]

In terms of Elinor Ostrom's eight design principles for successful common pool resource management, fisher IDs helped establish the first and most important principle, stated as "clearly defined boundaries: Individuals or households who have rights to withdraw resource units from the CPR must be clearly defined, as must the boundaries of the CPR itself" (Ostrom 1990, 90). Giving exclusive rights to marine resources as a conservation and development strategy also aligns with the neoclassical economic ideology advanced by Ronald Coase (2000 [1960]), which asserts that assigning individual or collective property rights to natural resources will help society reach its social, environmental, and economic optimum. According to both Ostrom and Coase, establishing exclusive rights over resources helps align individual and collective interests and allows for mutual accountability.

While this sounds enticing, significant challenges existed in conservation organizations' attempts to impose the commons in effective and just ways. As noted, although fishers in a given area theoretically had the right to fish in the multiuse zone of the MPAs, many women and the poorest fishers in a community were not able to exercise their rights given how the assignment of fisher IDs played out in practice. A further complication was the porous nature of community boundaries and who counted as an insider.

Although fishing eligibility requirements seemed straightforward, difficulties arose when fishing associations and international conservation organization field agents had to decide who was an insider or an outsider. A marine conservation director initially explained that who was eligible for an ID was simple: "IDs were only distributed to those who used the area prior to the implementation of the MPA." Yet when pressed on who decided this and how it was decided, the director said that in fact things were "very complex," given that some fishers had fished in the MPA region seasonally for their entire lives but did not have permanent residence in the area. The director explained that ultimately, "even if they are not living inside but used the area before the MPA, then they can benefit from the specific MPA–ID license as long as they are at least 18."[31]

An international conservation organization field agent in southwestern Madagascar explained that they informed fishers in numerous villages that the number of cards would be limited (*un nombre limité*).[32] The field agent said that when they came to register fishers, collect information, and take pictures, some fishers who did not reside in the target village obtained cards because they happened to be in the village on the days the conservation organization distributed cards and had friends in the local fishing association who vouched for them. However, the inverse was true as well. Some fishers interviewed who lived in the village but were away when the conservation organization distributed cards did not receive ID cards. It was difficult for people to obtain a card after the initial round of data collection occurred because visits to some villages were infrequent. As one village president lamented, "If you didn't get your card, you can go to the regional city to get your card. But [the conservation organization] hasn't come back yet."[33] The long and spatially dispersed bureaucratic process of obtaining a fishing card was an obstacle for some. The combined logistics of needing to be present on ID processing day, having a history of fishing in the area, securing a national identity card, being at least eighteen, and enrolling in a fisher's association meant that numerous fishers were left out. In addition, reliance on enrollment in a fishing association to obtain a fisher ID meant that association members had discretion over who they believed should or should not be allowed to fish. My interviews with fishing association leaders, fishing association members, and fishers who were not members of associations showed me that associations followed no set rules to determine who could join an association and thus get an ID card. Instead, membership was influenced by assumptions about what a fisher looked like and what kind of fishing was deemed economically and environmentally good or professional, which similarly plagued the SWIOFish2-supported fisher ID program. The new element to "good" or "professional" fisher was also spatialized, lending itself to even more exclusive notions of who was an insider.

Moreover, the exclusive rights strategy, on which spatially tied fisher IDs rely, were not defensible in practice. Across all three regions, fishers complained about well-funded export-oriented fishing ventures coming into local multiuse and community-use zones. These outsider fishers, some of whom were armed, were often tied to well-funded exporters. For example, in one comanaged MPA in northeastern Madagascar, where Madagascar National Parks worked in collaboration with a local fishing association and community-based management committee, wealthy boat-owners from port cities several hundred kilometers away fished within the MPA. Individuals on these boats often came armed and frequently left the same day they arrived. Some of the boat captains, working directly for exporters, would hire local men to dive for sea cucumbers or collect other lucrative products such as shark fins, seahorses, and lobster. Similarly, in northwestern Madagascar in a community-managed MPA established in 2015, numerous fishers emphasized that they could not monitor their community-based MPA because they lacked motorized boats. In one focus group, several elder fishers stated that in the past decade there was an increase in the number of fishers from outside their community fishing for lucrative organisms (primarily sea cucumbers, but also lobster, fish, squid, and sharks) in the waters next to their villages. They argued that to monitor and enforce their exclusive rights within the multiuse zone of the MPA, as well as the no-take zones, they would need a speedboat, binoculars, and guns (Baker-Médard, Rasoanandrasana, and Saula 2011). They stressed that they would also have to be backed by either private or governmental entities who would be more feared by transgressors and who would have contacts with people in positions of power better able to solve the problem of contravening MPA rules.

International conservation organizations working in both of these areas recognized this issue but were not sure how to address the problem. Two directors of marine conservation from these organizations said that it boiled down to a capacity issue and financial insufficiency. One said, "Yes, I know fishers from outside can be a menace. They used speedboats or other illegal fishing techniques. But that is why we utilize a community-based approach. It's for this reason one must go before the [local] managers to raise awareness [sensibiliser] that in our MPA it is forbidden to use illegal techniques."[34]

The question then arises about what motivates conservation organizations, if they know that incursions regularly occur from fishers backed by well-funded exporters, to continue with this hyperlocal construction of the commons. The drive to impose the commons in these seascapes goes back to the politics of the low-hanging fruit. Conservation organizations essentially pick the metaphorical low-hanging fruit by focusing their efforts at the local level. At this scale, conservation organizations can exert their financial and political power to change some people's environmental behavior. Conservation organizations' focus on sedenterizing marine resource users, rather than addressing ultimate drivers of fisheries decline such as global commodity chains, well-funded illicit extraction networks, foreign fishing, and more.

Resistance to Being Legible

Women are scared and don't want to get fisher ID cards. They call the ID system a "hook in the neck," a trap, something that'll be tied to a tax.

—*Ministry of Fisheries and Marine Resources agent, southwestern Madagascar, July 14, 2018*

To my surprise the lack of a fisher ID was not always seen as negative to certain fishers without IDs, particularly women. Some women indicated that being left out of the new fisher ID system was good. Although the lack of an ID had the potential to jeopardize one's long-term access to marine resources, it also allowed one to be less legible to the state apparatus and therefore freer. Some women were wary of recent governmental and non-governmental interventions in their lives. One woman in a village in which cards had recently been distributed said, "Things aren't clear, I don't know what they, the government or the project is doing, I don't want to get involved."[35] A women from a different village in the southwest also indicated that she was not upset about not having a fisher ID because it meant "I wouldn't be caught with the government's tax [*hetra fanjakana*]."[36] This concern was not groundless. According to a regional agent of the MRHP in 2008, due to a push from the World Bank, European Union, and FAO to establish minimum catch information requirements, fish collectors, who at the local level were primarily women, had to register as collectors and pay anywhere from 20,000–60,000 Ariary (US$5–15) per license. Local collectors called this a governmental tax.[37] As one elderly man declared in a mixed-gender focus group interview in southwestern Madagascar, "When the government counts something, they'll tax it." He explained that many years earlier "the government required everyone in our village to number their houses, then later began taxing each household based on their registered house number."[38]

An international conservation organization field agent who distributed the cards confirmed this resistance, explaining, "Yeah, some don't want taxes, they are afraid. It's not only [fear of] taxes. They are afraid maybe that we will take them to prison or they may have trouble with the government if they give this information." If an individual refused to provide all the necessary information, they did not receive a card. The field agent added that some fishers were fearful at first but then came around: "Some people change their minds. Sometimes they need time to think."[39] Another worker in the same office who was charged with distributing the cards said in a low voice so that his superiors wouldn't hear, "This job is very difficult [*sarotra mare*]." He said that he actually believed that a tax might one day be tied to the ID cards. When he visited each village, he continued, "we count the boats and everything." Echoing the elderly man from the focus group, he explained that "if the government does a census [*recensement fanjakana*] and they number each house, then later they'll collect taxes per house. This is the same thing."[40] Another MRHP worker seconded the difficulty of registering fishers due to fear of taxes. He said that this fear also applied to fishers joining fishing associations, a prerequisite for the card: "People are also afraid of being taxed if they are in association."[41]

Understanding the gendered practices regarding household finances put into context some of the gendered fears and resistance to registering for a fisher ID. Many women are the primary and often exclusive financial managers for their household. In the survey conducted with 889 people across three regions of the island in 2011, 86.2 percent responded that a woman in the household exclusively managed finances for the household. Of the remaining households, 28.1 percent reported that finances were jointly managed between spouses (*mpivady/mpivaly*). In other words, women's role as household financial manager might have made them more reluctant to enter in a system that could increase household costs. By understanding and being attentive to gendered intra-household dynamics, as well as societal gendered divisions of labor, conservation programming can be more feminist in its approach and push against misguided modernization solutions to fisheries management.

Revisiting the Paradox of Professionalization

The professionalization and modernizing strategies endorsed by the Malagasy government and carried out by numerous international conservation organizations powerfully shaped how fishers saw themselves and one another, thus shaping categories of gender, race, and class. Embedded in the logic of modernizing and professionalizing fisheries in Madagascar was the pursuit of making fisheries more "rational" and "organized." These framings disparaged current fishing practices as irrational, unorganized, and decidedly not modern. Taken together, the discursive and material strategies conservation organizations used rendered women and poorer fishers' fishing practices illegal, sedenterized previously itinerant fishers, and reshaped Malagasy fishing identity.

The purported gender-blindness of these programs exacerbated gendered inequalities. The ID system in particular was one of the most insidious yet powerful forces racializing Malagasy fishers as decided by not up to European standards, and marginalizing women and poor fishers. The professionalization and modernization strategies used by governmental and nongovernmental organizations that imposed a sedentary commons with a restricted number of users reconfigured notions of community, of who is an insider and ultimately of what constitutes a real commons. Women's tendency to have plural livelihood identities was incongruent with the new fisher identification system. Although many women living in the coastal areas fished (up to 80 percent in some villages) and fished frequently, few identified themselves primarily as fishers and did not attend meetings where ID photos were taken and cards distributed. Similarly, the biases that influenced who obtained national ID card were replicated in the fisher ID card system, which resulted in the poorest of each community not being eligible for a fisher ID.

Given the issues wrought by small-scale fisher professionalization and formalization, what would a more feminist approach to conservation look like in Madagascar? How might a conservation and development program focused on fisheries appear if self-determination were the starting point of the program instead of an added burden to consider in the pursuit of other objectives?

SIX

A Case for Transnational Feminist Conservation

The New World Order is best described as a process of recolonization.
Far from flattening the world into a network of interdependent circuits,
it has reconstructed it as a pyramidal structure, increasing inequalities
and social/economic polarization, and deepening the hierarchies that
have historically characterized the sexual and international division of
labor, which the anticolonial and the women's liberation movements
had undermined.

—*Silvia Federici, Revolution at Point Zero, 102*

What do the practices and processes of marine conservation in Madagascar show us about the potential for transnational feminist conservation? To explore what feminist conservation might look like in practice, this chapter is dedicated to deepening our understanding of the key lessons learned from the stories, experiences, and insights of fishers, conservation workers, and governmental officials. After presenting five principles central to feminist conservation, I introduce the concept of feminist commoning. I explore how national and transnational feminist networks demonstrate commoning across social, political, and geographic differences and represent an emergent form of feminist conservation. Ultimately, I argue that transnational feminist conservation is an important alternative to the current conservation paradigm because it centers the knowledge, values, and hopes of those most impacted by the current unjust and unsustainable political-economic system of natural resource extraction.

Despite facing creeping enclosure from marine protected areas and other forms of restrictions on their marine-based livelihoods, Malagasy fishers, in particular women and the poorest in the community, have found ways to cope and survive. Although sad that her favorite area to fish was now off-limits within a marine reserve, Tensy, an elderly woman in southwestern Madagascar, told me: "Even as I age, like everybody else I find a way to adapt and cope [*miotikotike*]. We will always find a way to live with the ocean, it is our livelihood [*fivelompan-po*] and our way of living [*fomba fiaina*]." Responding to the criminalization of their livelihoods, fishers find ways to continue working with and from the ocean through everyday acts of resistance. When asked how she copes, Tensy replied, "We find a way to live. Even though people are scared to be caught breaking the rules [*matahotse gijagija*], both women and men steal fish at night [*mangalatsy haly*]. We need to live so we do what is necessary like fishing at night with a flashlight."[1]

People's ability to cope and adapt is essential to the survival of communities pushed to the margins of an economic, political, and social system that is not meant to serve them. A feminist approach to conservation pushes back against these systems of marginalization. As a starting point, feminist conservation asserts that equality and sustainability are not mutually exclusive but are instead co-constitutive. Here I distill key findings from my research to expand conversations about social justice in conservation, sustainability, and environmental governance. Weaving my work together with research on marine management from around the world, I advance practices and principles that embody a feminist approach to conservation. Though neither exhaustive nor universally applicable, the following principles are intended as a starting point for scholars, practitioners, and activists alike to begin reimagining, and ultimately reshaping, conservation practice.

Principles of Feminist Conservation

Women will never be at the top or in charge [*moloha*], but we will always be dynamic, bold, and daring [*sirika*].

—*Middle-aged fisherwoman, southwestern Madagascar,*
August 20, 2022

Resist Enclosure

Based on my research on marine conservation in Madagascar, the first principle is the importance of halting the enclosure of the marine commons. Due to the failures in procedural justice described below, many Madagascar MPA policies have completely or partially enclosed key areas disproportionately fished by women and people with lower socioeconomic standing, thus impairing their access to resources. Managing the commons without full spatial enclosures will enable these community members to access the marine resources they depend on for their livelihoods and, by reducing disproportionate gender and class impacts, improve distributive justice.

As I have shown in chapters 1 and 2, the Aichi Biodiversity targets adopted in 2014 by the Malagasy president committed Madagascar to place 15 percent of marine and coastal zones under protection, a commitment that spurred conservation organizations rapidly to implement marine spatial enclosures across the island. Local people were consulted on where (but not whether) marine enclosures should exist. For these community consultations, conservation organizations selected a disproportionate number of men to represent the community, leaving women's interests largely unrepresented in MPA placement, an intracommunity procedural justice problem. In all the MPAs I researched across three regions of Madagascar, no-take zones enclosed key sections of reef that were shallow enough to enable fishing on foot during low tides. Given the diversity of fishing methods practiced by most men, partial or complete closures of shallow regions through MPAs did not prevent men from continuing to fish. However, due to cultural norms around fishing practices, lack of training in boat-based fishing techniques, and lower levels of boat ownership, women living near MPA enclosures of shallow reef areas had to either stop fishing altogether, fish illegally at night, or decrease their fishing efforts.

My research further identified knowledge enclosure as a key problem: Western scientific knowledge systems were centered and drove MPA planning and implementation. Often, international conservation organization personnel were not aware of, or in some cases looked down on, Malagasy fishing taboos that had previously formed the basis for local fisheries management and customary marine property. As a result, marine management systems initiated and led by conservation organizations largely failed to reflect or embody an understanding of the reciprocal socionatural relations between fishers and the reefs and other marine ecosystems. Instead, conservation organization personnel typically held views that positioned local resource users as threats to the marine environment.

Malagasy fishers' conception of causal links between fishing practices and ecological outcomes differed from the causal frameworks of international conservation organizations. This explains why some fishers were skeptical of if not wholeheartedly opposed to MPAs as a tool for enhancing fisheries production. In order to develop conservation practices that are more accountable to non-Western worldviews, it is important to understand that in many cases, local worldviews and beliefs do not support cordoning off areas or enclosing the commons to address decline in fisheries production.

My findings in Madagascar echo widespread community resistance to the enclosure of the marine commons around the world, including in Canada, Chile, Ecuador, Iceland, New Zealand, Malawi, Spain, Thailand, and the United States (Bennett and Dearden 2014; Copes and Pálsson 2000; Pinkerton 2017; Veuthey and Gerber 2012). For example, Sandra Veuthey and Julien-François Gerber (2012) detail the long-standing and powerful community resistance to privatization and enclosure of commonly managed mangrove areas in Muisne, Ecuador, where mestizo (of mixed European and Indigenous ancestry) women were the primary leaders of the protests and resistance movements. Given a gendered division of labor in which women collected shellfish and crabs in the mangroves and men fished beyond the mangrove area in boats, women were disproportionately affected by so-called sustainable development initiatives. Specifically, the transfer and loss of mangroves to privatized shrimp aquaculture created disproportionate, negative impacts on women's livelihoods. Women were also harassed more frequently than men by armed guards and dogs, preventing them from accessing estuaries for harvest. In 2003, however, after nearly fifteen years of protests and resistance, the Ecuadorian government designated 5,000 hectares of mangrove in Muisne as an extractive reserve to be collectively managed by the resource users themselves. In the newly established use area, privatized enclosure is banned and coastal communities may fish and collect (Veuthey and Gerber 2012, 618). This example shows the importance of collective resistance to privatization; preservation of the commons can help to ensure equity and environmental sustainability.

Address Structural Drivers of Oppression and Ecological Decline at Scale

The second principle requires engaging with the multiscalar and cross-boundary entanglements of people and natural resources as a central component of conservation policy. A narrow focus on local drivers of marine resource use and change perpetuates regressive and ineffective spatial solutions for problems that span large geographies with complex socioecological histories. In resource-dependent communities, such local fixes disproportionately and unjustly target women's livelihoods and means of production. A broader framework centering the power differentials and social inequities that drive marine resource use and management can forge greater accountability to and respect for local producers.

Policy solutions proposed at the international level often set narrowly focused targets, such as local protected areas, which facilitate goal measurement and performance monitoring. These solutions may then be embedded in national policies. However, the needs, values, and voices of individual farmers and fishers who are involved with production are typically left out. Without robust input and guidance from those engaged most directly in production, this procedural injustice perpetuates conservation policies that enable dispossession in the name of the common global good and promote protective measures that disproportionally affect the most economically and politically marginalized members of a community. Regulation that is focused primarily on local small-scale practices, such as fishing on foot, rather than interconnected global systems of production, consumption, trade, and waste means that conservation policies do not adequately address broader forces driving marine system degradation—political-economic relations such as global markets, multilateral aid, and global trade networks.

An important structural cause of local marine conservation problems is the global market for exports. In some regions of Madagascar, over 70 percent of marine products are exported out of country, underscoring the significant role that remote consumption plays in driving unsustainable harvest patterns. Another driver is the impact of greenhouse gas emissions from countries in the Global North on Madagascar marine systems. These impacts include ocean acidification, increased frequency and severity of storms, sea level rise, coral bleaching, shifts in upwellings and ocean current patterns, and more (Belhabib et al. 2018; Cai et al. 2014; Kroodsma et al. 2018). Negative impacts of global climate disruption on Madagascar's marine systems dwarf any impact arising from local use patterns such as fishing on foot. Faced with the important challenges of climate change and unsustainable consumption, international conservation organizations continue to avoid more politically complex problems and focus on small-scale fisher practices.

Despite this trend, many individuals, communities, and networks around the world, with a greater understanding of structural factors driving ecological decline, are pushing for broader social change. The notion of degrowth, which aims to curtail capitalist expansion and provide an alternative framework for reconnecting communities across space, has gained traction among academics and activists in the past decade (Nirmal and Rocheleau 2019). Degrowth is not a new idea; rather, it is rooted in concepts and practices such as *buen vivir*, conviviality, ecological *swaraj*, *ubuntu*, feminist ethics of care, solidarity economy, and food and energy sovereignty.[2] However, as feminist scholars Padini Nirmal and Dianne Rocheleau argue (2019, 470), putting degrowth concepts into practice requires "moving beyond imagined polarities of individualist materialism and voluntary simplicity, which some degrowth advocates have done," and to "com[e] to grips with territories and coloniality . . . to deal with intersections of gender with race, class, ethnicity, sexuality, religion, political affiliations, colonial positionality, and more." Thus degrowth could offer a politically powerful regional and transnational platform to advance collective resistance to the ecologically damaging and dehumanizing outcomes of capitalist economics and neoliberal and imperialist political regimes.

In the marine realm, "blue degrowth" directly challenges the pursuit of "blue growth" currently advanced by the World Bank, United Nations, FAO, and other international development organizations. To fight ongoing enclosure of marine commons that consolidates wealth in the hands of the most powerful, the blue degrowth movement opposes "injustices and inequalities taking place in marine/blue spaces such as the displacement of coastal and fisher communities, grabbing of their aquatic resources, and privatizations of the seas and coastlines limiting or preventing public use of a range of once common marine areas" (Ertör and Hadjimichael 2020, 5). Instead, blue degrowth advocates working outside a capitalist framework to protect the rights of coastal communities and advance cooperative management. Blue degrowth further links the issue of marine commons enclosure to food sovereignty movements in coastal communities, critiquing neoliberal paradigms that disconnect consumers from producers of marine food products (Barbesgaard 2018; Brent, Barbesgaard, and Pedersen 2020; Ertör and Hadjimichael 2020).

Blue degrowth overlaps with broader movements for fisheries justice that demand accountability for the disproportionate impacts of climate change on coastal and marine environments in developing countries and for the uneven distribution of food resources along the lines of class, race, and nationality. Such movements also challenge the protection and promotion of industrial fishing over the rights and interests of small-scale fishers (Le Manach et al. 2012; Mills 2018; Pinkerton 2017; Said and MacMillan 2020). As an example, small-scale fishers in South Africa successfully organized to overturn national fisheries policies favoring large-scale industrial fishing over small-scale fishers, a process documented by Moenieba Isaacs (2011), a fisheries policy scholar and blue justice advocate. In 2002, the South African Association of Artisanal Fishers and Masifundise community organization formed a grassroots network to challenge a 1988 policy introducing individual transferrable fishing quotas, or ITQs, to South Africa—a policy that excluded artisanal, subsistence, and small-scale fishers and distributed fishing rights to large, predominantly white-owned commercial enterprises. These groups protested the privatization and the criminalization of small-scale fishers' livelihoods in South African (Isaacs 2011; Salo 2007). When their organizing failed to change policy in their favor, they launched a class action lawsuit in 2004 against the Minister of Environmental Affairs and Tourism. After six years of negotiation, and with the involvement of international fisher networks such as the World Forum of Fisher Peoples (WFFP) and the ICSF (International Collective in

Support of Fishworkers), in 2010 a new small-scale fisheries policy was collectively drafted. This process was led by a national task team composed of representatives of the Association of Artisanal Fishers, Masifundise, commercial, artisanal, and subsistence small-scale fishers, and governmental representatives. The Policy for the Small-Scale Fisheries Sector in South Africa, completed in 2012, represented a "shift away from past management approaches to one which emphasises . . . a community-based approach to harvesting and managing marine living resources by sector," which directly opposed a property regime that favored large, mostly white-owned commercial business interests (Isaacs 2011, 77; Mills 2018).

Expand Just and Effective Participation in Decision-Making

The third principle focuses on local participation in decision-making as an important component of procedural justice that advances self-determination and sustainable local livelihoods. A feminist approach to conservation thus requires effective, not just nominal, participation in resource management for community members across all axes of difference. Gender, class, nationality, race, age, and ethnicity must all be factored into community representation in decision-making. My research findings clearly demonstrate how participation determined who had the political agency to shape—and to benefit from—conservation projects.

Even though many conservation institutions have moved toward a more collaborative and community-based orientation, international marine conservation projects have still reinforced gendered and classed divisions of labor, access to natural resources, and in some cases direct benefit through conservation payments. When local resource users were involved in decision-making, far more men and wealthier individuals participated, compared to other groups. The lack of participation in local conservation committees by women and by the community's poorest residents prevented them from obtaining indemnities from the conservation organizations, considered by many fishers to be the most direct benefit from marine conservation in their region. Important features of a more equitable and desirable future would include an increase both in women's public participation in decision-making and in pay for women's labor.

In order to realize effective change, however, women's participation in decision-making must occur in tandem with other broad and systemic changes, especially changes in leadership. As Ayana Elizabeth Johnson and Katherine Wilkinson (2021, xi) put it, "The climate crisis is a leadership crisis. . . . To transform society this decade—the clear task science has set before us—we need transformational leadership. We need feminine and feminist climate leadership, which is wide open to people of any gender. This is where possibility lives-possibility that we can turn away from the brink and move toward a life-giving future for all." Participatory justice is fundamental to marine conservation globally. Complex socioecological systems like our global climate and global seas require multiscalar, multidiscipline, and deeply creative collaborative action. New and differently positioned people in leadership can help us transform systems in a deeply unjust and interconnected world—and help us move beyond incrementalism to find new ways of relating to ourselves and our environments.

Decolonize Resource Management Regimes

The fourth principle is that organizations engaged in conservation and development initiatives must work toward decolonizing resource management regimes. This work includes moving beyond archaic notions and invocations of customary law, such as dina, that distort or in some cases fully supplant local interests and leadership while favoring foreign and male-centered conservation strategies. Although "customary law" was both named and developed in the context of colonization (Joireman 2008), conservation organizations have leveraged what they considered "local" customary law to legitimize marine enclosures and restrictions on fishing practices they deemed incompatible with Western conservation ideals. Conservation organizations have introduced and maintained a particular construct of customary rules to justify a socioracial and institutional hierarchy aligned with their goals of protected-area expansion and biodiversity conservation. These rules place a disproportionate burden on women and poorer community members, due to the stratification of different fishing practices by gender and class. As numerous feminist scholars have shown, customary law favors men's access to and claims over natural resources (Joireman 2008; Whitehead and Tsikata 2003).

An examination of history uncovers the social and political drivers behind these management frameworks and the hierarchies they create. What fishers consider valuable in the ocean, what they consider a fair price for fish, octopus, shark fins, or sea cucumbers, is shaped by a deep history of trade regulations. Given its colonial ties to nations that have either over-fished or strongly protected their own waters, Madagascar has historically sold fishing permits cheaply, far below market rates, to distant nations (Le Manach et al. 2013). Thus, reparations that make up for such historically unfair pricing and illegal unreported and unregulated fishing must be part of current and future conservation efforts.

The principle of decolonizing resource management regimes challenges the notion that self-determination and democratic decision-making is a Western feminist concept that should not be introduced into communities deemed to be traditional. Instead, by focusing on procedural justice in the form of inclusive and representative decision-making, individuals, communities, and organizations can advance their own frameworks of change, centering their own cosmologies and ontologies to define and guide conservation. This principle resonates with the postcolonial intersectional framework advanced by Sharlene Mollet and Caroline Faria (2013), calling for an explicitly anticolonial analytic that decenters hegemonic masculinist and Eurocentric ideas and ideologies of development (and, I would add, conservation). A postcolonial, intersectional understanding of conservation is particularly important in Madagascar, given that race and ethnicity, in addition to gender and class, have been and continue to be shaped by conservation narratives and strategies. By engaging a postcolonial intersectional framework, communities at the frontline of socioenvironmental challenges and change can reimagine and reconstitute new conservation futures that attend to their interests, values, experiences, and knowledge.

Important insights can be gained from a large literature on Indigenous epistemologies and from research methodologies that highlight Indigenous resistance to settler colonization, neocolonialism, and privatization and enclosure in marine conservation (George and Wiebe 2020; Hau'ofa 1998; Ingersoll 2016; Menon, Sowman, and Bavinck 2018; Sand 2012; Sowman and Sunde 2018; Vaughan 2018). Indigenous peoples may hold distinct worldviews regarding the compositions of and relationships among humans and the more-than-human world. As anthropologist Philippe Descola (2013, 391) argues, these differences among peoples invite us to dig deeper to understand why a "particular social fact, belief or custom [is] present in one place but not in another." We need to hold space for the differences among us, our cultures, and our knowledge systems, so that we may work toward rectifying histories of domination, engage in reparations, and reimagine a world that supports collective survival.

In Hawaii, as an example, native people have resisted co-optation and colonization of their marine resource management practices, relationships with the ocean, and socioecological worldview through a variety of everyday practices and legal battles (Ingersoll 2016; Vaughan 2018; Vaughan, Thompson, and Ayers 2017). In *Kaiāulu: Gathering Tides*, Mehana Blaich Vaughan illuminates the resistance to colonization that started shortly after the United States annexed Hawaii as a territory in 1900. Local-level fishing rights connected to customary land division practices (*ahupua'a*) were first challenged but ultimately upheld in *United States v. Damon* in 1904, establishing recognition for these rights within an ahupua'a (Vaughan 2018, 35). Vaughan documents the numerous challenges, from the early 1900s until the present, posed by settler colonization, privatization, and Western resource management ideologies, as well as the deep and ongoing resistance to these forces by native Hawaiians through collective action, storytelling, resource-sharing, adaptation, and activism.

As Vaughan explains, *kuleana*, a Hawaiian word that means rights as well as responsibilities, has guided human-nature relations and shaped Hawaiian land and seascapes for centuries. Kuleana departs from Western ideas of nature as separate from culture, instead emphasizing human-nature interconnection, interdependence, and mutual care.[3] Principles such as continuing to dwell on the land and sea (*noho papa*), eating from the land and sea (*kupa'ai au*), maintaining genealogical ties (*ēwe, 'ōwi*), perpetuating knowledge of place (*ho'okupa, ho'okama'aina*), and attending and caring for the land (*maka'āinana, mālama*) advance a worldview and path of resistance to settler colonization and Western-rooted resource management ideology and legislation. These principles are often enacted even when access to the land

and sea is difficult. Despite frequent challenges and disappointments, by working to pass rules that include the knowledge, values, and visions of native Hawaiians, communities "achieve far more, capturing the imagination and support of diverse groups across Hawai'i through their tireless work and sacrifice to care for their home" (Vaughan 2018, 156).

Efforts to decolonize conservation practices by centering local and Indigenous worldviews that include the pursuit of sovereignty is an essential component of a feminist approach to conservation. Similarly, new visions of human-nature relations that fundamentally reshape understandings of scarcity and "enough-ness" can edge us towards transformative justice with a feminist politics of care and commoning.

Contest Narrow Metrics of Development and Formalization

The fifth principle is that conservation should not require formalization and modernization of resource-dependent livelihoods as the only path available for community development. In Madagascar, for example, the World Bank, the Malagasy government, and international conservation organizations sought to formalize and modernize small-scale fishing by inscribing rights and conditions of marine resources access through place-based ID cards. This formalization process favored wealthy, mobile, and predominantly male fishers at the expense of the community at large. The use of such formalization instruments will tend to exacerbate uneven distribution of marine resources and associated benefits.

As we have seen, the ID-based formalization process shifted the way fishers saw themselves. Women were less likely to describe themselves as just fishers, despite regularly fishing. Some fishers without an ID were more hesitant to fish. Yet women and some of the poorest in a given community without birth certificates did not feel welcome at meetings where ID photos were taken and cards distributed. Such discursive and material strategies used by conservation organizations to formalize and modernize small-scale fishing in some regions thereby delegitimized women's roles as fishers and effectively rendered their work in the ocean illegal. Thus, fisher formalization, adopted according to principles of professionalization and modernization, further narrowed marine resource access for many in the community.

The push to formalize the small-scale fishing sector in Madagascar reflects the narrow metrics of development adopted by governmental and nongovernmental entities that privilege data collection, monitoring, and increased fisheries revenue, as measured by national GDP. Yet conservation and development organizations' focus on increasing GDP or the total number of fishers within a multiuse marine protection area obscures the vast array of relational values and practices that support coastal fisheries in Madagascar.

Furthermore, formalization processes that introduce metrics such as GDP as a primary measure of development progress are a highly masculinist endeavor, promoted by neoliberal modernization. Ecofeminist Vandana Shiva (1992, 208) argues that women's conservation and natural resource–related work is often unpaid and unrecognized within capitalist frameworks: "Recognition of what is and is not labour is exacerbated both by the great volume of work that women do and the fact that they do many chores at the same time. It is also related to the fact that although women work to sustain their families most of their work is not measured in wages." This argument aligns with a Marxist-feminist understanding of reproductive labor (raising children, caring for elders, cooking, cleaning, and other tasks) as being socially constructed and naturalized as women's work. As these scholars argue, social constructions of women's work set the foundation for the hierarchical and exploitative social and ecological relations intrinsic to capitalism (Dalla Costa 1996; Federici 1975, 2004, 2020; Toupin 2018).

Few studies in the marine literature analyze how social difference intersects with small-scale fisheries formalization in developing countries; this remains an important avenue of inquiry as efforts to formalize, modernize, and professionalize small-scale fishers expand globally.[4] Scholarship on formalization more generally suggests that it is imbued with power dynamics that advance social hierarchies shaped by patriarchy, racism, and imperialism. The formalization of small-scale fisheries through instruments such as fisher ID card registries that in effect block fisheries entry by gender and class could be considered the marine equivalent of land formalization, or the "practice by which state land managers document, legalize, register, title, and assign property rights in land through bureaucratic means" (Kelly and Peluso 2015, 437). Such formalization instruments unbalance place-based and social-ecological relations that are embedded within informal land use practices and norms (Meinzen-Dick and Mwangi 2009). Similar to land titling, where previously commonly held resources are divided and assigned to individuals, fishing licenses and other tools restricting access such as fisher IDs are a form of creeping enclosure, a powerful form of enclosure adapted to the fluid materiality of ocean spaces (Apostle, McCay, and Mikalsen 2002; McCay 1999).

Numerous feminist scholars have shown how land formalization has been profoundly classed, raced, and gendered (Archambault and Zoomers 2015; Fortmann and Bruce 1991; Kelly and Peluso 2015; Mollett 2010; Walker 2005). For example, Sharlene Mollet (2010), a feminist political ecologist, reveals how land formalization in Honduras, with the Cadastral and Land Regularization Project, undermined Indigenous women's ability to claim longstanding rights to family lands. Mollet explains how the Honduran state required people in Río Plátano, including the Miskito (the largest Indigenous group in the region), to individualize matrilineally bestowed and collective family land. Although the government framed the formalization process as a way to meet conservation and sustainable natural resource goals, Mollett argues that the process advanced Honduras's "history of state whitening projects designed to transform the racial and cultural composition" of the region (365). Moreover, the land titling undermined women's access to and control over land: Miskito men consolidated "a disproportionate number of parcels through registration, as land contracts [were] assigned in the names of the head of the household," and "75% of households [were] male-headed" (366). Mollett concludes that the land formalization process ultimately "devalu[ed] Miskito (Indigenous) tenure arrangements and land use systems, erasing Miskito women and their 'work' as 'farmers' from the land systems" (370).

It will not be easy, under the current model of conservation, to put into practice the principles outlined above as well as others that may emerge. The development of new forms of accountability, knowledge sharing, and collective goal setting will be essential. The emergence of grassroots networks of groups and communities taking collective action offers a hopeful alternative to the current conservation paradigm and fertile ground in which many of these principles can grow.

Seagrassroots Networks and Commoning

The five principles, outlined above, that underpin a feminist approach to conservation are increasingly being realized through feminist networks and associated commoning practices. Feminist commitment to network building and collective action involves taking on structural drivers of oppression and ecological decline, ensuring that these problems can be addressed by people with different vantage points and experiences. This work requires new forms of commoning, which—unlike a focus on the *commons*, a noun often used to describe spatially distinct places with clear social and ecological boundaries—engages with the multiscalar processes and everyday practices of repair, collaboration, and collective resistance (Diver et al. 2024). As feminist historian, researcher, and activist Silvia Federici (2012, 47) argues, "The production of commons requires first a profound transformation in our everyday life, in order to recombine what the social division of labor in capitalism has separated."

My formulation of commoning draws from Indigenous environmental scholarship, such as that of Mehana Blaich Vaughan (2018) and Kawika Winter and colleagues (2023) in Hawaii, of Ron Reed and Sibyl Diver (2023) in the Pacific Northwest, and Robin Michigiizhigookwe Clark and coworkers (2022) and Nicholas Reo and colleagues (2019) in the Great Lakes region of Canada and the United States.[5] These scholars challenge researchers, conservationists, and activists to move beyond the settler colonial paradigm of humans managing a land or seascape, in which the land or sea is seen as a passive recipient of human action, to a paradigm of respect, responsibility, and care that centers community and place-based social relationships as well as interspecies relationships connecting humans with the more-than-human world. Commoning also draws on feminist scholarship that argues that everyday practices of care, social reproduction, and collective action are fundamental ways to resist capitalist enclosure and protect the commons, thus forming the foundation for alternative modes of survival and sovereignty

(Bauhardt and Harcourt 2018; Clement et al. 2019; Federici 2018; Fisher and Tronto 1990; Gaard 2017; Harcourt 2019; Wichterich 2015).

With commoning, the pursuit of sustainability and socioecological repair can move beyond the hyperlocal focus of many conservation efforts to consider how people can be accountable to each other and other species to start addressing sociopolitical and economic hierarchies. This understanding of commoning requires robust processes to ensure both procedural and distributive justice. Not confined to the formal legal realm, procedural and distributive justice are also embedded in everyday ethics and processes that enable those marginalized in current social, political, and economic structures to engage in and transform decision-making, introducing new vantage points from which to understand and address problems that affect land, sea, and resources.

Commoning as a principle is intended to redress the deficiencies of the Ostrom-style common pool resource governance regimes created by many international conservation organizations. Elinor Ostrom's first principle of "clearly defined boundaries" disregards the social and ecological entanglements a given community and seascape has with people and places across the globe. The focus on local resource restrictions fails to address broader political economic relations such as global markets, multilateral aid, and trade networks that exacerbate racial, class, and gender hierarchies and contribute to environmental degradation (Bardhan and Ray 2006; Goldman 1998; Rocheleau 2008; Saunders 2014). Communities, including those in seemingly isolated places like coastal Madagascar, are deeply and increasingly globally connected through the exchange of goods, information, and waste. The global connections that small-scale fishers in Madagascar and elsewhere have through common pool resources are profoundly shaped by neoliberal governance and flows of capital across space, thereby requiring transnational organizing.

By bringing people together to navigate the complexity of interests regarding a given place and the resources it harbors, a feminist approach to conservation can start to create avenues for greater accountability across scales and across geographic, social, and economic differences. As the strands connecting people and places become more visible, transnational commoning strengthens networks among people and communities fighting to protect their rights. In *Female Well-Being: Toward a Global Theory of Social Change*, Carolyn Fluehr-Lobban and Janet Billson (2005, 383) argue that addressing gender inequities and inequality requires transboundary and transnational networks where women can build solidarity, share ideas, disagree, better understand their differences, collectively advocate for structural change at a macro level, and support each other in more localized efforts for progressive change.

A focus on feminist commoning encourages a deeper understanding of how power differentials persist across social and ecological boundaries.[6] In addition to structural connections of production, consumption, trade, and waste, people have intimate, embodied, and emotional connections to their community and environments, often tied to cultural and spiritual beliefs. Both the intimate ties and the structural links that connect people and places are essential starting points for a new ethic of commoning in which people understand their stakes in the social and ecological changes that result from these connections (Nightingale 2019). This ethic stands in stark contrast to the dominant modes of transnational accountability, which include market-based sustainability strategies such as eco-certification or green consumerism (Scales 2014b). Although green consumerism is enticing because it fits within a capitalist mode of production and consumption and dovetails nicely with dominant modes of international conservation efforts, it has been sharply criticized for its failure to address the vast rift between consumers and producers: consumers continue to have minimal knowledge of and interest in the outcomes of their detrimental consumptive choices (Eden 2010; Foley and Havice 2016; Ponte 2012; Scales 2014b). Other critiques emphasize imperialist processes that accompany eco-certification schemes and contribute to further marginalization of producers and governments in the Global South, facilitating the uneven accumulation of capital along gendered, raced, and classed lines (Castree 2008; Vandergeest and Unno 2012).

A feminist approach to conservation is rooted in commoning, or the everyday practices that strengthen social interactions, mutual understanding, and creative expression, which serves as the foundation on which people can organize across ecological and social divides and act collectively (Clement et al. 2019). Commoning thus opens a window of hope in an otherwise despairing world for us to imagine new ways to create community in places we reside and across social, political, and geographic boundaries to support social and environmental justice (Harcourt 2019).

Building Feminist Networks of Support: SSF Guidelines

Feminist commoning was in some ways supported by the 2014 "voluntary guidelines" for Securing Sustainable Small-Scale Fisheries in the Context of Food Security and Poverty Eradication (SSF Guidelines), created and adopted by member countries of the FAO. The SSF Guidelines marked a critical juncture for small-scale fishers in their long-standing movement for greater consideration and voice in decisions made at the local, regional, and international level regarding fisheries policies and standards of practice (Chuenpagdee 2019; Smith and Basurto 2019; Willmann et al. 2017). The SSF Guidelines were also the first international instrument to recognize the importance of women's marine resource use rights, their lack of representation in decision-making about fisheries and marine resource management, and their immense contribution to small-scale fisheries worldwide (Alonso-Población and Siar 2018).

In a section titled "Capacity Development," the SSF Guidelines advocate for the creation of women's fishing networks: "where appropriate and necessary, separate spaces and mechanisms should be provided to enable women to organize autonomously at various levels on issues of particular relevance to them" (FAO 2015, 17). The explicit focus on women's rights, inclusion in decision-making, and role in fisheries resulted from decades of women fishers and fish workers protesting, lobbying, and organizing globally (Alonso-Población and Siar 2018; Pictou 2018). Since the passage of the SSF Guidelines, with a rising tide of interest in small-scale fisheries (Smith and Basurto 2019), the number of small-scale fisher organizations has grown worldwide, particularly women fisher networks at the subnational and transnational level.

In 2021 I attended a panel titled "Gender Equality in the Seafood Value Chain," hosted by the International Institute for Environment and Development. Panelists included four women whose work focuses on addressing gender-based inequalities in fisheries in East Africa, East Asia, northern Europe, and Latin America.[7] I asked the panelists what they thought a feminist approach to fisheries management might look like. Kyoko Kusakabe, a professor of gender and development studies who researches fisheries in East and Southeast Asia, stressed the importance of supporting women's groups and letting them "decide their own fate, let them decide their own [management] design." Editrudith Lukanga, cofounder of African Women Fish Processors and Traders Network (AWFishNet), explained that a feminist approach to fisheries management requires working across multiple scales of social, economic, and political organization. Networks of women fishers need to work both at the "continental level where invisibility happens in policies, in strategies and in programs" and at the "local level where women are doing their day-to-day responsibilities." If women can organize across these scales, Lukanga argued, then women can "unify their voices, learn from each other, encourage each other, be empowered, which will lead to improved governance and also improve their situation in general."[8] Kusakabe's and Lukanga's comments, informed by their deep experience with these issues, emphasize the importance of developing a feminist network to address systemic and multiscalar issues that women and other marginalized identities face in fisheries.

Indigenous feminist scholar and activist Sherry Pictou (2018) argues that Indigenous relational understandings of land and water helped to move the SSF Guidelines away from neoliberal strategies of fisheries management (such as privatization and an emphasis on economic development) toward flexibility and consideration for the highly context-specific social, spiritual, and cultural relations that many peoples have with the marine environment. Pictou's emphasis on accommodating a wide variety of social and ecological contexts underscores the importance of a feminist and intersectional approach to shifting fisheries practices and fisheries management around the globe.

National Networks: Madagascar's Fisherwomen Leadership Forum

The Fisherwomen Leadership Program (FWLP) developed out of a national small-scale fishers' network in Madagascar. The group of ten women discussed in chapter 4, who approached the conservation committee president in southwestern Madagascar, exemplified collective action and resistance to conservation policies that closed access to established community fishing places. Although this interaction occurred at the village level, Malagasy women have been articulating discontent with existing marine conservation and fisheries management more broadly for years. In 2018 and 2019, a number of women fishers within the Madagascar small-scale fishers' network, MIHARI, approached a female conservation agent (the only one at the time) who was helping to coordinate the network to express grievances concerning their lack of involvement in making decisions.[9] The agent responded positively by securing funds and lobbying other organizations to support the creation of a national Fisherwomen Leadership Program (Baker-Médard et al. 2023). The first FWLP forum, held in October 2020 in Antananarivo, aimed to "empower women to fully enjoy their rights and to benefit from the offshoots of sustainable development through their participation in natural resources governance in their communities."

The forum brought together twenty women and ten men from six coastal regions around the island to launch a women fishers–focused program dedicated to: (1) building awareness around the ways women contribute to fisheries and marine resource management; (2) forming a network of political and social solidarity for people interested in making marine conservation and fisheries management more gender inclusive; and (3) sharing best practices and strategies to make gender-inclusive marine conservation and fisheries management a reality. Many of the women who attended the forum said that it opened their eyes to similarities in the experiences of women fishers in Madagascar despite significant ecological, political, and social differences that exist across the island. Even though all participants were active fishers, they were not well informed about or included in marine conservation, fisheries management, and fisheries development opportunities.

One young fisher from northwestern Madagascar said that the forum was important for her because "women are not seen as leaders or in charge. Since being here, I realize that marine management that has been done by daring [fahasahiana] and proactive [fahavonosana] women for a while now, functions quite well. Now it's well established that women can take charge [afaka mandray andraikitra] of marine and coastal management."[10]

A middle-aged fisher from northeastern Madagascar who also attended the forum said, "I came here to get more experience [*traikefa*] and encouragement [*risi-po*] regarding fishing and fisheries management." She emphasized, "Now I am invigorated. I am sharing and learning so much, and I will share what I have learned here with women fishers back home."[11]

All attendees underscored the simple yet profound impact of just knowing that their fishing experience was not unique. A fisher from northwestern Madagascar shared that she was "happy to be [at the forum] because I've learned that there are a lot of women fishers. I was surprised that it wasn't just us women [from her home region], so now I have got to know women fishers from all over Madagascar. So many! And that makes me happy!"[12] One of the men attending the forum said that he and other men "came here to stand in solidarity [*mitsangana miarakamin'zare*] with women to address this issue. . . . Everyone has a stake [*samby manana anjara*], we need to share responsibility, we need to try to be equals [*ezahana mitovy lenta*]."[13] Men educating other men can serve as a powerful antidote to potential backlash to gender-specific programming. By connecting women and their male allies across the island, the FWLP engaged a network model of change to address gender inequities in marine resource management and access to benefits from marine resources.

An important facet of the FWLP is the notion of strength in difference. Forum participants came from nearly every coastal region of the country; their ethnic, economic, and geographic contexts varied greatly. Some women were from regions where hundreds of women fish throughout the year, whereas in other regions an attendee might have been one of a handful of women fishers in a village who only fish seasonally. Some women were fairly wealthy, and others struggled to feed their families. Some participated in a diversity of income-generating activities, and others relied only on fishing for their livelihood. Although experience and interests varied from region to region and even from person to person, important common needs and goals also emerged.

One thread at the forum was the importance of gaining and maintaining access to marine resources. For example, one older fisher from southeastern Madagascar emphasized that if women have access to marine resources, then families have a better chance to survive severe weather changes. She reported, "The ocean is dynamic, and the climate is changing [*miovaova, toetra-anro*]. If it's bad weather, then a household will struggle to survive. But if a woman works independently [in the ocean], then she will be able to save her spouse and the household [*sauven vadiny anatin'ny tokatrano ao*]."[14] Another young woman from northeastern Madagascar who stressed the importance of access and rights noted her surprise that some women in her village and other villages "need convincing that they have a right [*manana zo*] to marine resources."[15]

Another thread was the importance of intracommunity collaboration, especially between men and women. Women wanted to be taken seriously as fishers and resource managers. A woman from northwestern Madagascar stated, "[Women and men] are equals, we have the same rights, so if we make decisions together, strategize together [*ho iray hevitra, iray tetika*] and a problem arises, then finding a solution will be easier [*maivana zegny famahana olana*]."[16] Another woman from western Madagascar echoed the sentiment, emphasizing, "We need to work together. Men and women need to share responsibility [*samy mandray anjara*] to protect [the marine environment] and to make things sustainable for our future."[17] A young fisher from southwestern Madagascar said that she was thankful for the FWLP because "we need to change things, our goal here is to figure out a way to change people's minds [*hanovana ity toe-tsaina*] so that men and women will be treated as equals, we need it for our survival."[18]

The last thread running through participants' comments was their dedication to ensuring that fish, octopus, mangroves, shrimp, bivalves, gastropods, and other marine organisms thrive, given women's dependence on these organisms. Women from across the island participating in FWLP emphasized the importance of having a healthy and thriving marine ecosystem. For example, a woman from southeastern Madagascar shared that in her region, "we [women] protect [*tahiry*] shrimp, fish, and crab. We ensure that the needs of the baby shrimp, fish, and crab are satisfied [*afa-po*]."[19] She underlined that the survival of these organisms meant the survival of her community. Another woman from northwestern Madagascar explained, "We [women] noticed things changing in the ocean, and we met to think about protecting and making things better for all the living things in the ocean. . . . For example, women are taking the lead because our mangrove is disappearing, and we are able to manage, protect, and improve marine ecosystems [*hitanana, hiaro, hanastara le volazavaboary an'dranomasina*] because it has [been] and will always be the source of our livelihood."[20] She stressed that her community's survival is contingent on the mangrove restoration. Central to many women's accounts of why they wanted to be involved in marine resource management was understanding the needs of both the human and more-than-human environment and articulating the intimate relationship between the two. This awareness of interconnectedness and the need for environmental care resonates with the idea of feminist commoning, which moves beyond human-human relations to interspecies interdependence and reciprocity.

Multispecies Networks: Interspecies Commoning

Women who fish on foot have their own octopus dens [*samby mana ty lavaky horitany*] that they know and visit each low tide. Women are used to [*mahazahatra*] these dens, and the octopuses, too, are used to these women.

—*Middle-aged woman fisher, southwestern Madagascar, May 20, 2019*

Feminist networks also make space for interspecies commoning. According to feminist political ecologists, interspecies relations are crucial to achieving more sustainable and just futures (Clement et al. 2019; Di Chiro 2017; Gaard 2017; Harcourt 2019; Harcourt and Nelson 2015; Mortimer-Sandilands and Erickson 2010; Nelson 2017). In her insightful work on community fishing rights and responsibilities held by Hawaiians, Mehana Blaich Vaughan (2018) advocates for moving beyond the unidirectional power of humans *over* nature to a framework of mutual care, mutual reliance, and reciprocity. Vaughan asserts (in Diver et al. 2019, 410) that "reciprocal relations are a means of relearning, reclaiming, and reasserting community connections to place. Reciprocal relations enhance future resource abundance, based on responsibility rather than ownership." Indigenous relational human-nature frameworks enable feminist scholars to look anew at the model of human-nature relations embedded in conservation strategies and institutions.

People deeply rooted in place, with knowledge, worldviews, and political motivations shaped by human-nature dependency, care, and reciprocity, serve as critical participants in building a multispecies commoning network (Nightingale 2019; Nirmal and Rocheleau 2019). Many Malagasy fishers, for example, understand the ocean, the reefs, and the organisms in relational and interdependent terms. They see marine organisms and marine ecologies as having agency, as active beings rather than passive objects, and as having value independent of market value. Many fishers I lived and fished with used the verb *tia*, "to love" or "to like," to explain how the ocean felt and thus provided more to some fishers than others based on this feeling. These intimate socionatural relations were contingent on both how the fisher behaved and how the ocean perceived a particular fisher. Actions fishers took or failed to take would affect how generous the ocean would feel toward them, whether it would enhance or diminish their catch.

By centering intimate human-nature reciprocity, Indigenous scholars and feminist environmental scholars argue that new or renewed patterns of social and ecological interactions can emerge; ensuring that humans and the more than-human-world can survive and ultimately thrive. Avenues for greater accountability and exchange with the more-than-human world challenge Western-rooted worldviews characterized by separation and hierarchies (Cajete 2000; Craft 2016; Shiva and Mies 1993; TallBear 2019; Vaughan 2018). Kim TallBear strikingly captures the danger of this hierarchical thinking in "Caretaking Relations, not American Dreaming":

> I propose an explicitly spatial narrative of caretaking relations—both human and other-than-human—as an alternative to the temporally progressive settler-colonial American Dreaming that is ever co-constituted with deadly hierarchies of life. A relational web as spatial metaphor requires us to pay attention to our relations and obligations here and now. It is a narrative that can help us resist those dreams

American flag painted on a fishing boat, southwestern Madagascar. Photograph by author.

> of progress toward a never-arriving future of tolerance and good that
> paradoxically requires ongoing genocidal and anti-Black violence, as
> well as violence toward many de-animated bodies. (TallBear 2019, 25)

TallBear emphasizes that Eurocentric and humancentric hierarchies are
used to justify both individual and structural violence against non-Euro-
pean and nonhuman beings. Indigenous relational frameworks, by resisting
these hierarchies, provide a starting point for intergenerational care and accountability across human and more-than-human communities.

National and Transnational Fisheries Networks

A transnational example of feminist commoning is the fisheries network
AWFishNet. Co-founded by Editruith Lukanga in 2017, AWFishNet connects women working across multiple African nations for greater recognition
in fisheries production and policy who are demanding greater transnational

accountability about the marginalization of women and the poor in small-scale fishing economies and fisheries management. The FWLP and its sister organization Réseau National des Femmes de la Pêche à Madagascar are connected to AWFishNet and in September 2023 sent a representative to attend the AWFishNet Bureau meeting in Abidjan, Côte d'Ivoire.

In an interview in 2019, Lukanga said that the network was launched to increase recognition for the political and economic work that women already do in fisheries and to ensure that women's experiences and perspectives inform regional and global efforts to develop fisheries in Africa.[21] Lukanga emphasized the need for a transnational network: many of the problems fisherwomen face across Africa are "not unique to one country," and in advocating for broader economic, political, and cultural change, "unity is our strength." She explained that by sharing information and organizational strategies across countries, fisherwomen are able to "secure a place at the decision-making table" and are able to demand for "services, resources and rights specific to women's needs in the [fishing] sector." Similarly, at the Seventh Global Conference on Gender in Aquaculture and Fisheries in Bangkok, Lukanga and her colleague Kafayat Fakoya, a Nigerian scholar and gender in fisheries activist, advocated for a movement across Africa for greater recognition and rights of women in fisheries. They asserted that across Africa "women do fish and are very active in post-harvest, but their position is stereotyped, their rights not protected, and gender relations and strategic gender needs ignored."[22]

A similar organization of small-scale fisherwomen in Europe, called AK-TEA, considers itself a network of "independent organisations acting at national or regional levels and representing wives of fishermen carrying out tasks linked to the fisheries enterprises (selling fish, administration, etc.), as well as fisherwomen, shellfish gatherers and net menders."[23] AKTEA launched in 2006 with a suite of participatory and distributive justice goals, including: "make the role of women in fisheries visible and recognized; employment statistics in the fisheries to reflect gender; women to have access to decision-making on fisheries management and coastal development; enhanced visibility of coastal and inland fishing communities and women's contributions to these communities; greater exchange of experiences and sharing of knowledge; . . . and access to vocational training." With an explicit focus on low-impact fisheries, AKTEA sees women's empowerment in the fisheries sector as inextricably tied to ecological sustainability.[24] At a network meeting in Belgium in 2019, the chair of AKTEA, Marja Bekendam-de Boer, observed that women's organizations like AKTEA tend to be at the helm of efforts in Europe to shift marine-focused environmental policies in a more progressive direction, explicitly advocating for "sustainable development of fisheries and aquaculture and thus the survival of coastal fishing communities" because women often bear the responsibility of "preserving local culture and tradition," which rely on healthy oceans.[25]

One of the longest-standing movements for women's rights in fisheries is found in Brazil, where fisherwomen (Mulheres Pescadoras) started mobilizing in the 1980s to be recognized as workers and thus to secure pension plans, maternity pay, and rights to unemployment benefits (Alencar 2013). Brazilian fisherwomen also lobbied for greater political representation in both governmental and nongovernmental fisheries organizations and greater recognition of fishing territorial rights (Alencar 2013; Inácio and Leitão 2012). After twenty-five years of struggle, Mulheres Pescadoras were able to secure much of what they fought for with the passage in 2006 of the Articulação Nacional das Mulheres Pescadoras (Fisher Women's National Law) and in 2009 of the Seguro Desemprego do Pescador Artesanal (Artisanal Fishers Unemployment Insurance) law. According to Edna Ferreira Alencar, Sandra Pereira Palheta, and Isabel Soares de Sousa (2015, 44), the fisherwomen's movement highlighted that the categories of woman and man were ripe for political and legal transformation to undo systemic subordination and create avenues for greater autonomy within the fisheries sector.[26] Brazilian fisheries management scholars Denise Almeida de Andrade, Roberta Laena Costa Jucá, and Tarin Cristino Mont (2019) show how the Indigenous rights and women's rights movements pushed for a more pluralist and participatory democracy in Brazil, which shaped progressive, rights-based fisheries laws, thereby contesting androcentric, ethnocentric, and elitist colonial paradigms of the modern state.[27]

The FWLP in Madagascar, AWFishNet, AKTEA, and Mulheres Pescadoras serve as transcommunal and transnational models for gender-based solidarity, advocacy, and support in fisheries. The work of these networks intersects with larger fisheries-focused networks such as the WFFP (World Forum of Fisher Peoples), the International Planning Committee on Food Sovereignty (IPC) Fisheries Working Group, and La Via Campesina's Fisherfolk network.

These global networks and social movements offer an important alternative to the current conservation paradigm in their explicit focus on centering the knowledge, values and voices of fishers and fishing communities. The World Forum of Fisher Peoples was founded in 1995 because the interests and needs of small-scale fishing communities were not being addressed by the World Trade Organization (Levkoe, Lowitt, and Nelson 2017). The WFFP calls itself a "mass-based social movement of small-scale fisher people from across the world," which "advocates for the rights of fisher people to access and manage fisheries resources, for human rights and for the protection of natural biodiversity." It comprises twenty-nine member organizations from twenty-three countries, representing approximately ten million fishers across the world.[28] The IPC describes itself as "an autonomous and self-organised global platform of small-scale food producers and rural workers organizations and grassroots/community based social movements" that advances a "food sovereignty agenda at the global and regional level."[29] Similar to the WFFP, the network is deeply committed to a human rights–based agenda and to uplifting the voices of women, Indigenous people, and ethnic minorities. The IPC functions primarily as transnational convener, bringing together key actors and representatives of regional and community-based networks to discuss, organize, and advocate for food sovereignty. It works closely with La Via Campesina, which describes itself as "an international movement which coordinates peasant organizations of small and middle-scale producers, agricultural workers, rural women, and Indigenous communities from Asia, Africa, America, and Europe." La Via Campesina is the largest network of smallholder producers globally and works across 180 organizations and eighty-one countries (Mann 2017); although most of its efforts are land-based, the organization also works with coastal communities and fishers on food sovereignty and resource use rights in the marine realm. The WFFP and the IPC were instrumental in shaping the SSF Guidelines to be more communally focused, guided by a human rights–based approach to fisheries management and attentive to gender equity issues and to injustices that Indigenous and ethnic minorities face in fisheries (Pictou 2018).

Reflections on Transnational Feminist Networks: Embracing Difference

Through solidarity and resistance to marginalization and to structural or physical violence, transnational feminist networks lay the groundwork for a commitment to intracommunity and intranetwork justice. Fishers and fish workers can begin to recognize how gender hierarchies are created through forms of trade, development policy, and conservation aid and to shift institutions and processes to be more socially and ecologically just.

An important tension in transnational networking and activism involves holding the necessity for collective action based on common interests alongside respect for and engagement with the substantial differences within and across communities globally. One need only look at the history of Western white feminist paradigms that advance the utopian ideal of a global sisterhood while ignoring systemic racism, classism, casteism, nationalism, ableism, and neocolonialism. Chandra Mohanty (1988, 2003) critiques the concept of a "third world woman" identified with victimhood in international conservation and development circles. She argues that this monolithic category of woman is not only inaccurate but dangerous because it advances the logic that gender is the origin of women's oppression rather than the historically embedded and context-specific political, economic, and social processes that produce gender categories.[30] Instead Mohanty (2003, 226) advocates for feminist scholars and activists around the world to find ways to work across social and geographic boundaries in ways that uplift instead of flatten differences: "In knowing differences and particularities, we can better see the connections and commonalities. . . . The challenge is to see how differences allow us to explain the connections and border crossings better and more accurately, how specifying difference allows us to theorize universal concerns more fully."

Mohanty (2003) advances what she calls a "feminist solidarity model" of educating ourselves and working in the world. This model focuses on mutuality, coresponsibility, and common interests across the borders of nation

and culture, highlighting how local and global processes exist simultaneously and constitute each other.[31] In a similar vein, Inderpal Grewal (2008,
192) notes that "while different feminist groups can enact solidarities and
collaborations, there are also conflicts and disconnects since there are so
many different agendas and languages that are being spoken." Grewal and
Caren Kaplan (1994, 18) argue that "transnational feminist practices
require[s] . . . comparative work rather than the relativistic linking of 'differences' undertaken by proponents of 'global feminism'; that is, to compare
multiple, overlapping, and discrete oppressions rather than to construct a
theory of hegemonic oppression under a unified theory of gender." Developing this line of thought, Richa Nagar and Amanda Swarr (2012, 14) in
Critical Transnational Feminist Praxis warn feminist scholars and activists to
"resist an impulse to celebrate collaboration as a panacea," reminding us
that "collaboration itself must be subjected to continuous critical scrutiny so
that it can oppose the paralyzing effects emanating from the institutionali-
zation of both academia and activism." They propose that transnational
feminisms are "necessarily open and contingent, rather than static and pre-
scriptive" (15).

There is no single model for transnational network building and solidarity. Not all small-scale women fishers have the same interests or face the
same oppressions. Yet there is common agreement that attending to how
women's lives differ across social, geopolitical, and environmental boundaries is the only way for transnational collaborations to resist what led them
to organize collectively in the first place.

A feminist approach to conservation within fisheries is both collective
and deeply accountable to difference. It includes multiple overlapping and
intersecting networks: geographically specific (Mulheres Pescadoras's Bra-
zil-based advocacy), regional and more topic-driven organizing networks
(AKTEA's work across Europe), and geographically expansive ones that
serve as touchpoints for other networks (IPC).

In a transnational networking strategy of change, individuals involved
with and accountable to networks can better shape the agendas and policy
proposals occurring at the local, national, and multinational-regional level,
thereby centering participatory and distributive justice. Because these net-

works are rooted in place, where the needs of the more-than-human world are clear and people have deep and historic reciprocal relations with the more-than-human world, commoning across difference and across scales can work.

Facing Our Collective Future

More work is needed to understand the ways in which extraction, transnational commodity trading, and conservation and development projects shape social and ecological seascapes. I have outlined the origins and consequences of conservation agendas that overlook intracommunity divisions and hierarchies within and across national boundaries. I have demonstrated how conservationists and governments focus almost exclusively on the local—while ignoring global drivers of ecological decline and neocolonial masculinist frameworks that favor foreign-driven biodiversity preservation strategies, notably the establishment of MPAs. I have further shown how such conservation policies marginalize Malagasy worldviews and the livelihoods of women and poorer small-scale fishers.

As an alternative, I advance a more feminist approach to conservation that resists the enclosure of common pool resources, focuses on structural drivers of oppression and ecological decline on a broader scale, expands just and effective participation in decision-making, decolonizes resource management regimes, and contests narrow metrics of development and formalization.

How should international conservation organizations engage with these challenges? I believe that these organizations could use their immense funding and power to confront key drivers of environmental injustices and ecological decline, including the privileging of capitalist accumulation and unsustainable consumption in wealthy countries. They also could acknowledge and redress ongoing neocolonial relations between heavily indebted countries in the Global South and wealthy countries in the Global North, as well as the systemic racism, classism, sexism, and ableism that pervades most international conservation leadership and development organizations. Given the current profile of conservation leaders and development donors, it may be most important to challenge elitist restrictions on who can participate in decision-making and in determining international national conservation agendas. The people currently leading international conversations and forging international agreements that concern fishers and the marine environment tend to be highly educated, located in the Global North, wealthier, predominantly male, and white. Ayana Elizabeth Johnson and Katherine Wilkinson's (2021) assertion that the climate crisis is a leadership crisis speaks to the importance of reaching beyond our current leaders and frameworks to address the marine environmental crisis. People experiencing firsthand the negative effects of our sociocultural and political economic systems need to be the key architects of how we change these systems, which is key not only to their survival but to our collective strategies for survival.

International conservation organizations could play a role in advancing this leadership change by funding transnational meetings of place-based and regional smallholder networks — if they can do so without imposing Western worldviews and narrow frameworks of desired outcomes. Centering women's and other marginalized people's rights, needs, values, interests, worldviews, and knowledge will require broad institutional and structural changes. Remaining within the Eurocentric, capitalist, colonial, and patriarchal framework of marine conservation as currently conceived will not affect the underlying drivers of social injustice and ecological decline in the marine environment. By embracing a place-based and grassroots network theory of change can we shift toward a more just and sustainable world. A transnational, decolonial feminist vision for the future sees our interdependence, both among humans and between humans and the nonhuman world, as a necessary starting point for greater respect, accountability, and care.

Feminist fisheries networks, especially those tied to broader transnational networks focused on small-scale fishers rights, smallholder rights, and food sovereignty, are a key avenue through which women and other marginalized identities in marine fisheries can shape a more intersectional and justice-oriented approach to managing the marine commons. This goal can be reached only if the networks can avoid being coopted by NGOs and thus tethered to capitalist and imperial processes and frameworks for change (Alvarez 2009; Hodžic 2014; Mohanty 2013; Nagar and Swarr 2012). To maintain the political, epistemic, and liberatory roots of grassroots feminist decolonial movements, the networks and institutional coalitions created at the nexus of feminist organizing and marine conservation must find ways to create accountability across difference and to respect people's situated experience. Despite these challenges, multiple movements have begun. It is now time to figure out our place in these movements and reimagine our collective future.

Chapter 1. Introduction

1. Kobalava and all other names of people and places in this book are pseudonyms unless otherwise noted. Pers. comm. with Zara, October 27, 2010.
2. Kobalava project report, fisher focus group Kobalava, October 25, 2010.
3. Village president, pers. comm., October 28, 2010, northeastern Madagascar.
4. Village elder and fisher, pers. comm., October 25, 2010, northeastern Madagascar.
5. A report written by an organization charged with conducting the biophysical and socioeconomic research on the Hoalankara area states that "reef top fishing should be banned outright until fishermen [sic] are properly educated so that they will make an effort to curb damage to the coral." Protected source, 106.
6. Hoalankara, pers. comm., October 25, 2010, northeastern Madagascar.
7. I learned later that the species was *Holothuria fuscogilva,* which can fetch high prices in centers of sea cucumber trade such as Hong Kong and Guangzhou, China. See Purcell, Williamson, and Ngaluafe 2018.
8. Although scholars disagree about the precise definition of *postmodernism,* most concur that it is situated in opposition to modernism and the universalist ideas, ideals, and metanarratives endemic to modernist projects. Instead, embedded in postmodernist ideals is a commitment to specificity and context. A postmodernist approach in conservation or development may focus, then, on searching for previously silenced voices to emphasize that these partial and localized accounts of the world will produce more meaningful and valuable interventions in specific locales. See Attwell and Cotterill 2000; and Marchand and Parpart 2003.
9. More relativistic and context-driven approaches to conservation broadly emerged from postmodernist thought. A parallel argument in relation to restructuring labor in education is made by Jill Blackmore, who uses the term *regendering* in discussing the management of educational work. Blackmore (1997, 443) argues that despite many institutions moving in the direction of "flatter, more collaborative, team-oriented and

flexible orientations," which purport to lay the groundwork to dismantle historically entrenched gendered divisions of labor, these efforts actually re-entrench and reassert these divisions. Attwell and Cotterill (2000) make a similar argument concerning biodiversity conservation.

10. Aligned with critical postcolonial literature, I am not conceiving of postcolonialism in Madagascar as a time after colonialism ceased following Independence Day (June 26, 1960), when the country gained political independence from France. Instead, postcolonialism is an engagement with the cultural, economic, political, and ecological legacy of imperialism, and an analysis of how these legacies continue to inform discourses, power structures, and social hierarchies. See Comaroff and Comaroff 2001; Mollett 2017; and Spivak 1999.

11. This definition build directly on bell hooks's (2000, 26) assertion that feminism is a "struggle to end sexist oppression, and therefore a struggle to eradicate the ideology of domination that permeates Western culture" and arguments by Lee Maracle (1996), Farhana Sultana (2022), and Kyle Whyte (2018) that ongoing settler colonial and neocolonial processes violently stratify and hierarchize communities and individuals within communities.

12. Although I make a case that these principles are deeply feminist in origin, the concerns underscored here are not specific to feminist thought. They are the concerns of theorists from a range of schools of thought, including Indigenous scholars, Marxists, postcolonial theorists, and scholars engaged in actor-network theory and indigenous scholarship.

13. Political ecology is an approach to understanding socioenvironmental relations. Key authors who summarize this diverse and growing field of inquiry include Farhana Sultana (2021), Paul Robbins (2020), and Michael Watts (2017).

14. For an eye-opening example of how foreign conservation organizations knowingly exclude local people's knowledge from conservation decision-making and actively or inadvertently marginalize local fishing practices in the process, see Walley 2004.

15. Ostrom's eight principles are: (1) *clearly defined boundaries:* individuals or households who have rights to withdraw resource units from the CPR must be clearly defined, as must the boundaries of the CPR itself; (2) *congruence between appropriation and provision rules and local conditions:* appropriation rules restricting time, place, technology, and/or quantity of resource units are related to local conditions and to provision rules requiring labor, material, and/or money; (3) *collective-choice arrangements:* most individuals affected by the operational rules can participate in modifying the operational rules; (4) *monitoring:* monitors, who actively audit CPR conditions and appropriator behavior, are accountable to the appropriators or are the appropriators; (5) *graduated sanctions:* appropriators who violate operational rules are likely to be assessed graduated sanctions (depending on the seriousness and context of the offense) by other appropriators, by officials accountable to these appropriators, or both; (6) *conflict-resolution mechanisms:* appropriators and their officials have rapid access

to low-cost local arenas to resolve conflicts among appropriators or between appropriators and officials; (7) *minimal recognition of rights to organize:* the rights of appropriators to devise their own institutions are not challenged by external governmental authorities; and (8), for CPRs that are parts of larger systems, *nested enterprises:* appropriation, provision, monitoring, enforcement, conflict resolution, and governance activities are organized in multiple layers of nested enterprises.

16. Although Zofia Łapniewska applauds Ostrom for not engaging in explicitly sexist language that portrays women as sex objects or judges them based on their appearance instead of intellectual performance and competencies, she emphasizes that universalist expressions, underpinned by universal assumptions about actors and community members, pervade Ostrom's writings. Łapniewska (2016, 140) shows that Ostrom's most frequently used terms are undifferentiated across gender, class, caste, and race, citing how often the following terms are used throughout Ostrom's writing: "they" (3,508), "their" (3,332), "rights" (1,353), "community" (863), "them" (809), "human" (740), "people" (474), "communities" (320), "members" (265), "communal" (220), "person" (196), and "humans" (185).

17. Kalpana Wilson's (2006, 25) work in India, shows that involving communities in a World Bank irrigation management scheme allows the bank to "portray privatization and the dismantling of public services as 'empowering' the community, while simultaneously extending NGO control over 'civil society,' " which ultimately "reinforces inequalities within the community."

18. Resistance is sometimes passive, depending on physical properties or location (e.g., distant from political and economic centers), or active, where individuals and communities have worked hard to exist outside state authority. See Steinberg 2018.

19. As geographer and legal scholar Nicholas Blomley (2003, 124) argues, "The construction of that which is deemed law thus rests on the definition of a violent world of nonlaw. The inscription of a frontier which may be figurative, temporal and spatial is integral to this process." Blomley further explains that inextricably linked to the frontier framework are white mythologies that justify colonial property regimes, where the state is the paladin of modernity held in opposition to a zone of savagery.

20. The ease with which governmental and nongovernmental conservation organizations can lay claim to new areas in the name of conservation is evidenced by the spate of large MPAs established worldwide in the past decade where heads of state around the globe have taken turns establishing the next world's largest MPA (Gray et al. 2017; Gruby et al. 2017).

21. Property is broadly defined as the right (or bundle of rights) to benefit from things and is a salient driver of racialized and gendered economic, social, and political inequities within and between communities. See Agarwal 1994; Fortmann 1995; Fortmann, Antinori, and Nabane 1997; Li 1996; and Lund 2008.

22. Christian Lund (2008, 155) argues that "laws, regulations, and policies do not determine access and use of resources as such but erect a structure of opportunities

for negotiation of these rights." These understandings of resource access and rights draw on a Foucauldian notion of power, which emphasizes the importance of one's social and political position in gaining and maintaining access to resources (Foucault 1978). The particular social positions and political configurations in which access and rights exist inevitably change over space and time, influenced both by shifts in the broader political economy and in governance structures, including decentralization, colonization, and political upheaval. (Sikor and Lund 2009).

23. "Il s'agit d'instaurer veritablement une 'politique de peche.' Elle devient du meme coup une politique de races" (Petit 1930, 349).

24. Colonial conservation policies introduced a suite of gear restrictions and enclosed the marine commons in either privatized marine concessions (e.g., oyster and pearl concessions along the western coast) available to French male colonists only or marine protected areas (e.g., dugong refuges in the eastern and northwestern regions of the island). At the same time, the colonial state encouraged the use of larger synthetic nets, larger motorized boats, and the development of an industrial fleet (Petit 1930).

25. Georges Petit linked fisheries management to colonial pronatalism by arguing that French colonial fisheries management would help to fight nitrogen deficiency, thus improving birthrates and preventing stillbirths (1930, 349). Merrill Baker-Médard and Jade Sasser (2020) provide a historical and up-to-date analysis of how pro- and antinatalism currently relates to conservation in Madagascar.

26. Another author who offers a trenchant critique of foreign investment in terrestrial conservation in Madagascar is Nadia Horning (2008).

27. Several authors elucidate the origin and frameworks used for the collective turn toward MPAs as a marine conservation strategy in Madagascar; see Cinner et al. 2009; Corson and MacDonald 2012; Harris 2011; Le Manach et al. 2012; and Oliver et al. 2015.

28. Senior official at the Ministry of Fisheries and Marine Resources (now Ministry of Fisheries and the Blue Economy), pers. comm., July 13, 2018, Antananarivo.

29. Marine director, internation conservation NGO, pers. comm., April 17, 2019, Antananarivo.

30. The age breakdown of these data are: 18–20, 9 percent; 21–30, 29 percent; 31–40, 33 percent; 41–50, 14 percent; 51–60, 11 percent; and over 61, 4 percent. People under the age of 18 were not surveyed. Given the fluidity of some people's ethnicity in Madagascar, we asked informants for their place of origin. If it was not the target village, we also collected the length of time the informant had lived in the village and the distance traveled from their place of origin. Of the women surveyed, 47 percent were not from the target village, came from an average 48 kilometers away, and lived in the target village on average fourteen years. Of the men surveyed, 37 percent were not from the target village, came from on average 42 kilometers away, and have lived in the target village on average twelve years. Surveys were randomized by estimating the number of houses from Google Earth maps or recent village census data available at district government offices, assigning

a number to each house, and then generating a random number table online at stattrek.com (thirty numbers/houses for villages of more than two hundred houses, fifteen for villages of fewer than two hundred houses) to select a house. Each survey team, stratified by gender with separate number tables, surveyed the first willing female or male respondent over age 18 in each randomly selected house.

31. Students were trained in survey methods as well as semistructured interview methods. Training consisted of five days of classroom-based theory and discussion, one week of pilot survey testing, and two weeks of field-based training where all students were given extensive one-on-one feedback while they learned to conduct semistructured interviews and effectively administer and record surveys. All students were also trained to enter and analyze data in Excel and thus were involved in some of the preliminary analysis of results and the dissemination of these preliminary results to local community members, governmental and nongovernmental organization personnel, and groups of university students in Madagascar.

Chapter 2. Enclosure

1. International conservation organization field agent, pers. comm., September 1, 2011, southwestern Madagascar.
2. Middle-aged fisher, pers. comm., July 9, 2015, southwestern Madagascar.
3. Christine Walley (2004, 16) makes a similar argument: "Ultimately, the social drama of the Mafia Island Marine Park suggests a reality in which history is both structured by existing power relationships and open-ended, and in which everyday social relationships consist of practices and ideas with multiple historical and social genealogies."
4. Senior international conservation organization agent, pers. comm., July 17, 2018, Antananarivo.
5. As Doreen Massey (1994, 4) points out, any given place can be seen in terms of "the ever-shifting geometry of social/power relations." Similarly, Gillian Hart (2002, 14) explains that one should think of place "not as a bounded unit, but as always formed through relations and connections with dynamics at play in other places," and in wider regional, national, and transnational arenas.
6. Across all sites, the average distance traveled frequently (daily, weekly, or monthly) was 26.2 kilometers for men versus 14.2 kilometers for women (p< 0.01), and the average distance traveled infrequently (one to two times a year or once every several years) was 48.3 kilometers for men versus 30.1 kilometers for women (p<0.01).
7. Ribot and Peluso (2003) foundational article regarding the theory of access contains a longer list of structural and relational access mechanisms.
8. Net fishing also includes trap (vovo) fishing. Diving includes skin diving and/or diving with an oxygen tank.

9. Both reports, *Réserve de Biosphère Mananara-Nord, 2001: Plan de gestion de la réserve de biosphère, 2002–2006* (DEC), and *Plan de gestion de la conservation—Parc National Mananara Nord* (ANGAP-European Union/IC, 2003; (ANGAP 2003; Huttle, Trouber and Clusener-Godt 2002) were hard copies provided to me by the director of Mananara National Park.

10. International conservation organization agent, pers. comm., February 10, 2011, northeastern Madagascar.

11. International conservation organization agent, pers. comm., October 12, 2010, southwestern Madagascar.

12. International conservation organization agent, pers. comm., November 2, 2010, northeastern Madagascar.

13. Women's focus group, pers. comm., October 25, 2010, northeastern Madagascar.

14. Fisher focus group, pers. comm., July 4, 2015, southwestern Madagascar.

15. Fisher focus group, pers. comm., August 1, 2011, northwestern Madagascar.

16. Fisher, pers. comm., November 12, 2011, northeastern Madagascar.

17. Village elder, pers. comm., September 13, 2010, southwestern Madagascar.

18. To place these eight fisheries in context, consider that WWF works in approximately one hundred countries; more than seventy of these contain marine conservation initiatives, corresponding to hundreds of fisheries worldwide. Also in 2016, WWF launched its Markets Institute Initiative, which is dedicated to "optimizing global food sector sustainability." Although the program is in its initial stage, this initiative promises to address marine resource decline with a multiscalar, multisector approach. See "The Markets Institute," WWF, https://www.worldwildlife.org/pages/markets-institute-change-at-the-speed-of-life; and a new WWF-guided global Seafood Investor Collaboration: WWF, "New Investor Collaboration Will Engage the Seafood Sector on Key Nature Risks and Impacts," press release, February 27, 2023, https://www.worldwildlife.org/press-releases/new-investor-collaboration-will-engage-the-seafood-sector-on-key-nature-risks-and-impacts.

19. Quotations are taken from eight separate interviews conducted with governmental and nongovernmental workers, March 2011–August 2012. Some informants knew that Nosy Tanikely marine reserve was established more than fifty years ago in 1968 (Nosy Be province).

20. International conservation organization marine director, pers. comm., June 18, 2018, Antananarivo.

21. Alasdair Harris, director of Blue Ventures, describes this "demonstration effect" in a promotional video (Blue Ventures 2018).

22. International conservation organization field agent, pers. comm., October 24, 2010, northeastern Madagascar.

23. Local conservation committee members, pers. comm., March 13, 2011, southwestern Madagascar.

24. International conservation organization field agents, pers. comm., March 2, 2011, July 2, July 14, 2015; marine conservation directors, pers. comm., March 12, 2011, June 27, 2015, July 2, 2018.

25. International conservation organization field agent, pers. comm., June 27, 2018, southwestern Madagascar.

26. For example, surveys indicate that in northeastern Madagascar approximately 41 percent (n=429) of coastal populations reported fishing, whereas in southwestern Madagascar 72 percent (n=461) reported fishing. Similarly, of those who reported fishing, the average fishing frequency in southwestern Madagascar ranged from never (rank of 0, or "never fish") to every day (rank of 6, or "fish one or more times a day"). The average score for southwestern Madagascar was 4.7 versus 2.0 in northeastern Madagascar.

27. Philip Steinberg and Kimberley Peters (2016, 247) propose that wet ontology is a way to "endorse the perspective of a world of flows, connections, liquidities, and becomings, but also to propose a means by which the sea's material and phenomenological distinctiveness can facilitate the reimagining and re-enlivening of a world ever on the move." See also the discussion of wet ontology in Sammler 2020.

28. Village elder and fisher, pers. comm., August 14, 2022, southwestern Madagascar.

29. Fisher, pers. comm., March 20, 2011, southwestern Madagascar.

30. "There are a lot of taboos" fisher, pers. comm., June 14, 2011, southwestern Madagascar; "If you don't follow" fisher, pers. comm., April 22, 2011, northeastern Madagascar; "Fishers who don't follow" fisher, pers. comm., July 26, 2011, northwestern Madagascar.

31. Male fisher, pers. comm., July 1, 2015, southwestern Madagascar. In this case the spirit was considered a predominantly land-based spirit (*tambahoaky*), but these spirits can affect people at sea. Other informants reporting the outcome of transgressing taboo emerged from open-ended survey responses collected by Malagasy research assistants: fishers in northeastern Madagascar, April 19, May 24, 29, June 7, 9, 18, 2011; and fishers in southwestern Madagascar, April 14, 23, May 2, June 4, 15, 2011.

32. Frank Muttenzer (2020, 113) argues that conservationists and Vezo fishers engage in marine conservation strategies such as temporary octopus closures "despite shared doubt about its efficacy" because "conservation efforts are motivated neither by what they both know about the fishery nor by what the other party wants, but by each party's desire to be ethical persons. The desire to save face by signaling the will to improve the fishery is rooted in the party's respective political-economic interest in conservation. A moral commitment to conservation, then, is signaled by local fishers, exporters, and conservation NGOs irrespective of either party's commitment to manage fisheries." This moral signaling, what Muttenzer (2020, 183) calls "an empty commitment to the other's goals," allows community-based marine conservation projects to persist despite fundamental differences in what people think drives both social and ecological change, and most important, what to do about it.

33. For an excellent, nuanced analysis of the tensions, convergences, and opportunities that emerge when different worldviews of and relations with nature exist in relation to marine conservation efforts, see Lowe 2006.

34. International conservation organization marine director, pers. comm., November 4, 2011, Antananarivo.

35. International conservation organization regional representative, pers. comm., June 20, 2011, Toliara.

Chapter 3. Self-Determination

1. The Ministry for Environment, Ecology, Oceans and Forests was formerly the Ministry of Agriculture, Livestock and Fisheries; the fishing portion was briefly called the Ministry of Marine Resources and Fishing and as of 2024 is called the Ministry of Fisheries and the Blue Economy.

2. For a detailed history of the ethnic-based political and economic divisions and hierarchies in Madagascar, see Campbell 2005.

3. International conservation organization agent, pers. comm., July 17, 2018, Antananarivo.

4. Silvia Federici (2018, 108) argues, for example, that "grassroots women's communalism today leads to the production of a new reality, shapes a collective identity, constitutes a counterpower in the home and the community, and opens a process of self-valorization and self-determination from which there is much that we can learn." Similar arguments are made by Carolyn Merchant (1996) and Vandana Shiva (1989).

5. One of the four gender-variant individuals I spoke with in southwestern Madagascar recalled being surveyed. Statistically speaking, it is highly likely that data from other *sarindahy* or *sarin'ampela/sarimbavy* were captured in the dataset. Additionally, the Malagasy students I worked with to administer the surveys also commented that they believe some of the survey respondents were *sarindahy* and *sarin'ampela/sarimbavy* but did not mark the "other" category because the decision was up to the respondent.

6. Teliny, like all other names in this book, is a pseudonym used to protect the informant's identity. Pers. comm., July 6, 2015, southwestern Madagascar.

7. Rivike, pers. comm., July 11, 2015, southwestern Madagascar.

8. The French verb *animer* was frequently used, which directly translates as "to animate" but, more colloquially, translates as "to motivate," "to enliven," or "to invigorate." Conservation agent, pers. comm., September 26, 2010, northwestern Madagascar; conservation agent, pers. comm., November 18, 2010, northeastern Madagascar; conservation agent, pers. comm., March 22, 2011, southwestern Madagascar; conservation agent, pers. comm., June 30, 2015, southwestern Madagascar.

9. In participant observation and interviews, local people talked about these individuals in their communities as "knowledgeable" (*mahay*) or as people who "get things

done" (*mahavita*), yet it wasn't clear if they were seen as knowledgeable and effective because they had been approached by development organizations in the past or whether this predated their involvement.

10. For an excellent overview of how "social identity" becomes a mechanism of access to natural resources, see Ribot and Peluso (2003, 170).

11. Following Filmer and Pritchett 2001, a wealth index includes assets belonging to three categories: household ownership of consumer durables, characteristics of the household dwelling, and house and land ownership was created. Factor loadings for each asset was obtained from a principal component analysis (PCA). Factor loadings were then summed from the first principal component to assign each survey respondent with a national and a regional wealth score. Generalized linear models with a logistic error distribution (that is, logistic regression) were then run to see if participation in conservation, coded as a binary variable, was correlated with each survey participant's national wealth score. Pearson residuals were examined with each model to verify model assumptions. All models were run in R version 1.3.1093.

12. International conservation organization agents, pers. comm., June 22, 2018, southwestern Madagascar; July 1, 2018, southwestern Madagascar; April 17, 2019, Antananarivo.

13. The largest number of survey informants finished some or all elementary school, *école primaire*, which included one to five years of formal education ($n=441$). Individuals in this category had the lowest level of participation across any management category, with 22 percent involved "in any capacity" with the marine conservation project, 18 percent involved in monitoring, 10 percent involved in decision-making, and 8 percent involved in enforcement. Individuals who finished some or all middle school, "college," corresponding to six to nine years of formal education ($n=137$), had a medium level of participation, including 35 percent involved "in any capacity," 27 percent involved in monitoring, 22 percent involved in decision-making, and 19 percent involved in enforcement. Individuals who started or completed high school, corresponding to ten to twelve years of formal education ($n=35$), had the highest level of participation, including 40 percent involved "in any capacity," 28 percent involved in monitoring, 25 percent involved in decision-making, and 23 percent involved in enforcement.

14. Field agents from three international conservation organizations, pers. comm., September 10, 2010, March 31, April 9, May 1, June 10, 22, 2011.

15. Ostrom also cautions readers that if differences between resource users are too great, a CPR management regime might fail. She provides the example of the CPR failure for fishers in the Bay of Izmir and Bodrum, Turkey, explaining: "Internally, these were large groups that were characterized by severe heterogeneity of interests and of relevant time horizons. Given the different technologies in use, any rules that were defined to limit use would tend to benefit one subgroup over another, rather than benefit all in a similar manner" (1990, 146).

16. The full list of members includes BirdLife International, Conservation International, Fauna and Flora International, the Nature Conservancy, the International Union for the Conservation of Nature, the Wildlife Conservation Society, and the Worldwide Fund for Nature. These organizations are the largest in terms of finances, geographic distribution, and number of programs.

17. A blog on the CIHR site echoes a key finding of this chapter: "Whilst men generally dominate decision-making forums in communities in which conservation organizations work, they are not the only people who affect and are affected by conservation. Women are also farmers, fishers and foresters" (Anthem 2018). This seemingly straightforward observation is echoed incisively by the national WCS director of Fiji, who states, "It is critical to understand 'intersectionality,' where social categorizations such as ethnicity, class, and gender can overlap and can compound inequalities. Beyond a moral issue, inequalities can create obstacles that—if not understood and addressed—will ultimately make biodiversity and fisheries interventions ineffective. And if we are not careful, the very interventions we use can reinforce or exacerbate inequalities. For example, if a marine protected area is placed where women glean, this can impact food security, as the women will need to travel further or work harder to feed their families" (Mangubhai 2019). Taken together, these observations from people working within international conservation organizations illustrate the difficulty of going beyond rhetoric to implementation.

18. International conservation organization workers, pers. comm., October 22, November 28, 2010, November 6, 2011, July 17, 2018.

19. This relates to a Weberian notion of legitimacy born from one's ethical responsibility (Starr 1999).

20. Fishers, pers. comm., September 12, 2010, southwestern Madagascar; August 10, 2011, northwestern Madagascar; July 10, 2015, southwestern Madagascar.

21. Village president, pers. comm., September 6, 2010, southwestern Madagascar.

22. Local conservation committee member, pers. obs., June 30, 2018, southwestern Madagascar.

23. Focus group international conservation organization workers, pers. comm., September 25, 2010, northeastern Madagascar.

24. Fisher, pers. comm., September 6, 2010, southwestern Madagascar.

25. Verbal fight between international conservation organization agent and village conservation committee president, pers. obs., September 10, 2010, southwestern Madagascar.

26. Women's focus group, pers. comm., July 3, 2015, southwestern Madagascar.

27. Fisher and member of women's association, pers. comm., July 5, 2011, northwestern Madagascar.

28. Fisher and member of women's association, pers. comm., October 16, 2020, Antananarivo.

29. Fisher and village leader, pers. comm., Oct 16, 2020, Antananarivo. "Tsy mataho toly" implies an element of destiny or fate. In other words, it implies that these men are not afraid of judgment or being punished by larger forces, even though they are treating women poorly.

30. Fisher and member of women's association, pers. comm., October 16, 2020, Antananarivo.

31. These scholars emphasize the need to dismantle current political economic power structures in order to redress how a large number of women workers are underpaid or unpaid in the formal sector or are not recognized for their immense contributions within informal economies and sectors of care where women's labor dominates. See Ellerby 2017; Federici 2020; and True 2012. Feminist political economist Jacqui True (2012, 188) warns, however, that "global economic processes can cause women to get jobs over men or migrate for them—which may be economically empowering for them on the one hand but which may involve workplace abuse and lead to heightened domestic violence on the other hand." True (2012, 188) argues that this happens because labor opportunities presented to women function within a zero-sum game framework, where "men simultaneously are disempowered by the same globalizing process." Thus, True argues that women's economic empowerment needs to be supported by the organizations funding and rolling out programs oriented toward women with robust human rights protection policies and processes that protect against gendered discrimination at the local and national levels. See also Fluehr-Lobban and Billson 2005.

32. Fisherwomen Leadership Program (FWLP) organizer, pers. comm., June 17, 2021, Antananarivo.

33. FWLP organizer, pers. comm., September 9, 2021, online interview.

34. FWLP participants, pers. comm., October 16, 2020, Antananarivo.

Chapter 4. Customary Law and Imposed Tradition

1. Elinor Ostrom (1990, 69) specifically mentions "customary practices" in relation to the Spanish Huerta irrigation institutions.

2. *Fokonolona* is translated in the *Diksionera Malagasy-Anglisy* (1974) as "the community group; its organization; applied to people of the same district," and is described in the Malagsy Encyclopedic Dictionary (malagasyword.org) as "firaisam-pileovana sy fitondran' ny mponina amin' ny tanàna iray na amin' ny vohitra madinika mifanakaiky ka manan-jo eo anatrehan' ny fanjakana izany fileovana izany" or "union or collective of people in a single village or small neighboring villages which are governed by it and have rights before the state."

3. "Dia fsy hevitra natao ny Zanakandrianato hampanana'ny an'Andrianampoinimerina vanja sy basy: 'Avia isika, ho izy: ny manan'andevo iray dia mividy angalisa; ny manan'omby valo, dia mividy marovy; ary ny manan'omby

fito, dia mividy tsifidianana-anaram-basy izany.'—Dia nifaneky Zanakandrianato nanao hoe: 'raha hanompoa'nay ny olona tahak'anay aza, dia tsy avela nay tsy ho tanteraka izany.' Ary no lazaina tamy ny Andrianampoinimerina izao dina sy faekena izao" (Callet 1908, 487–488, my translation).

4. Décret du 9 Mars 1902 portant organization de l'administration indigene de l'Imerina.

5. Dina workshop, pers. obs., July 9, 2009, Toliara.

6. "Ohatra, fokonolo? Sarotry mireaka amy fokonolo. Komitinpokontany? Olobe an-tanana? Aja aman'ampela?" asked the first man in the cluster. Pers. obs., July 10, 2009, Toliara.

7. "Alika no mamany eto, dina 5,000 Ar." These rules are respected by some but actively flouted by others. This fact was used in 2009 by Gothlieb, a comedian who has a regular standup gig that airs on national radio. He announced that he would write on several walls around his house, "Do not drop off televisions and radios here, you are a dog, and in accordance with *dina* you will pay 5,000 Ar." He maintained that, after several weeks, his house would be full of TVs and radios.

8. Regional fishing association president, pers. comm., August 3, 2009, southwestern Madagascar.

9. Conservation organization field agent, pers. comm., November 18, 2010, northeastern Madagascar.

10. Zebu (*Bos indicus*) is a species of cattle prevalent in Madagascar.

11. International conservation organization field agent, pers. comm., July 18, 2015, Antananarivo.

12. See Réglementant la pêche maritime côtière dans la colonie de Madagascar et Dépendances, June 5, 1922. The original text in French (Petit 1930) reads: "Sont prohibés les filets fixes don't la plus petite maille aura moins de 25 millimètres en carré" (300); "interdit de jeter . . . toutes substances solides ou liquids, produits d'usine ou autres, toutes plantes ou latex de plantes capables d'enivrer ou d'empoisonner les poisons" (302).

13. In the original Malagasy text: "Tsy azo atao ny mandehandeha eny ambonin'ny vatoharana"; "Tsy azo atao ny mamadibadika, mamakivaky sy ny mamindrafindra ny vatoharana"; and "Tsy azo ampiasaina ny harato latsaky roa tondro (maille étirée moins de 2,5 cm) anisan'izany ny laity na tulle moustiquaire."

14. May be called *tarikaky,* makarakara, ramikoko, draoto, karaoke, or other names depending on the size and pocket of the net, the harvest method, and region in which it is used. Some literature exists that examines the ecological impacts of beach seine use. See McClanahan 2010; McClanahan and Mangi 2001; and Nunoo and Azumah 2015.

Chapter 5. Professionalization, Identity, and Persuasion

1. "Tsy mira lenta" here can be interpreted in several ways, such as women do not have the same "consideration," "value," "level," or "equality" as men.

2. For example, the law passed on June 5, 1922, is far reaching, with twenty-one articles in eight sections of regulations ranging from the definition of what marine activities constitute fishing to where, when, and how marine products can be harvested across Madagascar (Décret du 5 Juin 1922). This particular law focuses on harvest rules pertaining not only to fish but also to oysters, mussels, sponges, sea cucumbers, crabs, and shrimp. The law from 1922 is referenced in a law passed in 1986 (Arrêté du 5 Mars 1986) pertaining to the extraction of lobsters, crabs, sea cucumbers, and algae, which is then again referenced in a law of 1992 (Décret du 3 Mai 1992) pertaining to fishing and aquaculture rules. Each layer adds greater specificity to the rules established in 1922 pertaining to the extraction of these organisms. The laws of 1986 and 1992 are then referenced in several other more recently established laws pertaining to net fishing, lobster harvest, sea cucumber harvest, and other extractions. Another colonial maritime law dating to 1953 (Décret 192 du 14 Mars 1953) is similarly cited in a law passed in 2007 (Décret 1254 du 21 Août 2007) delineating the exclusive economic zone, or jurisdictional reach of a coastal nation over both living and nonliving resources, between Madagascar and Réunion Island. A report written by the FAO in 1992 attests to the perpetuation of colonial law in Madagascar marine resource use legislation and states that "no special provision was made in Malagasy law to abolish the legislation prior to 1960, and as a result legal text that has not been explicitly repealed is still in effect" (Andrianaivojaona, Kasprzyk, and Dasylva 1992).

3. In 1923, during the First International Congress on the Protection of Nature in Paris, General Secretary of the Congress Raoul de Clermont (1926, iv) defined *conservation* even more directly as an act of refinement or civility, in discursive opposition to savage acts of destruction.

4. Formed in 1854 as the Société impériale zoologique d'acclimation, initially focused on wildlife preservation and then expanded to include the protection of plants and landscapes (Matagne 1998).

5. International conservation organization worker, pers. comm., June 30, 2018, southwestern Madagascar.

6. International conservation organization workers, pers. comm., July 17, 2018, Antananarivo; June 30, 2018, southwest Madagascar; June 18, 2018, Antananarivo.

7. MRHP agent, pers. comm., July 14, 2018, Antananarivo.

8. International conservation organization worker, pers. comm., June 30, 2018, southwestern Madagascar.

9. MRHP agent, pers. comm., June 27, 2018, southwestern Madagascar.

10. MRHP agent, pers. comm., June 27, 2018, southwestern Madagascar.

11. Women's focus group, pers. comm., July 3, 2018, southwestern Madagascar.

12. Conservation organization regional director, pers. comm., October 12, 2010, southwestern Madagascar.

13. Conservation organization director, pers. comm., March 10, 2011, Antananarivo.

14. International conservation organization agent, pers. comm., November 2, 2010, northeastern Madagascar.
15. MRHP agent, pers. comm., July 14, 2018, Antananarivo.
16. International conservation organization agent, pers. comm., July 17, 2018, Antananarivo.
17. MRHP agent, pers. comm., June 27, 2018, southwestern Madagascar.
18. International conservation organization agent, pers. comm., July 2, 2018, southwestern Madagascar.
19. Fisher, male, pers. comm., March 29, 2019, southwestern Madagascar.
20. Village president, pers. comm., July 3, 2018, southwestern Madagascar.
21. Men's focus group, pers. comm., June 23, 2018, southwestern Madagascar.
22. In northwestern Madagascar, 24 percent of survey informants reporting fishing as the primary reason they migrated, and in northeastern Madagascar, 6 percent reported fishing as the primary reason they migrated.
23. International conservation organization agent, pers. comm., June 30, 2018, southwestern Madagascar.
24. International conservation organization director, pers. comm., July 17, 2018, Antananarivo.
25. International conservation organization agent, pers. comm., June 30, 2018, southwestern Madagascar.
26. Other key authors offer similar insight regarding territoriality (Murphy 2012; Scott 1998). In particular, Robert Sack (1986, 19) defines territoriality as an "attempt by an individual or group to affect, influence, or control people, phenomena, and relationships by delimiting and asserting control over a geographic area."
27. International conservation organization marine director, pers. comm., July 17, 2018, Antananarivo.
28. Fisher, pers. comm., June 30, 2018, southwestern Madagascar.
29. International conservation organization field agent, pers. comm., July 17, 2018, Antananarivo.
30. International conservation organization marine director, pers. comm., July 19, 2018, Antananarivo.
31. International conservation organization marine director, pers. comm., July 17, 2020, Antananarivo.
32. Conservation agent, pers. comm., southwestern Madagascar, July 2, 2018.
33. Village president, pers. comm., southwestern Madagascar, July 3, 2018.
34. International conservation organization marine director, pers. comm., July 19, 2018, Antananarivo.
35. Fisher, pers. comm., June 23, 2018, southwestern Madagascar.
36. Fisher, pers. comm., July 3, 2018, southwestern Madagascar.
37. MPRH agent, pers. comm., June 27, 2018, southwestern Madagascar.
38. Fisher, pers. comm., June 23, 2018, southwestern Madagascar.

39. International conservation organization field agent, pers. comm., June 28, 2018, southwestern Madagascar.
40. MPRH agent, pers. comm., June 27, 2018, southwestern Madagascar.
41. MPRH agent, pers. comm., July 14, 2018, Antananarivo.

Chapter 6. A Case for Transnational Feminist Conservation

1. Elder fisher, pers. comm., August 14, 2022, southwestern Madagascar.
2. Multiple scholars explore the rich intersection between feminist ethics and degrowth; see Bauhardt and Harcourt 2018; Demaria and Kothari 2017; and Martínez-Alier 2012.
3. Mehana Blaich Vaughan carefully documents the variety of ways Hawaiian fishers maintain kuleana in the face of ongoing challenges. They resist, Vaughan (2018, 112) writes, "through everyday practices that perpetuate relationships with the land and sea." They maintain their presence and enact kuleana by "fighting to keep family lands, perpetuating genealogical connections by gathering as a family and caring for grave sites, continuing to eat fish and eat from their home areas [within *ahupua'a*], teaching future generations knowledge of these areas, and continuing to care for them" (112). On occasion, local fishers take more direct measures against fishing actions not aligned with kuleana such as "cut[ting] lay nets left unattended overnight, calling them 'death traps,' for any fish swimming by" and confiscating gear of "community members or outsiders harvesting too much" (144).
4. A study of a fisher identification registration program in Somalia showed significant geographic bias related to the distribution of fisher IDs. While the analysis was not explicitly focused on race, class, or gender, the research helped underscore the deeply political nature of the process of formalizing and registering fishers (Gilmer 2016).
5. Kyle Powys Whyte and Chris J. Cuomo (2017) provide an excellent summary of the relationship between feminist and indigenous understandings of care as it relates to commoning for environmental change.
6. An excellent Special Issue in the *International Journal of the Commons*, summarized by Floriane Clement and colleagues (2019), explores the concept of commoning in relation to environmental management and beyond.
7. Editrudith Lukanga, cofounder of African Women Fish Processors and Traders Network (AWFishNET), Kyoko Kusakabe, a professor of gender and development studies at the Department of Development and Sustainability, School of Environment, Resources and Development, Asian Institute of Technology in Thailand; Madeleine Gustavsson, researcher at Ruralis in Norway; and Bertha del Carmen Martínez Villalobos, a business entrepreneur with expertise in seafood product development and marketing.
8. Also see (starting at 41:00) "Fish Night 7: Gender Equality in the Seafood Value Chain," IIED, March 8, 2021, https://www.youtube.com/watch?v=Fnijifamgu8.

9. MIHARI stands for "MItantana HArena an-dRanomasina avy eny Ifotony," which literally translates to "marine resource management from the foundation/base," or more generally, locally managed marine conservation. It is a network created in 2012 to bring together communities involved in locally managed marine areas in Madagascar.

10. FWLP forum participant, young woman fisher from northwestern Madagascar, pers. comm., October 16, 2020, Antananarivo.

11. FWLP forum participant, middle-aged woman fisher from northeastern Madagascar, pers. comm., October 16, 2020, Antananarivo.

12. FWLP forum participant, middle-aged woman fisher from northwestern Madagascar, pers. comm., October 16, 2020, Antananarivo.

13. FWLP forum participant, middle-aged man from northeastern Madagascar, pers. comm., October 16, 2020, Antananarivo.

14. FWLP forum participant, older woman fisher from southeastern Madagascar, pers. comm., October 16, 2020, Antananarivo.

15. FWLP forum participant, young woman fisher from northeastern Madagascar, pers. comm., October 16, 2020, Antananarivo.

16. FWLP forum participant, woman fisher from northwestern Madagascar, pers. comm., October 16, 2020, Antananarivo.

17. FWLP forum participant, woman fisher from western Madagascar, pers. comm., October 16, 2020, Antananarivo.

18. FWLP forum participant, young woman fisher from southwestern Madagascar, pers. comm., October 16, 2020, Antananarivo.

19. FWLP forum participant, woman fisher from southeastern Madagascar, pers. comm., October 16, 2020, Antananarivo.

20. FWLP forum participant, woman fisher from northwestern Madagascar, pers. comm., October 16, 2020, Antananarivo.

21. Interview conducted by Yajaira Hernández, social activist from Tegucigalpa, Honduras, September 3, 2019. https://peoples-sovereignty-lab.org/en/common_library/i47/Interview-with-Editrudith-Lukanga-The-Struggles-for-the-Rights-of-Fishing-Women-in-Africa.html.

22. Editrudith Lukanga and Kafayat Fakoya, presentation at Gender in Aquaculture and Fisheries 2018 (GAF7), Bangkok, October 18–21, 2018, in Williams et al. 2019, 51.

23. European network of fisherwomen's organizations. AKTEA's name derives from the goddess of Hellenic mythology symbolizing the shore. See http://akteaplatform.eu/.

24. "Low impact" isn't a formal certification but follows several policies and practices that in theory contribute to more sustainable fishing (Percy and O'Riordan 2020).

25. See Marja Bekendam-de Boer's AKTEA presentation on the Low Impact Fishers of Europe website: https://lifeplatform.eu/wp-content/uploads/2020/02/Aktea_Marja_Bekendam.pdf.

26. Numerous Brazilian fisheries scholars argue that the fisherwomen rights movement in Brazil was fundamentally a fight about personhood and basic human rights, from which some were barred based on gender and others based on race (Alencar, Palheta, and de Sousa 2015; de Andrade, Jucá, and Mont 2019; Inácio and Leitão 2012).

27. The relative success of fisherwomen networks and advocacy work in Brazil, however, requires constant vigilance and ongoing work given frequent attempts by conservative forces in the Brazilian government to roll back these progressive policies (Alencar, Palheta, and de Sousa 2015; de Andrade, Jucá, and Mont 2019).

28. See https://worldfishers.org/.

29. See https://www.foodsovereignty.org/.

30. Chandra Mohanty maintains that kinship structures, colonialism, the organization of labor and a suite of other social relations emerge dialectically with categories of gender. She argues that "women are produced through these very relations as well as being implicated in forming these relations" (1988, 65).

31. With her concept "radical postmodernism," bell hooks similarly underscores the importance of recognizing differences and creating empathy across these differences in coalition building. hooks (1991, 514) argues that "radical postmodernism calls attention to those shared sensibilities which cross the boundaries of class, gender, race, etc., that could be fertile ground for the construction of empathy—ties that would promote recognition of common commitments, and serve as a base for solidarity and coalition."

REFERENCES

Abesamis, Rene A., and Garry R. Russ. 2005. "Density-Dependent Spillover from a Marine Reserve: Long-Term Evidence." *Ecological Applications* 15 (5):1798–1812. https://doi.org/10.1890/05-0174.

Adams, W. M., and D. Hulme. 2001. "If Community Conservation Is the Answer in Africa, What Is the Question?" *Oryx* 35 (3):193–200. https://doi.org/10.1046/j.1365-3008.2001.00183.x.

Adams, William M., and Jon Hutton. 2007. "People, Parks and Poverty: Political Ecology and Biodiversity Conservation." *Conservation and Society* 5 (2):147–183. https://www.jstor.org/stable/26392879.

Afflerbach, Jamie C., Sarah E. Lester, Dawn T. Dougherty, and Sarah E. Poon. 2014. "A Global Survey of 'TURF-Reserves,' Territorial Use Rights for Fisheries Coupled with Marine Reserves." *Global Ecology and Conservation* 2:97–106. http://dx.doi.org/10.1016/j.gecco.2014.08.001.

Agardy, T. M. 1994. "Advances in Marine Conservation: The Role of Marine Protected Areas." *Trends in Ecology and Evolution* 9 (7):267–270. http://dx.doi.org/10.1016/0169-5347(94)90297-6.

Agarwal, Bina. 1994. "Gender, Resistance and Land: Interlinked Struggles over Resources and Meanings in South Asia." *Journal of Peasant Studies* 22 (1):81–125. https://doi.org/10.1080/03066159408438567.

——. 2010. *Gender and Green Governance: The Political Economy of Women's Presence within and beyond Community Forestry.* Oxford: Oxford University Press.

Agrawal, Arun, and Clark C. Gibson. 1999. "Enchantment and Disenchantment: The Role of Community in Natural Resource Conservation." *World Development* 27 (4):629–649. https://doi.org/10.1016/S0305-750X(98)00161-2.

Alaimo, Stacy. 2008. "Trans-Corporeal Feminisms and the Ethical Space of Nature." *Material Feminisms* 25 (2):237–264.

Alencar, Edna Ferreira. 2013. "As Mulheres pescadoras e a conservação de recursos pesqueiros na Reserva de Desenvolvimento Sustentável Mamirauá." In *Trabalhadores e trabalhadoras na pesca: Ambiente e reconhecimento*, edited by Elenise Scherer, 21–49. Rio de Janeiro: Garamond.

Alencar, Edna Ferreira, Sandra Pereira Palheta, and Isabel Soares de Sousa. 2015. "Trabalho na Pesca, ação política e identidade: As mulheres da Colônia de Pescadores Z-32 de Maraã, Amazonas." In *"Aquí estamos nós": Entre as águas dos mares, nas águas dos rios, nas terras de trabalho na pesca artesanal*, edited by Elenise Scherer, 39–69. Garamond: Rio de Janeiro.

Allnutt, Thomas F., Timothy R. McClanahan, Serge Andréfouët, Merrill Baker, Richard K. F. Unsworth, Erwann Lagabrielle, et al. 2012. "Comparison of Marine Spatial Planning Methods in Madagascar Demonstrates Value of Alternative Approaches." *PLOS ONE* 7 (2):e28969. https://doi.org/10.1371/journal.pone.0028969.

Alonso-Población, Enrique, and Susana V. Siar. 2018. "Women's Participation and Leadership in Fisherfolk Organizations and Collective Action in Fisheries: A Review of Evidence on Enablers, Drivers and Barriers." *FAO Fisheries and Aquaculture Circular* (C1159):I-48.

Alvarez, Sonia E. 2009. "Beyond NGO-ization? Reflections from Latin America." *Development* 52 (2):175–184. https://doi.org/10.1057/dev.2009.23.

Amia, Hajira. 2014. "Madagascar Impresses Global Conservation Congress with Community-Controlled Marine Protection Plans." *Seychelles News Agency*, December 5. http://www.seychellesnewsagency.com/articles/1885/Madagascar+impresses+global+conservation+congress+with+community-controlled+marine+protection+plans.

Andersen, Margaret Cook. 2010. "Creating French Settlements Overseas: Pronatalism and Colonial Medicine in Madagascar." *French Historical Studies* 33 (3):417–444. https://doi.org/10.1215/00161071-2010-004.

Andrade, Denise Almeida de, Roberta Laena Costa Jucá, and Tarin Cristino Mont. 2019. "Uma reflexão sobre as mulheres pescadoras Brasileiras a partir do pensamento descolonial." *Dom Helder Revista de Direito* 2 (4):65–87.

Andrade, Gustavo S. M., and Jonathan R. Rhodes. 2012. "Protected Areas and Local Communities an Inevitable Partnership toward Successful Conservation Strategies?" *Ecology and Society* 17 (4):14. https://www.jstor.org/stable/26269207.

Andriamahefazafy, Mialy, Megan Bailey, Hussain Sinan, and Christian A. Kull. 2020. "The Paradox of Sustainable Tuna Fisheries in the Western Indian Ocean: Between Visions of Blue Economy and Realities of Accumulation." *Sustainability Science* 15 (1):75–89. https://doi.org/10.1007/s11625-019-00751-3.

Andriamalala, Gildas, and Charlie J. Gardner. 2010. "L'utilisation du dina comme outil de gouvernance des ressources naturelles: Leçons tirés de Velondriake, sud-ouest de Madagascar." *Tropical Conservation Science* 3 (4):447–472. https://doi.org/10.1177/194008291000300409.

Andrianaivojaona, Charles, Zbigniew Kasprzyk, and Germain Dasylva. 1992. *Pêches et aquaculture à Madagascar: Bilan Diagnostic*. Antananarivo: FAO.

ANGAP. 2003. *Plan de gestion de la conservation–Parc National Mananara Nord*. Mananara, Madagascar: Association Nationale pour la Gestion des Aires Protégées – European Union.

Anthem, Helen. 2018. "International Women's Day: Press for Progress." CIHR, March 6, 2018, http://www.thecihr.org/blog/2018/3/5/international-womens-day-press-for-progress-t8abr.

Apostle, Richard A., Bonnie J. McCay, and Knut H. Mikalsen. 2002. *Enclosing the Commons: Individual Transferable Quotas in the Nova Scotia Fishery*. St. John's, NL: ISER Books.

Arbousset, Francis. 1950. *Le fokon'olona à Madagascar*. Paris: Domat Montchrestien.

Archambault, Caroline S., and Annelies Zoomers, eds. 2015. *Global Trends in Land Tenure Reform: Gender Impacts*. London: Routledge.

Archives nationales d'Outre-mer. 1920. "Principales exportations des produits du cru de Madagascar pour les trois premiers mois de l'année 1920." Box 925, folder 2878 [#DSCN0143].

Arora-Jonsson, Seema. 2011. "Virtue and Vulnerability: Discourses on Women, Gender and Climate Change." *Global Environmental Change* 21 (2):744–751. https://doi.org/10.1016/j.gloenvcha.2011.01.005.

———. 2012. *Gender, Development and Environmental Governance: Theorizing Connections*. London: Routledge.

Astuti, Rita. 1995. *People of the Sea: Identity and Descent among the Vezo of Madagascar*. Cambridge: Cambridge University Press.

Atkinson, Paul, and Martyn Hammersley. 1998. "Ethnography and Participant Observation." *Strategies of Qualitative Inquiry*, edited by Norman K. Denzin and Yvonna S. Lincoln, 248–261. Thousand Oaks, CA: Sage.

Attwell, C. A. M., and F. P. D. Cotterill. 2000. "Postmodernism and African Conservation Science." *Biodiversity and Conservation* 9 (5):559–577. https://doi.org/10.1023/A:1008972612012.

Baker-Médard, Merrill. 2017. "Gendering Marine Conservation: The Politics of Marine Protected Areas and Fisheries Access." *Society and Natural Resources* 30 (6):723–737. https://doi.org/10.1080/08941920.2016.1257078.

———. 2019. "Conservation in a Crisis Marine Resource Management Authority and Legitimacy during Political Instability in Madagascar." *Conservation and Society* 17 (4):331–342. https://doi.org/10.2307/26869204.

———. 2020. "Of Whales and Dugongs: Examining the Rise of Colonial Conservation as Development in Madagascar's Marine History." *Environment and History*. https://doi.org/10.3197/096734019X15755402985622.

Baker-Médard, Merrill, Thomas F. Allnutt, Marissa L. Baskett, Reg A. Watson, Erwinn Lagabrielle, and Claire Kremen. 2019. "Rethinking Spatial Costs and Benefits of

Fisheries in Marine Conservation." *Ocean and Coastal Management* 178:104824. https://doi.org/10.1016/j.ocecoaman.2019.104824.

Baker-Médard, Merrill, and Kristina Natalia Ohl. 2019. "Sea Cucumber Management Strategies: Challenges and Opportunities in a Developing Country Context." *Environmental Conservation* 46 (4):276–277. https://doi.org/10.1017/S037689291 9000183.

Baker-Médard, Merrill, Vatosoa Rakotondrazafy, Marianne Randriamihaja, Prisca Ratsimbazafy, and Ivonne Juarez-Serna. 2023. "Gender Equity and Collaborative Care in Madagascar's Locally Managed Marine Areas: Reflections on the Launch of a Fisherwomen's Network." *Ecology and Society* 28 (2). https://doi.org/10.5751/ ES-13959-280226.

Baker-Médard, Merrill, Hortensia Rasoanandrasana, and Floris Saula. 2011. *Socio-Economic Overview of the Marine and Coastal Protected Area Ankarea and Ankivonjy*. Antananarivo: Wildlife Conservation Society.

Baker-Médard, Merrill, and Jade Sasser. 2020. "Technological (Mis)Conceptions: Examining Birth Control as Conservation in Coastal Madagascar." *Geoforum* 108:12–22. https://doi.org/10.1016/j.geoforum.2019.11.004.

Ban, Natalie C., Georgina Grace Gurney, Nadine A. Marshall, Charlotte K. Whitney, Morena Mills, Stefan Gelcich, Nathan J. Bennett, et al. 2019. "Well-Being Outcomes of Marine Protected Areas." *Nature Sustainability* 2 (6):524–532. https://doi.org/10.1038/s41893-019-0306-2.

Ban, Natalie C., Gretchen J. A. Hansen, Michael Jones, and Amanda C. J. Vincent. 2009. "Systematic Marine Conservation Planning in Data-Poor Regions: Socioeconomic Data Is Essential." *Marine Policy* 33 (5):794–800. https://doi.org/10.1016/j.marpol.2009.02.011.

Barbesgaard, Mads. 2018. "Blue Growth: Savior or Ocean Grabbing?" *Journal of Peasant Studies* 45 (1):130–149. https://doi.org/10.1080/03066150.2017.1377186.

Bardhan, Pranab, and Isha Ray. 2006. "Methodological Approaches to the Question of the Commons." *Economic Development and Cultural Change* 54 (3):655–676. https://doi.org/10.1086/500032.

Barnes, David K. A., and Kate A. Rawlinson. 2009. "Traditional Coastal Invertebrate Fisheries in South-Western Madagascar." *Journal of the Marine Biological Association of the United Kingdom* 89 (8):1589–1596. https://doi.org/10.1017/S0025315409000113.

Barnett, R. 1996. "Shark Fisheries and Trade in East and Southern Africa." In *The World Trade in Sharks: A Compendium of Traffic's Regional Studies*, edited by N. T. Marshall and R. Barnett, 329–340. Cambridge: Traffic International.

Baskett, Marissa L. 2006. "Prey Size Refugia and Trophic Cascades in Marine Reserves." *Marine Ecology Progress Series* 328:285–293. https://doi.org/10.3354/meps328285.

Bauhardt, Christine, and Wendy Harcourt, eds. 2018. *Feminist Political Ecology and the Economics of Care: In Search of Economic Alternatives*. London: Routledge.

Belhabib, Dyhia, Raouf Dridi, Allan Padilla, Melanie Ang, and Philippe Le Billon. 2018. "Impacts of Anthropogenic and Natural 'Extreme Events' on Global Fisheries." *Fish and Fisheries* 19 (6):1092–1109. https://doi.org/10.1111/faf.12314.

Benda-Beckmann, Franz von, Keebet von Benda-Beckmann, and Melanie Wiber, eds. 2006. *Changing Properties of Property*. New York: Berghahn Books.

Bennett, Nathan James, and Philip Dearden. 2014. "Why Local People Do Not Support Conservation: Community Perceptions of Marine Protected Area Livelihood Impacts, Governance and Management in Thailand." *Marine Policy* 44:107–116. https://doi.org/10.1016/j.marpol.2013.08.017.

Bennett, Nathan J., Robin Roth, Sarah C. Klain, Kai Chan, Patrick Christie, Douglas A. Clark, Georgina Cullman, et al. 2017. "Conservation Social Science: Understanding and Integrating Human Dimensions to Improve Conservation." *Biological Conservation* 205:93–108. https://doi.org/10.1016/j.biocon.2016.10.006.

Berg-Schlosser, Dirk, and Norbert Kersting, eds. 2003. *Poverty and Democracy: Self-Help and Political Participation in Third World Cities*. London: Zed Books.

Berger, Michael F., Vincent Caruso, and Emily Peterson. 2019. "An Updated Orientation to Marine Conservation Funding Flows." *Marine Policy*:103497. https://doi.org/10.1016/j.marpol.2019.04.001.

Berkes, Fikret. 1994. "Property Rights and Coastal Fisheries." In *Community Management and Common Property of Coastal Fisheries in Asia and the Pacific: Concepts, Methods and Experiences*, edited by R. S. Pomeroy, 51–62. Manila: ICLARM.

——. 2004. "Rethinking Community-Based Conservation / Repensando la Conservación Basada en Comunidades." *Conservation Biology* 18 (3):621–630. https://doi.org/10.1111/j.1523-1739.2004.00077.x.

——. 2007. "Community-Based Conservation in a Globalized World." *Proceedings of the National Academy of Sciences* 104 (39):15188–15193. https://doi.org/10.1073/pnas.0702098104.

——. 2018. *Sacred Ecology*. 4th ed. New York: Routledge.

Berry, Sara. 1992. "Hegemony on a Shoestring: Indirect Rule and Access to Agricultural Land." *Africa* 62 (3):327–355.

——. 1993. *No Condition Is Permanent: The Social Dynamics of Agrarian Change in Sub-Saharan Africa*. Madison: University of Wisconsin Press.

Blackmore, Jill. 1997. "Level Playing Field? Feminist Observations on Global/Local Articulations of the Re-Gendering and Restructuring of Educational Work." *International Review of Education* 43 (5–6):439–461. https://doi.org/10.1023/a:1003038021606.

Blaikie, Piers, and Harold Brookfield, eds. 1987. *Land Degradation and Society*. London: Methuen.

Blomley, Nicholas. 2003. "Law, Property, and the Geography of Violence: The Frontier, the Survey, and the Grid." *Annals of the Association of American Geographers* 93 (1):121–141. https://doi.org/10.1111/1467-8306.93109.

Blue Ventures. 2018. "Blue Ventures Conservation—Our Approach." Video. https://vimeo.com/289853579.

——. 2019. "Pioneering Action Plan Launched for the Octopus Fishery of Southwest Madagascar." Blue Ventures, February 20. https://blueventures.org/pioneering-action-plan-launched-for-the-octopus-fishery-of-southwest-madagascar/.

Borrini-Feyerabend, Grazia, and Christoper B. Tarnowski. 2005. "Participatory Democracy in Natural Resource Management: A 'Columbus's Egg'?" In *Communities and Conservation: Histories and Politics of Community-Based Natural Resource Management*, edited by J. Peter Brosius, Anna Lowenhaupt Tsing, and Charles Zerner, 69–90. Lanham, MD: Alta Mira.

Botosoamananto, Radonirina Lebely, Gildas Todinanahary, Andriamanjato Razakandrainy, Mahery Randrianarivo, Lucie Penin, and Mehdi Adjeroud. 2021. "Spatial Patterns of Coral Community Structure in the Toliara Region of Southwest Madagascar and Implications for Conservation and Management." *Diversity* 13 (10):486. https://doi.org/10.3390/d13100486.

Bradshaw, Sarah, Sylvia Chant, and Brian Linneker. 2017. "Gender and Poverty: What We Know, Don't Know, and Need to Know for Agenda 2030." *Gender, Place and Culture* 24 (12):1667–1688. https://doi.org/10.1080/0966369X.2017.1395821.

Braidotti, Rosi. 1994. *Women, the Environment and Sustainable Development: Towards a Theoretical Synthesis*. London: Zed Books.

Bräutigam, A., M. Callow, I. R. Campbell, M. D. Camhi, A. S. Cornish, N. K. Dulvy, S. V. Fordham, et al. 2015. *Global Priorities for Conserving Sharks and Rays: A 2015–2025 Strategy*. Global Sharks and Rays Initiative.

Braverman, Irus, and Elizabeth R. Johnson. 2020. "Blue Legalities: Governing More-Than-Human Oceans." In *Blue Legalities: The Life and Laws of the Sea*, edited by Irus Braverman and Elizabeth Johnson, 1–24. Durham, NC: Duke University Press.

Brenner, Neil. 2001. "The Limits to Scale? Methodological Reflections on Scalar Structuration." *Progress in Human Geography* 25 (4):591–614. https://doi.org/10.1191/030913201682688959.

Brent, Zoe W., Mads Barbesgaard, and Carsten Pedersen. 2020. "The Blue Fix: What's Driving Blue Growth?" *Sustainability Science* 15 (1):31–43. https://doi.org/10.1007/s11625-019-00777-7.

Breuil, Christophe, and Damien Grima. 2014. *Baseline Report Madagascar: SmartFish Programme of the Indian Ocean Commission*. Ebene, Mauritius: Fisheries Management FAO Component.

Brockington, Dan. 2002. *Fortress Conservation: The Preservation of Mkomazi Game Reserve Tanzania*. Bloomington: Indiana University Press.

Brockington, Dan, Rosaleen Duffy, and Jim Igoe. 2008. *Nature Unbound: Conservation, Capitalism and the Future of Protected Areas*. London: Routledge.

Brockington, Daniel, and James Igoe. 2006. "Eviction for Conservation: A Global Overview." *Conservation and Society* 4 (3):424–470. https://www.jstor.org/stable/26396619.

Brosius, J. Peter, Anna Lowenhaupt Tsing, and Charles Zerner. 2005. *Communities and Conservation: Histories and Politics of Community-Based Natural Resource Management*. Lanham, MD: AltaMira.

Brown, Mervyn. 2002. *A History of Madagascar.* Princeton, NJ: Markus Wiener.

Bruggemann, J. Henrich, Martine Rodier, Mireille M. M. Guillaume, Serge Andréfouët, Robert Arfi, Joshua E. Cinner, Michel Pichon, et al. 2012. "Wicked Social-Ecological Problems Forcing Unprecedented Change on the Latitudinal Margins of Coral Reefs: The Case of Southwest Madagascar." *Ecology and Society,* 17 (4):47. https://doi.org/10.5751/es-05300-170447.

Bruno, John F., Amanda E. Bates, Chris Cacciapaglia, Elizabeth P. Pike, Steven C. Amstrup, Ruben van Hooidonk, Stephanie A. Henson, and Richard B. Aronson. 2018. "Climate Change Threatens the World's Marine Protected Areas." *Nature Climate Change* 8 (6):499–503. https://doi.org/10.1038/s41558-018-0149-2.

Buchan, Dianne. 2003. "Buy-In and Social Capital: By-Products of Social Impact Assessment." *Impact Assessment and Project Appraisal* 21 (3):168–172. https://doi.org/10.3152/147154603781766266.

Burawoy, Michael. 1998. "The Extended Case Method." *Sociological Theory* 16 (1):4–33. https://doi.org/10.1111/0735-2751.00040.

Cabral, Reniel B., Steven D. Gaines, May T. Lim, Michael P. Atrigenio, Samuel S. Mamauag, Gerold C. Pedemonte, and Porfirio M. Aliño. 2016. "Siting Marine Protected Areas Based on Habitat Quality and Extent Provides the Greatest Benefit to Spatially Structured Metapopulations." *Ecosphere* 7 (11):e01533. https://doi.org/10.1002/ecs2.1533.

Cabral, Reniel B., Benjamin S. Halpern, Sarah E. Lester, Crow White, Steven D. Gaines, and Christopher Costello. 2019. "Designing MPAs for Food Security in Open-Access Fisheries." *Scientific Reports* 9 (1):8033. https://doi.org/10.1038/s41598-019-44406-w.

Cai, Wenju, Agus Santoso, Guojian Wang, Evan Weller, Lixin Wu, Karumuri Ashok, Yukio Masumoto, and Toshio Yamagata. 2014. "Increased Frequency of Extreme Indian Ocean Dipole Events Due to Greenhouse Warming." *Nature* 510 (7504):254–258. https://doi.org/10.1038/nature13327.

Cajete, Gregory. 2000. *Native Science: Natural Laws of Interdependence.* Santa Fe, NM: Clear Light.

Callet, François. 1908. *Tantara ny Andriana eto Madagascar: Documents historiques d'après les manuscrits malgaches.* Vol. 2. Antananarivo: Imprimerie Officielle.

Campbell, Gwyn. 2005. *An Economic History of Imperial Madagascar, 1750–1895: The Rise and Fall of an Island Empire.* New York: Cambridge University Press.

Campbell, Lisa. 2002. "Conservation Narratives in Costa Rica: Conflict and Co-Existence." *Development and Change* 33 (1):29–56. https://doi.org/10.1111/1467-7660.00239.

Castree, Noel. 2008. "Neoliberalising Nature: The Logics of Deregulation and Reregulation." *Environment and Planning A: Economy and Space* 40 (1):131–152. https://doi.org/10.1068/a3999.

Cetas, Elijah R., and Maï Yasué. 2017. "A Systematic Review of Motivational Values and Conservation Success in and around Protected Areas." *Conservation Biology* 31 (1):203–212. https://doi.org/10.1111/cobi.12770.

Chaboud, Christian. 2006. "Gérer et valoriser les ressources marines pour lutter contre la pauvreté." *Études Rurales* (178):197–212. https://doi.org/10.4000/etudesr urales.8388.

Chaboud, Christian, and Florence Galletti. 2007. "Les aires marines protégées, catégorie particulière pour le droit et l'économie?" *Mondes en Développement* 138 (2):27–42. https://doi.org/10.3917/med.138.0027.

Chanock, Martin. 1991. "Paradigms, Policies and Property: A Review of the Customary Law of Land Tenure." *Law in Colonial Africa* 61:84.

Chhotray, Vasudha. 2004. "The Negation of Politics in Participatory Development Projects, Kurnool, Andhra Pradesh." *Development and Change* 35 (2):327–352. https://doi.org/10.1111/j.1467-7660.2004.00354.x.

Chuenpagdee, Ratana. 2019. "Too Big to Ignore—A Transdisciplinary Journey." In *Transdisciplinarity for Small-Scale Fisheries Governance: Analysis and Practice*, edited by Ratana Chuenpagdee and Svein Jentoft, 15–31. Berlin: Springer.

CI. 2016. "Conservation International's Corporate Partners: McDonald's." Conservation International. http://www.conservation.org/partners/Pages/mcdonalds.aspx.

———. 2017. "Le Programme Marin." Conservation International. https://www. conservation.org/global/madagascar/nos-activites/marine/Pages/marine.aspx.

———. 2019. *Guidelines for Integrating Gender and Social Equity Into Conservation Programming*. Arlington, VA: Conservation International.

CIHR. 2020. "The Conservation Initiative on Human Rights." CIHR. http://www. thecihr.org/.

Cinner, Joshua E. 2007. "The Role of Taboos in Conserving Coastal Resources in Madagascar." *Traditional Marine Resource Management and Knowledge Information Bulletin* 22:15–23.

Cinner, Joshua E., Andrew Wamukota, Herilala Randriamahazo, and Ando Rabearisoa. 2009. "Toward Institutions for Community-Based Management of Inshore Marine Resources in the Western Indian Ocean." *Marine Policy* 33 (3):489–496. http:// dx.doi.org/10.1016/j.marpol.2008.11.001.

Cisney, Vernon W., and Nicolae Morar, eds. 2015. *Biopower: Foucault and Beyond*. Chicago: University of Chicago Press.

Clark, Ann Marie, Elisabeth J. Friedman, and Kathryn Hochstetler. 1998. "The Sovereign Limits of Global Civil Society: A Comparison of NGO Participation in UN World Conferences on the Environment, Human Rights, and Women." *World Politics* 51 (1):1–35. https://doi.org/10.1017/S0043887100007772.

Clark, Robin Michigiizhigookwe, Nicholas J. Reo, Joshua E. Hudson-Niigaanwewiidan, Laura E. Waawaashkeshikwe Collins-Downwind, and Waabshkaa Asinekwe. 2022. "Gathering Giizhik in a Changing Landscape." *Ecology and Society* 27 (4). https:// doi.org/10.5751/ES-13605-270429.

Claudet, J., C. W. Osenberg, P. Domenici, F. Badalamenti, M. Milazzo, J. M. Falcón, I. Bertocci, et al. 2010. "Marine Reserves: Fish Life History and Ecological Traits Matter." *Ecological Applications* 20 (3):830–839. https://doi.org/10.1890/08-2131.1.

Cleaver, Frances. 2002. "Reinventing Institutions: Bricolage and the Social Embeddedness of Natural Resource Management." *European Journal of Development Research* 14 (2):11–30. https://doi.org/10.1080/714000425.

——. 2007. "Understanding Agency in Collective Action." *Journal of Human Development* 8 (2):223–244. https://doi.org/10.1080/14649880701371067.

Clement, Floriane, Wendy Jane Harcourt, Deepa Joshi, and Chizu Sato. 2019. "Feminist Political Ecologies of the Commons and Commoning." *International Journal of the Commons* 13 (1):1–15. http://dx.doi.org/10.18352/ijc.972.

Clermont, Raoul de. 1926. "Avant propos." In *Premier congrès international pour la protection de la nature: Faune et flore, sites et monuments naturels: (Paris 31 mai–2 juin 1923). . . .* N.p.

Coase, Ronald H. 2000. "The Problem of Social Cost" 2000 [1960]. In *Classic Papers in Natural Resource Economics*, edited by Chennat Gopalakrishnan, 87–137. New York: St. Martin's.

Collard, Marie, Igor Eeckhaut, Frank Dehairs, and Philippe Dubois. 2014. "Acid–Base Physiology Response to Ocean Acidification of Two Ecologically and Economically Important Holothuroids from Contrasting Habitats, *Holothuria scabra* and *Holothuria parva*." *Environmental Science and Pollution Research* 21 (23):13602–13614. https://doi.org/10.1007/s11356-014-3259-z.

Comaroff, Jean, and John L. Comaroff. 2001. "Naturing the Nation: Aliens, Apocalypse, and the Postcolonial State." *Social Identities* 7 (2):233–265. https://doi.org/10.1080/13504630120065301.

Comaroff, John L., and Simon Roberts. 1986. *Rules and Processes: The Cultural Logic of Dispute in an African Context*. Chicago: University of Chicago Press.

Convention on Biological Diversity. 2010. "Aichi Biodiversity Targets." Convention on Biological Diversity. September 18, 2020. https://www.cbd.int/sp/targets/.

——. 2015. "Madagascar—National Targets." https://www.cbd.int/countries/targets/?country=mg.

Cooley, Sarah R., Noelle Lucey, Hauke Kite-Powell, and Scott C. Doney. 2012. "Nutrition and Income from Molluscs Today Imply Vulnerability to Ocean Acidification Tomorrow." *Fish and Fisheries* 13 (2):182–215. https://doi.org/10.1111/j.1467-2979.2011.00424.x.

Cooper, Caren B., Janis Dickinson, Tina Phillips, and Rick Bonney. 2007. "Citizen Science as a Tool for Conservation in Residential Ecosystems." *Ecology and Society* 12 (2):11. https://www.jstor.org/stable/26267884.

Copes, Parzival, and Gísli Pálsson. 2000. "Challenging ITQs: Legal and Political Action in Iceland, Canada and Latin America: A Preliminary Overview." Paper presented at the Tenth Biennial Conference of the International Institute of Fisheries Economics and Trade: Microbehavior and Macroresults, Corvallis, OR. July 10–14, https://ir.library.oregonstate.edu/collections/1g05fh931?locale=en.

Cornwall, Andrea, Elizabeth Harrison, and Ann Whitehead, eds. 2007. *Feminisms in Development: Contradictions, Contestations and Challenges*. London: Zed Books.

Cornwall, Andrea, and Althea-Maria Rivas. 2015. "From 'Gender Equality' and 'Women's Empowerment' to Global Justice: Reclaiming a Transformative Agenda for Gender and Development." *Third World Quarterly* 36 (2):396–415. https://doi.org/10.1080/01436597.2015.1013341.

Corson, Catherine. 2011a. "From Rhetoric to Practice: How High-Profile Politics Impeded Community Consultation in Madagascar's New Protected Areas." *Society and Natural Resources* 25 (4):336–351. https://doi.org/10.1080/08941920.2011.565454.

———. 2011b. "Territorialization, Enclosure and Neoliberalism: Non-State Influence in Struggles over Madagascar's Forests." *Journal of Peasant Studies* 38 (4):703–726. https://doi.org/10.1080/03066150.2011.607696.

———. 2016. *Corridors of Power: The Politics of Environmental Aid to Madagascar.* New Haven: Yale University Press.

Corson, Catherine, and Kenneth Iain MacDonald. 2012. "Enclosing the Global Commons: The Convention on Biological Diversity and Green Grabbing." *Journal of Peasant Studies* 39 (2):263–283. https://doi.org/10.1080/03066150.2012.664138.

Costello, Mark J., and Bill Ballantine. 2015. "Biodiversity Conservation Should Focus on No-Take Marine Reserves: 94% of Marine Protected Areas Allow Fishing." *Trends in Ecology and Evolution* 30 (9):507–509. https://doi.org/10.1016/j.tree.2015.06.011.

Craft, Aimée. 2016. "Giving and Receiving Life from Anishinaabe Nibi Inaakonigewin (Our Water Law) Research." In *Methodological Challenges in Nature-Culture and Environmental History Research,* edited by Jocelyn Thorpe, Stephanie Rutherford, and L. Anders Sandberg, 105–119. London: Routledge.

Cripps, G., A. Harris, F. Humber, S. Harding, and T. Thomas. 2015. *A Preliminary Value Chain Analysis of Shark Fisheries in Madagascar.* Vol. SF/2015/34. Ebène, Mauritius: Programme for the Implementation of a Regional Fisheries Strategy for the Eastern and Southern Africa–Indian Ocean Region.

Cripps, Garth. 2009. *Understanding Migration amongst Small-Scale Fishers in Madagascar.* Blue Ventures Conservation Report for ReCoMaP.

Cripps, Garth, and Charlie J. Gardner. 2016. "Human Migration and Marine Protected Areas: Insights from Vezo Fishers in Madagascar." *Geoforum* 74:49–62. http://dx.doi.org/10.1016/j.geoforum.2016.05.010.

Cronon, William. 1996. *Uncommon Ground: Rethinking the Human Place in Nature.* New York: W. W. Norton.

Crowder, L. B., S. J. Lyman, W. F. Figueira, and J. Priddy. 2000. "Source-Sink Population Dynamics and the Problem of Siting Marine Reserves." *Bulletin of Marine Science* 66 (3):799–820.

Dalla Costa, Mariarosa. 1996. "Capitalism and Reproduction." *Capitalism Nature Socialism* 7 (4):111–121. https://doi.org/10.1080/10455759609358712.

Darboux, G., J. Cotte, P. Stephan, and F. Van Gaver. 1906. *L'industrie des pêches aux colonies.* Vol. 2: *La pêche dans les diverses colonies.* Marseille: Barlatier.

Davies, T. E., N. Beanjara, and T. Tregenza. 2009. "A Socio-Economic Perspective on Gear-Based Management in an Artisanal Fishery in South-West Madagascar." *Fisheries Management and Ecology* 16 (4):279–289. https://doi.org/10.1111/j.1365-2400.2009.00665.x.

Davis, Dona Lee, and Jane Nadel-Klein. 1992. "Gender, Culture, and the Sea: Contemporary Theoretical Approaches." *Society and Natural Resources* 5 (2):135–147. https://doi.org/10.1080/08941929209380782.

de Andrade, Denise Almeida, Roberta Laena Costa Jucá, and Tarin Cristino Mont. 2019. "Uma reflexão sobre as mulheres pescadoras Brasileiras a partir do pensamento descolonial." *Dom Helder Revista de Direito* 2 (4):65–87.

de la Torre-Castro, Maricela. 2006. "Beyond Regulations in Fisheries Management: The Dilemmas of the 'Beach Recorders' *Bwana Dikos* in Zanzibar, Tanzania." *Ecology and Society* 11 (2). http://dx.doi.org/10.5751/ES-01876-110235.

Deci, Edward L., and Richard M. Ryan, eds. 2004. *Handbook of Self-Determination Research.* Rochester, NY: University of Rochester Press.

Deloria, Vine, Jr. 2001. "American Indian Metaphysics." In *Power and Place: Indian Education in America,* edited by Vine Deloria Jr. and Daniel R. Wildcat, 57–65. Golden, CO: Fulcrum.

Delteil, Pierre. 1931. *Le Fokon'olona (Commune malgache) et les conventions de Fokon'olona.* Paris: Éditions Domat-Montchrestien.

Demaria, Federico, and Ashish Kothari. 2017. "The Post-Development Dictionary Agenda: Paths to the Pluriverse." *Third World Quarterly* 38 (12):2588–2599. https://doi.org/10.1080/01436597.2017.1350821.

Deschamps, Hubert. 1961. *Mondes d'outre-mer: Histoire de Madagascar.* Paris: Berger-Levrault.

———. 1971. "French Colonial Policy in Tropical Africa between the Two World Wars." In *France and Britain in Africa: Imperial Rivalry and Colonial Rule,* edited by Prosser Gifford and Wm. Roger Louis, 543–570. New Haven: Yale University Press.

Descola, Philippe. 2013. *Beyond Nature and Culture.* Translated by Janet Lloyd. Chicago: University of Chicago Press.

Dhital, Narayan, Randrianjafy Rasoloarisoa Vololomboahangy, and Damase P. Khasa. 2015. "Issues and Challenges of Forest Governance in Madagascar." *Canadian Journal of Development Studies* 36 (1):38–56. https://doi.org/10.1080/02255189.2015.989197.

Di Chiro, Giovanna. 2017. "Welcome to the White (M)Anthropocene? A Feminist-Environmentalist Critique." In *Routledge Handbook of Gender and Environment,* edited by Sherilyn MacGregor, 487–505. London: Routledge.

Di Ciommo, Regina C., and Alexandre Schiavetti. 2012. "Women Participation in the Management of a Marine Protected Area in Brazil." *Ocean and Coastal Management* 62:15–23. http://dx.doi.org/10.1016/j.ocecoaman.2012.02.010.

Diksionera Malagasy-Anglisy. 1974. Antananarivo: Trano Printy Loterana.

Di Lorenzo, Manfredi, Paolo Guidetti, Antonio Di Franco, Antonio Calò, and Joachim Claudet. 2020. "Assessing Spillover from Marine Protected Areas and Its Drivers: A Meta-Analytical Approach." *Fish and Fisheries* 21 (5):906–915. https://doi.org/10.1111/faf.12469.

Diver, Sibyl, M. Blaich Vaughan, and M. Baker-Medard. 2024. "Collaborative Care in Environmental Governance: Restoring Reciprocal Relations and Community Self-Determination." *Ecology and Society* 29 (1). doi: 10.5751/ES-14488-290107.

Diver, Sibyl, Mehana Blaich Vaughan, Merrill Baker-Médard, and Heather Lukacs. 2019. "Recognizing 'Reciprocal Relations' to Restore Community Access to Land and Water." *International Journal of the Commons* 13 (1):400–429. https://doi.org/10.18352/ijc.881.

Donlan, Josh. 2005. "Re-Wilding North America." *Nature* 436 (7053):913–914. https://doi.org/10.1038/436913a.

Dressler, Wolfram, Bram Büscher, Michael Schoon, Dan Brockington, Tanya Hayes, Christian A. Kull, James McCarthy, and Krishna Shrestha. 2010. "From Hope to Crisis and Back Again? A Critical History of the Global CBNRM Narrative." *Environmental Conservation* 37 (1):5–15. https://doi.org/10.1017/S0376892910000044.

Dudley, Nigel, Peter Shadie, and Sue Stolton. 2013. *Guidelines for Applying Protected Area Management Categories including IUCN WCPA Best Practice Guidance on Recognising Protected Areas and Assigning Management Categories and Governance Types.* Gland, Switzerland: IUCN.

Dueri, Sibylle. 2017. *Impacts of Climate Change and Ocean Acidification on Indian Ocean Tunas.* Paris: Institute for Sustainable Development and International Relations.

Duffy, Rosaleen. 2005. "Global Environmental Governance and the Challenge of Shadow States: The Impact of Illicit Sapphire Mining in Madagascar." *Development and Change* 36 (5):825–843. https://doi.org/10.1111/j.0012-155X.2005.00437.x.

Eden, Sally. 2010. "The Politics of Certification: Consumer Knowledge, Power, and Global Governance in Ecolabeling." In *Global Political Ecology*, edited by Richard Peet, Paul Robbins, and Michael Watts, 183–198. London: Routledge.

Edgar, Graham J., Rick D. Stuart-Smith, Trevor J. Willis, Stuart Kininmonth, Susan C. Baker, Stuart Banks, Neville S. Barrett, et al. 2014. "Global Conservation Outcomes Depend on Marine Protected Areas with Five Key Features." *Nature* 506 (7487):216–220. https://doi.org/10.1038/nature13022.

Eger, Aaron M., and Julia K. Baum. 2020. "Trophic Cascades and Connectivity in Coastal Benthic Marine Ecosystems: A Meta-Analysis of Experimental and Observational Research." *Marine Ecology Progress Series* 656:139–152. https://doi.org/10.3354/meps13430.

Ellerby, Kara. 2017. *No Shortcut to Change: An Unlikely Path to a More Gender Equitable World.* New York: New York University Press.

Elmhirst, Rebecca. 2011. "Introducing New Feminist Political Ecologies." *Geoforum* 42 (2):129–132. https://doi.org/10.1016/j.geoforum.2011.01.006.

Ertör, I., and M. Hadjimichael. 2020. "Editorial: Blue Degrowth and the Politics of the Sea: Rethinking the Blue Economy." *Sustainability Science* 15 (1):1–10. https://doi.org/10.1007/s116250-019-00772-y.

Escobar, Arturo. 2006. "Difference and Conflict in the Struggle over Natural Resources: A Political Ecology Framework." *Development* 49 (3):6–13. https://doi.org/10.1057/palgrave.development.1100267.

Esmail, Talib. 1997. *Designing and Scaling-Up Productive Natural Resource Management Programs: Decentralization and Institutions for Collective Action.* Washington, DC: World Bank, Rural Development Department.

Fairbanks, Luke, Lisa M. Campbell, Noëlle Boucquey, and Kevin St. Martin. 2018. "Assembling Enclosure: Reading Marine Spatial Planning for Alternatives." *Annals of the American Association of Geographers* 108 (1):144–161. https://doi.org/10.1080/24694452.2017.1345611.

FAO. 1982. *La pêche maritime à Madagascar.* Edited by J. C. Rey. Antananarivo, Madagascar: Food and Agriculture Organization of the United Nations.

——. 2008. *South West Indian Ocean Fisheries Commission Report of the Second Working Party on Fisheries Data and Statistics.* Mombasa, Kenya: Food and Agriculture Organization of the United Nations.

——. 2015. *Voluntary Guidelines for Securing Sustainable Small-Scale Fisheries in the Context of Food Security and Poverty Eradication.* Rome: Food and Agriculture Organization of the United Nations.

——. 2020. *The State of World Fisheries and Aquaculture, 2020: Sustainability in Action.* Rome: Food and Agriculture Organization of the United Nations.

Federici, Silvia. 1975. *Wages against Housework.* Bristol, UK: Falling Wall Press.

——. 2004. *Caliban and the Witch: Women, the Body, and Primitive Accumulation.* Brooklyn, NY: Autonomedia.

——. 2012. "Feminism and the Politics of the Commons." In *The Wealth of the Commons: A World beyond Market and State*, edited by David Bollier and Silke Helfrich, 45–54. Amherst, MA: Levellers Press.

——. 2018. *Re-Enchanting the World: Feminism and the Politics of the Commons.* Oakland, CA: PM Press.

——. 2020. *Revolution at Point Zero: Housework, Reproduction, and Feminist Struggle.* Oakland, CA: PM Press.

Feeley-Harnik, Gillian. 1995. "Plants and People, Children or Wealth: Shifting Grounds of 'Choice' in Madagascar." *PoLAR: Political and Legal Anthropology Review* 18 (2):45–64. https://doi.org/10.1525/pol.1995.18.2.45.

Ferse, Sebastian Ca, María Máñez Costa, Kathleen Schwerdtner Máñez, Dedi S. Adhuri, and Marion Glaser. 2010. "Allies, Not Aliens: Increasing the Role of

Local Communities in Marine Protected Area Implementation." *Environmental Conservation* 37 (1):23–34.

Filmer, Deon. 2020. *The Structure of Social Disparities in Education: Gender and Wealth.* Washington, DC: World Bank.

Filmer, Deon, and Lant H. Pritchett. 2001. "Estimating Wealth Effects without Expenditure Data—Or Tears: An Application to Educational Enrollments in States of India." *Demography* 38 (1):115–132. https://doi.org/10.2307/3088292.

Fisher, Berenice, and Joan Tronto. 1990. "Toward a Feminist Theory of Caring." In *Circles of Care: Work and Identity in Women's Lives,* edited by Emily K. Abel and Margaret K. Nelson, 35–62. Albany, NY SUNY Press.

Flacourt, Etienne de. 1661. *Histoire de la Grande Île de Madagascar.* Reprinted as vols. 8 and 9 in *Collection des ouvrages anciens concernant Madagascar,* edited by A. Grandidier et al., 9 vols. Paris: Comité de Madagascar, 1903–1920.

Flint, Courtney G., Al E. Luloff, and James C. Finley. 2008. "Where Is 'Community' in Community-Based Forestry?" *Society and Natural Resources* 21 (6):526–537. https://doi.org/10.1080/08941920701746954.

Flood, Michael, Molly Dragiewicz, and Bob Pease. 2018. *Resistance and Backlash to Gender Equality: An Evidence Review.* Brisbane, Australia: QUT Crime and Justice Research Centre.

Fluehr-Lobban, Carolyn, and Janet Mancini Billson. 2005. *Female Well-Being: Toward a Global Theory of Social Change.* London: Bloomsbury.

Fokontany Akany Sambatra. 1973. *Dinam-Pokonolona.* Edited by Kantao Ambohidrapeto. Antananarivo: Imprimerie Takariva Dépôt légal No. 57–74.

Foley, Paul, and Elizabeth Havice. 2016. "The Rise of Territorial Eco-Certifications: New Politics of Transnational Sustainability Governance in the Fishery Sector." *Geoforum* 69:24–33. https://doi.org/10.1016/j.geoforum.2015.11.015.

Forsyth, Tim, and Craig Johnson. 2014. "Elinor Ostrom's Legacy: Governing the Commons, and the Rational Choice Controversy." *Development and Change* 45 (5):1093–1110. https://doi.org/10.1111/dech.12110.

Fortmann, Louise. 1995. "Talking Claims: Discursive Strategies in Contesting Property." *World Development* 23 (6):1053–1063. https://doi.org/10.1016/0305-750X(95)00024-7.

Fortmann, Louise, Camille Antinori, and Nontokozo Nabane. 1997. "Fruits of Their Labor: Gender, Property Rights, and Tree Planting in Two Zimbabwe Villages." *Rural Sociology* 63 (3):295–314. https://doi.org/10.1111/j.1549-0831.1997.tb00653.x.

Fortmann, Louise, and John Bruce. 1991. "You've Got to Know Who Controls the Land and Trees People Use: Gender, Tenure and the Environment." *Center for Applied Social Science* 1:1–17. https://opendocs.ids.ac.uk/opendocs/handle/20.500.124 13/7574.

Foucault, Michel. 1978. "On Governmentality: Lecture at the Collège de France." In *The Foucault Effect: Studies in Governmentality,* edited by Graham Burchell, Colin Gordon, and Peter Miller, 87–104. Hemel Hempstead, UK: Harvester Wheatsheaf.

———. 2003. "The Birth of Biopolitics." In *The Essential Foucault: Selections from the Essential Works of Foucault, 1954–1984*, edited by Paul Rabinow and Nikolas Rose, 202–207. New York: New Press.

Freeman, Carla. 2001. "Is Local:Global as Feminine:Masculine? Rethinking the Gender of Globalization." *Signs: Journal of Women in Culture and Society* 26 (4):1007–1037. doi: 10.1086/495646.

Fritz-Vietta, Nadine V., Christiane Röttger, and Susanne Stoll-Kleemann. 2009. "Community-Based Management in Two Biosphere Reserves in Madagascar—Distinctions and Similarities: What Can Be Learned from Different Approaches?" *Madagascar Conservation and Development* 4 (2):86–97.

Gaard, Greta. 2017. "Posthumanism, Ecofeminism, and Inter-Species Relations." In *Routledge Handbook of Gender and Environment*, edited by Sherilyn MacGregor, 115–129. London: Routledge.

Gago, Verónica. 2020. *Feminist International: How to Change Everything*. London: Verso.

Gaines, Steven D., Crow White, Mark H. Carr, and Stephen R. Palumbi. 2010. "Designing Marine Reserve Networks for Both Conservation and Fisheries Management." *Proceedings of the National Academy of Sciences* 107 (43):18286–18293. https://doi.org/10.1073/pnas.0906473107.

Ganzhorn, Jörg U., Lucienne Wilmé, and Jean-Luc Mercier. 2014. "Explaining Madagascar's Biodiversity." In *Conservation and Environmental Management in Madagascar*, edited by Ivan R. Scales, 17–43. London: Routledge.

Gardner, Charlie J., Garth Cripps, Liz Prémesmil Day, Katrina Dewar, Charlotte Gough, Shawn Peabody, Gilde Tahindraza, and Alasdair Harris. 2020. "A Decade and a Half of Learning from Madagascar's First Locally Managed Marine Area." *Conservation Science and Practice* 2 (12):e298. https://doi.org/10.1111/csp2.298.

Geertz, Clifford. 2008. "Thick Description: Toward an Interpretive Theory of Culture." In *The Cultural Geography Reader*, edited by Timothy Oakes and Patricia L. Price, 41–51. London: Routledge.

George, Rachel Yacaaʔał, and Sarah Marie Wiebe. 2020. "Fluid Decolonial Futures: Water as a Life, Ocean Citizenship and Seascape Relationality." *New Political Science* 42 (4):498–520. https://doi.org/10.1080/07393148.2020.1842706.

Giakoumi, Sylvaine, Jennifer McGowan, Morena Mills, Maria Beger, Rodrigo H. Bustamante, Anthony Charles, Patrick Christie, et al. 2018. "Revisiting 'Success' and 'Failure' of Marine Protected Areas: A Conservation Scientist Perspective." *Frontiers in Marine Science* 5 (223). https://doi.org/10.3389/fmars.2018.00223.

Gilmer, Brittany. 2016. "Fishermen, Pirates, and the Politics of Aid: An Analysis of the Somali Fishermen Registration Programme." *Geoforum* 77:106–113. https://doi.org/10.1016/j.geoforum.2016.10.017.

Gissi, E., M. E. Portman, and A. K. Hornidge. 2018. "Un-Gendering the Ocean: Why Women Matter in Ocean Governance for Sustainability." *Marine Policy* 94:215–219. https://doi.org/10.1016/j.marpol.2018.05.020.

Gjerde, Kristina M., Lora L. Nordtvedt Reeve, Harriet Harden-Davies, Jeff Ardron, Ryan Dolan, Carole Durussel, Sylvia Earle, et al. 2016. "Protecting Earth's Last Conservation Frontier: Scientific, Management and Legal Priorities for MPAs beyond National Boundaries." *Aquatic Conservation: Marine and Freshwater Ecosystems* 26 (S2):45–60. https://doi.org/10.1002/aqc.2646.

Goldman, Michael. 1997. " 'Customs in Common': The Epistemic World of the Commons Scholars." *Theory and Society* 26 (1):1–37. https://www.jstor.org/stable/658067.

———. 1998. *Privatizing Nature: Political Struggles for the Global Commons.* London: Pluto.

Gough, Charlotte L. A., Katrina M. Dewar, Brendan J. Godley, Erude Zafindranosy, and Annette C. Broderick. 2020. "Evidence of Overfishing in Small-Scale Fisheries in Madagascar." *Frontiers in Marine Science* 7. https://doi.org/10.3389/fmars.2020.00317.

Govan, Hugh, et al. 2009. *Status and Potential of Locally Managed Marine Areas in the Pacific Island Region: Meeting Nature Conservation and Sustainable Livelihood Targets through Wide-Spread Implementation of LMMAs.* 2nd ed. SPREP/WWF/WorldFish-Reefbase/CRISP. New Caledonia: Coral Reef Initiatives for the Pacific.

Gramsci, Antonio. 1971. *Selections from the Prison Notebooks of Antonio Gramsci.* Edited and translated by Quintin Hoare and Geoffrey Nowell Smith. New York: International Publishers.

Grandcourt, E., C. Andrianarivo, L. Rene de Roland, and R. Rajaonarison. 1999. *Status and Management of the Marine Protected Areas in Madagascar.* International Coral Reef Action Network, UNEP/FAO.

Grandidier, A., C. Delhorbe, H. Froideaux, and G. Grandidier, eds. 1903. *Extrait d'ouvrages Portugais.* In *Collection des ouvrages anciens concernant Madagascar: 1500–1613.* Vol. 1. Paris: Paul Brodard.

Gray, Noella J., Nathan J. Bennett, Jon C. Day, Rebecca L. Gruby, T. 'Aulani Wilhelm, and Patrick Christie. 2017. "Human Dimensions of Large-Scale Marine Protected Areas: Advancing Research and Practice." *Coastal Management* 45 (6):407–415. https://doi.org/10.1080/08920753.2017.1373448.

Gray, Noella J., Rebecca L. Gruby, and Lisa M. Campbell. 2014. "Boundary Objects and Global Consensus: Scalar Narratives of Marine Conservation in the Convention on Biological Diversity." *Global Environmental Politics* 14 (3):64–83. https://doi.org/10.1162/GLEP_a_00239.

Green, Alison L., Leanne Fernandes, Glenn Almany, Rene Abesamis, Elizabeth McLeod, Porfirio M. Aliño, Alan T. White, Rod Salm, John Tanzer, and Robert L. Pressey. 2014. "Designing Marine Reserves for Fisheries Management, Biodiversity Conservation, and Climate Change Adaptation." *Coastal Management* 42 (2):143–159. https://doi.org/10.1080/08920753.2014.877763.

Grewal, Inderpal. 2008. "The Transnational in Feminist Research: Concept and Approaches." In *Mehrheit am Rand?*, edited by Heike Brabandt, Bettina Roß, and Susanne Zwingel, 189–199. Wiesbaden: Springer.

Grewal, Inderpal, and Caren Kaplan. 1994. "Introduction: Transnational Feminist Practices and Questions of Postmodernity." In *Scattered Hegemonies: Postmodernity and Transnational Feminist Practices*, edited by Caren Kaplan and Inderpal Grewal, 1–33. Minneapolis: University of Minnesota Press.

Griffiths, Laura L., Dominic A. Andradi-Brown, Gabby N. Ahmadia, Purwanto Purwanto, Awaludinnoer Ahmad, Dale Bryan-Brown, and Christopher J. Brown. 2022. "Linking Historical Fishing Pressure to Biodiversity Outcomes to Predict Spatial Variation in Marine Protected Area Performance." *Marine Policy* 139:105024. https://doi.org/10.1016/j.marpol.2022.105024.

Gruby, Rebecca L., Luke Fairbanks, Leslie Acton, Evan Artis, Lisa M. Campbell, Noella J. Gray, Lillian Mitchell, Sarah Bess Jones Zigler, and Katie Wilson. 2017. "Conceptualizing Social Outcomes of Large Marine Protected Areas." *Coastal Management* 45 (6):416–435. https://doi.org/10.1080/08920753.2017.1373449.

Haley, Michael, and Anthony Clayton. 2003. "The Role of NGOs in Environmental Policy Failures in a Developing Country: The Mismanagement of Jamaica's Coral Reefs." *Environmental Values* 12 (1):29–54. https://doi.org/10.3197/096327103129341216.

Hall, Derek, Philip Hirsch, and Tania M. Li. 2011. *Powers of Exclusion: Land Dilemmas in Southeast Asia*. Honolulu: University of Hawai'i Press.

Halpern, Benjamin S. 2003. "The Impact of Marine Reserves: Do Reserves Work and Does Reserve Size Matter?" *Ecological Applications* 13 (sp1):117–137. https://doi.org/10.1890/1051-0761(2003)013[0117:TIOMRD]2.0.CO;2.

Haraway, Donna. 1988. "Situated Knowledges: The Science Question in Feminism and the Privilege of Partial Perspective." *Feminist Studies* 14 (3):575–599. https://doi.org/10.2307/3178066.

Haraway, Donna. 2015. "Anthropocene, Capitalocene, Plantationocene, Chthulucene: Making Kin." *Environmental Humanities* 6 (1):159–165.

Harcourt, Wendy. 2019. "Feminist Political Ecology Practices of Worlding: Art, Commoning and the Politics of Hope in the Class Room." *International Journal of the Commons* 13 (1). http://dx.doi.org/10.18352/ijc.929

Harcourt, Wendy, Ana Agostino, Rebecca Elmhirst, Marlene Gómez, and Panagiota Kotsila, eds. 2023. *Contours of Feminist Political Ecology*. London: Palgrave Macmillan.

Harcourt, Wendy, and Ingrid L. Nelson. 2015. "Introduction: Are We 'Green' Yet? And the Violence of Asking Such a Question." In *Practicing Feminist Political Ecologies: Moving Beyond the "Green Economy,"* edited by Wendy Harcourt and Ingrid L. Nelson, 1–26. London: Zed.

Hardin, Garrett. 1968. "The Tragedy of the Commons." *Science* 162 (3859):1243–1248. https://doi.org/10.1126/science.162.3859.1243.

Harper, Sarah, Marina Adshade, Vicky W. Y. Lam, Daniel Pauly, and U. Rashid Sumaila. 2020. "Valuing Invisible Catches: Estimating the Global Contribution by Women to Small-Scale Marine Capture Fisheries Production." *PLOS ONE* 15 (3):e0228912. https://doi.org/10.1371/journal.pone.0228912.

Harris, Alasdair R. 2011. "Out of Sight but No Longer Out of Mind: A Climate of Change for Marine Conservation in Madagascar." *Madagascar Conservation and Development* 6 (1):7–14. http://dx.doi.org/10.4314/mcd.v6i1.68058.

Harris, Cheryl I. 1993. "Whiteness as Property." *Harvard Law Review* 106 (8):1707–1791. https://doi.org/10.2307/1341787.

Harrison, Elizabeth A., and Elizabeth E. Watson. 2012. "Mind the Gap: Disciplinary Dissonance, Gender, and the Environment." *Society and Natural Resources* 25 (9):933–944. https://doi.org/10.1080/08941920.2011.633597.

Hart, Gillian. 2002. *Disabling Globalization: Places of Power in Post-Apartheid South Africa.* Berkeley: University of California Press.

Hartmann, Betsy. 2014. "Converging on Disaster: Climate Security and the Malthusian Anticipatory Regime for Africa." *Geopolitics* 19 (4):757–783. https://doi.org/10.1080/14650045.2013.847433.

Hau'ofa, Epeli. 1998. "The Ocean in Us." *Contemporary Pacific* 10 (2):391–410.

Henkels, Diane M. 1999. "Une vue de près du droit l'environnement Malgache." *African Studies Quarterly* 3 (2):30–46.

Hilborn, Ray. 2014. "Introduction to Marine Managed Areas." In *Advances in Marine Biology,* vol. 69, edited by Magnus L. Johnson and Jane Sandell, 1–13. Amsterdam: Elsevier.

Hilborn, Ray, and Michel J. Kaiser. 2022. "A Path Forward for Analysing the Impacts of Marine Protected Areas." *Nature* 607 (7917):E1–E2. https://doi.org/10.1038/s41586-022-04775-1.

Hilborn, Ray, and Daniel Ovando. 2014. "Reflections on the Success of Traditional Fisheries Management." *ICES Journal of Marine Science* 71 (5):1040–1046. https://doi.org/10.1093/icesjms/fsu034.

Hilborn, Ray, Kevin Stokes, Jean-Jacques Maguire, Tony Smith, Louis W. Botsford, Marc Mangel, José Orensanz, et al. 2004. "When Can Marine Reserves Improve Fisheries Management?" *Ocean and Coastal Management* 47 (3–4):197–205. https://doi.org/10.1016/j.ocecoaman.2004.04.001.

Hodžic, Saida. 2014. "Feminist Bastards: Toward a Posthumanist Critique of NGOization." In *Theorizing NGOs,* edited by Bernal Victoria and Grewal Inderpal, 221–247. Durham, NC: Duke University Press.

hooks, bell. 1991. "Postmodern Blackness." In *Modern Literary Theory: A Reader,* edited by Philip Rice and Patricia Waugh, 511–518. London: Arnold.

———. 2000. *Feminist Theory: From Margin to Center.* 2nd ed. London: Pluto.

Horning, Nadia Rabesahala. 2008. "Strong Support for Weak Performance: Donor Competition in Madagascar." *African Affairs* 107 (428):405–431. https://doi.org/10.1093/afraf/adn036.

——. 2009. "Bridging the Gap between Environmental Decision-Makers in Madagascar." In *Governing Africa's Forests in a Globalized World*, edited by Laura A. German, Alain Karsenty, and Anne-Marie Tiani, 234–252. London: Earthscan.

Hufty, Marc, and Frank Muttenzer. 2002. "Devoted Friends: The Implementation of the Convention on Biological Diversity in Madagascar." In *Governing Global Biodiversity*, edited by P. Le Prestre, 279–309. London: Ashgate.

Humber, Frances, Mialy Andriamahefazafy, Brendan John Godley, and Annette Cameron Broderick. 2015. "Endangered, Essential and Exploited: How Extant Laws Are Not Enough to Protect Marine Megafauna in Madagascar." *Marine Policy* 60:70–83. http://dx.doi.org/10.1016/j.marpol.2015.05.006.

Humphreys, John, and Robert W. E. Clark. 2020. "A Critical History of Marine Protected Areas." In *Marine Protected Areas: Science, Policy and Management*, edited by John Humphreys and Robert W. E. Clark, 1–12. Amsterdam: Elsevier.

Huttle, Charles, Luc Touber, and Miguel Clusener-Godt. 2002. "La Réserve de Biosphère de Mananara-Nord: Un Défi Pour la Conservation et le Développement Intégrés." Antananrivo: UNESCO & ANGAP.

Igoe, Jim, Katja Neves, and Dan Brockington. 2010. "A Spectacular Eco-Tour around the Historic Bloc: Theorising the Convergence of Biodiversity Conservation and Capitalist Expansion." *Antipode* 42 (3):486–512. https://doi.org/10.1111/j.1467-8330.2010.00761.x.

Iida, Taku. 2005. "The Past and Present of the Coral Reef Fishing Economy in Madagascar: Implications for Self-Determination in Resource Use." *Senri Ethnological Studies* 67:237–258.

Imbiki, Anaclet. 2011. *Le fokonolona et le dina: Institutions traditionnelles modernisées au service de la sécurité publique et de la justice populaire à Madagascar*. Antananarivo: Jurid'ika.

Inácio, Pedro Henrique Dias, and Maria do Rosário de Fátima Andrade Leitão. 2012. "Pesca, gênero e políticas públicas: Uma introdução à história da articulação de mulheres pescadoras de Pernambuco." In *Gênero e trabalho: Diversidade de experiências em educação e comunidades tradicionais*, edited by Maria do Rosário de Fátima Andrade Leitão and Maria Helena Santana Cruz, 171–191. Ilha de Santa Catarina, Brazil: Editora Mulheres.

Ingersoll, Karin Amimoto. 2016. *Waves of Knowing: A Seascape Epistemology*. Durham, NC: Duke University Press.

Isaacs, Moenieba. 2011. "Individual Transferable Quotas, Poverty Alleviation and Challenges for Small-Country Fisheries Policy in South Africa." *MAST* 10 (2):63–84.

IUCN General Assembly. 1988. "Resolution 17.38: Protection of the Coastal and Marine Environment." https://portals.iucn.org/library/sites/library/files/resrecfiles/GA_17_REC_038_Protection_of_the_Coastal_and_Marine.pdf.

Jackson, Cecile. 1993. "Doing What Comes Naturally? Women and Environment in Development." *World Development* 21 (12):1947–1963. https://doi.org/10.1016/0305-750X(93)90068-K.

Jarosz, Lucy. 1996. "Defining Deforestation in Madagascar." In *Liberation Ecologies: Environment, Development, Social Movements*, edited by Richard Peet and Michael Watts, 148–164. New York: Routledge.

Johannes, R. E. 1978. "Traditional Marine Conservation Methods in Oceania and Their Demise." *Annual Review of Ecology and Systematics* 9:349–364. https://doi.org/10.2307/2096753.

———. 2002. "The Renaissance of Community-Based Marine Resource Management in Oceania." *Annual Review of Ecology and Systematics* 33 (1):317–340. https://doi.org/10.1146/annurev.ecolsys.33.010802.150524.

Johnson, Ayana Elizabeth, and Katharine K. Wilkinson. 2021. *All We Can Save: Truth, Courage, and Solutions for the Climate Crisis*. New York: One World.

Joireman, S. F. 2008. "The Mystery of Capital Formation in Sub-Saharan Africa: Women, Property Rights and Customary Law." *World Development* 36 (7):1233–1246. https://doi.org/10.1016/j.worlddev.2007.06.017.

Julien, G. 1931. "Foreword." In Pierre Deltiel, *Le Fokon'olona (Commune malagache) et les conventions de Folkon'olona*. Paris: Éditions Domat-Montchrestien.

Jürg, Brand, and Mora Willy. 2009. *Capitalisation de 7 ans d'expériences en conservation et développement, 2003–2009: Parc National Mananara-Nord Reserve de Biosphere*. Antananarivo: Madagascar National Parks.

Kaplan, Katherine A., Lauren Yamane, Louis W. Botsford, Marissa L. Baskett, Alan Hastings, Sara Worden, and J. Wilson White. 2019. "Setting Expected Timelines of Fished Population Recovery for the Adaptive Management of a Marine Protected Area Network." *Ecological Applications* 29 (6):e01949. https://doi.org/10.1002/eap.1949.

Kellert, Stephen R., Jai N. Mehta, Syma A. Ebbin, and Laly L. Lichtenfeld. 2000. "Community Natural Resource Management: Promise, Rhetoric, and Reality." *Society and Natural Resources* 13 (8):705–715. http://dx.doi.org/10.1080/089419200750035575.

Kelly, Alice B. 2011. "Conservation Practice as Primitive Accumulation." *Journal of Peasant Studies* 38 (4):683–701. https://doi.org/10.1080/03066150.2011.607695.

Kelly, Alice B., and Nancy Lee Peluso. 2015. "Frontiers of Commodification: State Lands and Their Formalization." *Society and Natural Resources* 28 (5):473–495. https://doi.org/10.1080/08941920.2015.1014602.

Kerr, Rachel Bezner. 2014. "Lost and Found Crops: Agrobiodiversity, Indigenous Knowledge, and a Feminist Political Ecology of Sorghum and Finger Millet in Northern Malawi." *Annals of the Association of American Geographers* 104 (3):577–593. https://doi.org/10.1080/00045608.2014.892346.

Kerwath, Sven E., Henning Winker, Albrecht Götz, and Colin G. Attwood. 2013. "Marine Protected Area Improves Yield without Disadvantaging Fishers." *Nature Communications* 4 (1):2347. https://doi.org/10.1038/ncomms3347.

Kimmerer, Robin Wall. 2013. *Braiding Sweetgrass: Indigenous Wisdom, Scientific Knowledge, and the Teachings of Plants*. Minneapolis, MN: Milkweed Editions.

Kinlan, Brian P., and Steven D. Gaines. 2003. "Propagule Dispersal in Marine and Terrestrial Environments: A Community Perspective." *Ecology* 84 (8):2007–2020. https://doi.org/10.1890/01-0622.

Kleiber, Danika, Leila Harris, and Amanda C. J. Vincent. 2018. "Gender and Marine Protected Areas: A Case Study of Danajon Bank, Philippines." *Maritime Studies* 17:163–175. https://doi.org/10.1007/s40152-018-0107-7.

Kothari, Uma. 2002. "Feminist and Postcolonial Challenges to Development." In *Development Theory and Practice: Critical Perspectives*, edited by Uma Kothari and Martin Minogue, 35–51. Houndmills, UK: Palgrave.

Kovach, Margaret. 2010. "Conversation Method in Indigenous Research." *First Peoples Child & Family Review* 5 (1):40-48. doi: https://doi.org/10.7202/1069060ar.

Kroodsma, David A., Juan Mayorga, Timothy Hochberg, Nathan A. Miller, Kristina Boerder, Francesco Ferretti, Alex Wilson, et al. 2018. "Tracking the Global Footprint of Fisheries." *Science* 359 (6378):904–908. https://doi.org/10.1126/science.aao5646.

Kull, Christian A. 1996. "Evolution of Conservation Efforts in Madagascar." *International Environmental Affairs* 8 (1):50–86.

———. 2000. "Deforestation, Erosion, and Fire: Degradation Myths in the Environmental History of Madagascar." *Environment and History* 6 (4):423–450. https://doi.org/10.3197/096734000129342361.

———. 2002. "Empowering Pyromaniacs in Madagascar: Ideology and Legitimacy in Community-Based Natural Resource Management." *Development and Change* 33 (1):57–78. https://doi.org/10.1111/1467-7660.00240.

———. 2004. *Isle of Fire: The Political Ecology of Landscape Burning in Madagascar.* Chicago: University of Chicago Press.

———. 2014. "The Roots, Persistence, and Character of Madagascar's Conservation Boom." In *Conservation and Environmental Management in Madagascar*, edited by Ivan R. Scales, 146–171. London: Routledge.

LaDuke, Winona. 1999. *All Our Relations: Native Struggles for Land and Life.* Cambridge, MA: South End Press.

Laffoley, Dan, John M. Baxter, Jon C. Day, Lauren Wenzel, Paula Bueno, and Katherine Zischka. 2019. "Marine Protected Areas." In *World Seas: An Environmental Evaluation*, vol. 3, 2nd ed., edited by Charles Sheppard, 549–569. Cambridge, MA: Academic Press.

Lagoin, Y. 1961. "Peche et utilization des requins." *Bulletin de Madagascar* (183):647–665.

Lambin, Eric F., B. L. Turner, Helmut J. Geist, Samuel B. Agbola, Arild Angelsen, John W. Bruce, Oliver T. Coomes, et al. 2001. "The Causes of Land-Use and Land-Cover Change: Moving beyond the Myths." *Global Environmental Change* 11 (4):261–269. https://doi.org/10.1016/s0959-3780(01)00007-3.

Langley, Josephine. 2006. *Vezo Knowledge: Traditional Ecological Knowledge in Andavadoaka, Southwest Madagascar.* London: Blue Ventures Conservation.

Łapniewska, Zofia. 2016. "Reading Elinor Ostrom through a Gender Perspective." *Feminist Economics* 22 (4):129–151. https://doi.org/10.1080/13545701.2016.1171376.

Latour, Bruno. 1993. *We Have Never Been Modern*. Translated by Catherine Porter. Cambridge, MA: Harvard University Press.

———. 2005. *Reassembling the Social: An Introduction to Actor-Network-Theory*. Oxford: Oxford University Press.

Laurent, Louis. 1906. "L'industrie des pêches aux colonies: Nos richesses coloniales, 1900–1905." In *Collection des ouvrages: Exposition coloniale de Marseille*, edited by G. Darboux, J. Cotte, P. Stephan, and F. van Gaver 221–250. Marseille: Barlatier.

Leach, Melissa. 2007. "Earth Mother Myths and Other Ecofeminist Fables: How a Strategic Notion Rose and Fell." *Development and Change* 38 (1):67–85. https://doi.org/10.1111/j.1467-7660.2007.00403.x.

Leach, Melissa, and Cathy Green. 1997. "Gender and Environmental History: From Representation of Women and Nature to Gender Analysis of Ecology and Politics." *Environment and History* 3 (3):343–370. https://www.jstor.org/stable/20723052.

Leach, Melissa, Robin Mearns, and Ian Scoones. 1999. "Environmental Entitlements: Dynamics and Institutions in Community-Based Natural Resource Management." *World Development* 27 (2):225–247. https://doi.org/10.1016/S0305-750X(98)00141-7.

Leach, Melissa, Lyla Mehta, and Preetha Prabhakaran. 2015. "Sustainable Development: A Gendered Pathways Approach." In *Gender Equality and Sustainable Development*, edited by Melissa Leach 1–33. New York: Routledge.

Lele, Sharachchandra, Peter Wilshusen, Dan Brockington, Reinmar Seidler, and Kamaljit Bawa. 2010. "Beyond Exclusion: Alternative Approaches to Biodiversity Conservation in the Developing Tropics." *Current Opinion in Environmental Sustainability* 2 (1–2):94–100. http://dx.doi.org/10.1016/j.cosust.2010.03.006.

Le Manach, Frédéric, Mialy Andriamahefazafy, Sarah Harper, Alasdair Harris, Gilles Hosch, Glenn-Marie Lange, Dirk Zeller, and Ussif Rashid Sumaila. 2013. "Who Gets What? Developing a More Equitable Framework for EU Fishing Agreements." *Marine Policy* 38:257–266. http://dx.doi.org/10.1016/j.marpol.2012.06.001.

Le Manach, Frédéric, Charlotte Gough, Alasdair Harris, Frances Humber, Sarah Harper, and Dirk Zeller. 2012. "Unreported Fishing, Hungry People and Political Turmoil: The Recipe for a Food Security Crisis in Madagascar?" *Marine Policy* 36 (1):218–225. https://doi.org/10.1016/j.marpol.2011.05.007.

Le Manach, Frédéric, Charlotte Gough, Frances Humber, Sarah Harper, and Dirk Zeller. 2011. "Reconstruction of Total Marine Fisheries Catches for Madagascar (1950–2008)." In *Fisheries Catch Reconstructions: Islands, Part II*, edited by Sarah Harper and Dirk Zeller, 21–37. Vancouver: University of British Columbia.

Lester, Sarah E., Benjamin S. Halpern, Kristen Grorud-Colvert, Jane Lubchenco, Benjamin I. Ruttenberg, Steven D. Gaines, Satie Airame, and Robert R. Warner. 2009. "Biological Effects within No-Take Marine Reserves: A Global Synthesis." *Marine Ecology Progress Series* 384:33–46. https://doi.org/10.3354/meps08029.

Levkoe, Charles Z., Kristen Lowitt, and Connie Nelson. 2017. " 'Fish as Food': Exploring a Food Sovereignty Approach to Small-Scale Fisheries." *Marine Policy* 85:65–70. https://doi.org/10.1016/j.marpol.2017.08.018.

Leymarie, Philippe. 1975. "Le Fokonolona: La voie malgache du socialisme?" *Revue Française d'Études Politiques Africaines* 10 (112):42–62.

Li, Tania Murray. 1996. "Images of Community: Discourse and Strategy in Property Relations." *Development and Change* 27 (3):501–527. https://doi.org/10.1111/j.1467-7660.1996.tb00601.x.

———. 2002. "Engaging Simplifications: Community-Based Resource Management, Market Processes and State Agendas in Upland Southeast Asia." *World Development* 30 (2):265–283. https://doi.org/10.1016/S0305-750X(01)00103-6.

Lilette, Valérie. 2006. "Mixed Results: Conservation of the Marine Turtle and the Red-Tailed Tropicbird by Vezo Semi-Nomadic Fishers." *Conservation and Society* 4 (2):262–286. https://www.jstor.org/stable/26396661.

Lima, André L. R., Linda M. Eggertsen, Jessyca L. S. Teixeira, Alexandre Schiavetti, Fabiana C. Félix-Hackradt, and Carlos W. Hackradt. 2023. "The Influence of Marine Protected Areas on the Patterns and Processes in the Life Cycle of Reef Fishes." *Reviews in Fish Biology and Fisheries* 33:893–913. https://doi.org/10.1007/s11160-023-09761-y.

Little Bear, Leroy. 2000. "Jagged Worldviews Colliding." In *Reclaiming Indigenous Voice and Vision*, edited by Marie Battiste, 77–85. Vancouver, BC: University of British Columbia Press.

Long, Stephen. 2017. "Short-Term Impacts and Value of a Periodic No-Take Zone (NTZ) in a Community-Managed Small-Scale Lobster Fishery, Madagascar." *PLOS ONE* 12 (5):e0177858. https://doi.org/10.1371/journal.pone.0177858.

Louw, Simone, and Markus Bürgener. 2020. *Sea Cucumber Trade from Africa to Asia.* Cambridge, UK: TRAFFIC International.

Lowe, Celia. 2006. *Wild Profusion: Biodiversity Conservation in an Indonesian Archipelago.* Princeton, NJ: Princeton University Press.

Lubchenco, Jane, and Kirsten Grorud-Colvert. 2015. "Making Waves: The Science and Politics of Ocean Protection." *Science* 350 (6259):382–383. https://doi.org/10.1126/science.aad5443.

Lund, Christian. 2002. "Negotiating Property Institutions: On the Symbiosis of Property and Authority in Africa." In *Negotiating Property in Africa*, edited by Kristine Juul and Christian Lund, 11–43. Portsmouth, NH: Heinemann.

———. 2006. "Twilight Institutions: Public Authority and Local Politics in Africa." *Development and Change* 37 (4):685–705. https://doi.org/10.1111/j.1467-7660.2006.00497.x.

———. 2008. *Local Politics and the Dynamics of Property in Africa.* Cambridge: Cambridge University Press.

Lund, Christian, and Catherine Boone. 2013. "Introduction: Land Politics in Africa—Constituting Authority over Territory, Property and Persons." *Africa* 83 (1):1–13. https://doi.org/10.1017/S000197201200068X.

Lynch, Melody, and Sarah Turner. 2022. "Rocking the Boat: Intersectional Resistance to Marine Conservation Policies in Wakatobi National Park, Indonesia." *Gender, Place and Culture* 29 (10):1376–1398. https://doi.org/10.1080/0966369X.2021.1 971630.

Maestro, María, M. Luisa Pérez-Cayeiro, Juan Adolfo Chica-Ruiz, and Harry Reyes. 2019. "Marine Protected Areas in the 21st Century: Current Situation and Trends." *Ocean and Coastal Management* 171:28–36. https://doi.org/10.1016/j.ocecoaman. 2019.01.008.

Malagasy Government. 1973a. Ordonnance no 73–9 du 24 mars 1973 portant structuration du monde rural pour une maîtrise populaire du développement. Antananarivo: Journal Officiel.

——. 1973b. Ordonnance no 73–10 du 24 mars 1973 portant organisation et fonctionnement des "fokontany." Antananarivo: Journal Officiel.

——. 1973c. Ordonnance no 73–73 du 1er décembre 1973 portant orientation du développement rural. Antananarivo: Journal Officiel.

Máñez, Kathleen Schwerdtner, and Annet Pauwelussen. 2016. "Fish Is Women's Business Too: Looking at Marine Resource Use through a Gender Lens." In *Perspectives on Oceans Past: A Handbook of Marine Environmental History*, edited by Bo Poulsen and Kathleen Schwerdtner Máñez, 193–211. Berlin: Springer.

Mangi, S. C., and C. M. Roberts. 2006. "Quantifying the Environmental Impacts of Artisanal Fishing Gear on Kenya's Coral Reef Ecosystems." *Marine Pollution Bulletin* 52 (12):1646–1660. https://doi.org/10.1016/j.marpolbul.2006.06.006.

Mangubhai, Sangeeta. 2019. "Promoting Gender Equity and Social Inclusion in Fisheries." WCS, November 19. https://medium.com/wcs-marine-conservation-program/making-it-happen-implementing-joint-food-security-and-conservation-objectives-d7f05469a508.

Mann, Alana. 2017. "Food Sovereignty and the Politics of Food Scarcity." In *Global Resource Scarcity: Catalyst for Conflict or Cooperation?*, edited by Marcelle C. Dawson, Christopher Rosin, and Nave Wald, 131–145. London: Routledge.

Mansourian, Stephanie, and Nigel Dudley. 2008. *Protected Areas for a Living Planet— Delivering on CBD Commitments*. Gland, Switzerland: WWF International.

Maracle, Lee. 1996. *I Am Woman: A Native Perspective on Sociology and Feminism*. Vancouver, BC: Press Gang.

Marchand, Marianne H., and Jane L. Parpart, eds. 2003. *Feminism/Postmodernism/ Development*. London: Routledge.

Marine Conservation Institute. 2023. "The Marine Protection Atlas." http://mpatlas.org.

Martell, Steven J. D., Timothy E. Essington, Bob Lessard, James F. Kitchell, Carl J. Walters, and Christofer H. Boggs. 2005. "Interactions of Productivity, Predation Risk, and Fishing Effort in the Efficacy of Marine Protected Areas for the Central Pacific." *Canadian Journal of Fisheries and Aquatic Sciences* 62 (6):1320–1336. https://doi.org/10.1139/f05-114.

Martínez-Alier, Joan. 2012. "Environmental Justice and Economic Degrowth: An Alliance between Two Movements." *Capitalism Nature Socialism* 23 (1):51–73. https://doi.org/10.1080/10455752.2011.648839.

Massey, Doreen. 1994. *Space, Place, and Gender.* Minneapolis: University of Minnesota Press.

Matagne, Patrick. 1998. "The Politics of Conservation in France in the Nineteenth Century." *Environment and History* 4 (3):359–367. https://doi.org/10.2307/20723081.

Matsuda, H., Y. Takemoto, and T. Katsukawa. 2016. "Design and Evaluation of Offshore Marine Protected Areas." Paper presented at the 2016 Techno-Ocean Conference, Kobe, Japan, October 6–8, 2016.

Matthews, Elizabeth, Jamie Bechtel, Easkey Britton, Karl Morrison, and Caleb McClennen. 2012. *A Gender Perspective on Securing Livelihoods and Nutrition in Fish-Dependent Coastal Communities; Report to the Rockefeller Foundation.* Bronx, NY: Wildlife Conservation Society.

Maxwell, Sara M., Kristina M. Gjerde, Melinda G. Conners, and Larry B. Crowder. 2020. "Mobile Protected Areas for Biodiversity on the High Seas." *Science* 367 (6475):252–254. 10.1126/science.aaz9327.

May, Ann Mari, and Gale Summerfield. 2012. "Creating a Space Where Gender Matters: Elinor Ostrom (1933–2012) Talks with Ann Mari May and Gale Summerfield." *Feminist Economics* 18 (4):25–37. https://doi.org/10.1080/13545701.2012.739725.

Mayol, Taylor Lee. 2013. "Madagascar's Nascent Locally Managed Marine Area Network." *Madagascar Conservation and Development* 8 (2):91–95. https://doi.org/10.4314/mcd.v8i2.8.

McCay, Bonnie J. 1999. " 'That's Not Right': Resistance to Enclosure in a Newfoundland Crab Fishery." In *Fishing People, Fishing Places: Issues in Canadian Small-Scale Fisheries,* edited by D. Newell and R. Ommer, 301–320. Toronto: University of Toronto Press.

McClanahan, Timothy R. 2010. "Effects of Fisheries Closures and Gear Restrictions on Fishing Income in a Kenyan Coral Reef." *Conservation Biology* 24 (6):1519–1528. https://doi.org/10.1111/j.1523-1739.2010.01530.x.

McClanahan, Timothy R., Mebrahtu Ateweberhan, Emily S. Darling, Nicholas A. J. Graham, and Nyawira A. Muthiga. 2014. "Biogeography and Change among Regional Coral Communities across the Western Indian Ocean." *PLOS ONE* 9 (4):e93385. https://doi.org/10.1371/journal.pone.0093385.

McClanahan, T. R., and S. Mangi. 2001. "The Effect of a Closed Area and Beach Seine Exclusion on Coral Reef Fish Catches." *Fisheries Management and Ecology* 8 (2):107–121. https://doi.org/10.1046/j.1365-2400.2001.00239.x.

McEwan, Cheryl. 2001. "Postcolonialism, Feminism and Development: Intersections and Dilemmas." *Progress in Development Studies* 1 (2):93–111. https://doi.org/10.1177/146499340100100201.

McSween, Terry E., Wanda Myers, and Tod C. Kuchler. 1990. "Getting Buy-In at the Executive Level." *Journal of Organizational Behavior Management* 11 (1):207–221. https://doi.org/10.1300/J075v11n01_13.

MEDD. 2019. "Elargir et consolider le réseau des aires marines protégées de Madagascar Cadre de Gestion Environnemental et Social (CGES) et Cadre des Procédures (CP)." Antananarivo: Ministère de l'Environnement et du Développement Durable.

MEF. 2010. "Plan de sauvegarde sociale et environnementale de l'aire protégée marine Nosy Ve-Androka." In *Programme environnemental III. Report No. 240 V7*, edited by Madagascar National Parks. Antananarivo: Ministère de l'Environnement et des Forêts.

Meinzen-Dick, Ruth, and Esther Mwangi. 2009. "Cutting the Web of Interests: Pitfalls of Formalizing Property Rights." *Land Use Policy* 26 (1):36–43. https://doi.org/10.1016/j.landusepol.2007.06.003.

Meinzen-Dick, Ruth, and Margreet Zwarteveen. 2001. "Gender Dimensions of Community Resource Management: The Case of Water Users' Associations in South Asia." In *Communities and the Environment: Ethnicity, Gender, and the State in Community-Based Conservation*, edited by Arun Agrawal and Clark Gibson, 63–88. New Brunswick, NJ: Rutgers University Press.

Menon, Ajit, Merle Sowman, and Maarten Bavinck. 2018. "Rethinking Capitalist Transformation of Fisheries in South Africa and India." *Ecology and Society* 23 (4). https://www.jstor.org/stable/26796870.

Merchant, Carolyn. 1980. *The Death of Nature: Women, Ecology and the Scientific Revolution*. London: Harper and Row.

———. 1996. *Earthcare: Women and the Environment.* New York: Routledge.

Merry, Sally Engle. 2011. "Measuring the World: Indicators, Human Rights, and Global Governance." *Current Anthropology* 52 (S3):S83–S95. https://doi.org/10.1086/657241.

———. 2016. *The Seductions of Quantification: Measuring Human Rights, Gender Violence, and Sex Trafficking.* Chicago: University of Chicago Press.

Micheli, Fiorenza, Benjamin S. Halpern, Louis W. Botsford, and Robert R. Warner. 2004. "Trajectories and Correlates of Community Change in No-Take Marine Reserves." *Ecological Applications* 14 (6):1709–1723.

Mickey, S. 2018. "Cosmology and Ecology." In *The Encyclopedia of the Anthropocene*, edited by Dominick A. Dellasala and Michael I. Goldstein, 151–157. Oxford: Elsevier.

Mills, Elyse N. 2018. "Implicating 'Fisheries Justice' Movements in Food and Climate Politics." *Third World Quarterly* 39 (7):1270–1289. https://doi.org/10.1080/0143659 7.2017.1416288.

Mohan, Giles, and Kristian Stokke. 2000. "Participatory Development and Empowerment: The Dangers of Localism." *Third World Quarterly* 21 (2):247–268.

Mohanty, Chandra. 1988. "Under Western Eyes: Feminist Scholarship and Colonial Discourses." *Feminist Review* 30 (1):61–88. https://doi.org/10.1057/fr.1988.42.

——. 2003. *Feminism without Borders: Decolonizing Theory, Practicing Solidarity.* Durham, NC: Duke University Press.

——. 2013. "Transnational Feminist Crossings: On Neoliberalism and Radical Critique." *Signs: Journal of Women in Culture and Society* 38 (4):967–991. https://doi.org/10.1086/669576.

Mollett, Sharlene. 2010. "Está Listo (Are You Ready)? Gender, Race and Land Registration in the Río Plátano Biosphere Reserve." *Gender, Place and Culture* 17 (3):357–375. https://doi.org/10.1080/09663691003737629.

——. 2017. "Feminist Political Ecology, Postcolonial Intersectionality, and the Coupling of Race and Gender." In *Routledge Handbook of Gender and Environment*, edited by Sherilyn MacGregor, 146–158. London: Routledge.

Mollett, Sharlene, and Caroline Faria. 2013. "Messing with Gender in Feminist Political Ecology." *Geoforum* 45:116–125. https://doi.org/10.1016/j.geoforum.2012.10.009.

——. 2018. "The Spatialities of Intersectional Thinking: Fashioning Feminist Geographic Futures." *Gender, Place and Culture* 25 (4):565–577.

Molloy, Philip P., Ian B. McLean, and Isabelle M. Côté. 2009. "Effects of Marine Reserve Age on Fish Populations: A Global Meta-Analysis." *Journal of Applied Ecology* 46 (4):743–751. https://doi.org/10.1111/j.1365-2664.2009.01662.x.

Momsen, Janet Henshall. 2001. "Backlash: Or How to Snatch Failure from the Jaws of Success in Gender and Development." *Progress in Development Studies* 1 (1):51–56. https://doi.org/10.1177/146499340100100105.

Moore, Sally Falk. 1986. *Social Facts and Fabrications: "Customary" Law on Kilimanjaro, 1880–1980.* Cambridge: Cambridge University Press.

——. 1988. "Legitimation as a Process: The Expansion of Government and Party in Tanzania." In *State Formation and Political Legitimacy*, edited by Ronald Cohen and Judith D. Toland, 155–172. New Brunswick, NJ: Transaction Books.

Mortimer-Sandilands, Catriona, and Bruce Erickson. 2010. *Queer Ecologies: Sex, Nature, Politics, Desire.* Bloomington: Indiana University Press.

Moser, Caroline, and Annalise Moser. 2005. "Gender Mainstreaming since Beijing: A Review of Success and Limitations in International Institutions." *Gender and Development* 13 (2):11–22. https://doi.org/10.2307/20053145.

Mosse, David. 1997. "The Symbolic Making of a Common Property Resource: History, Ecology and Locality in a Tank-Irrigated Landscape in South India." *Development and Change* 28 (3):467–504. https://doi.org/10.1111/1467-7660.00051.

Murphy, Alexander B. 2012. "Entente Territorial: Sack and Raffestin on Territoriality." *Environment and Planning D: Society and Space* 30 (1):159–172. doi: 10.1068/d4911.

Muttenzer, Frank. 2020. *Being Ethical among Vezo People: Fisheries, Livelihoods, and Conservation in Madagascar.* London: Lexington Books.

Mwangi, Esther, Ruth Meinzen-Dick, and Yan Sun. 2011. "Gender and Sustainable Forest Management in East Africa and Latin America." *Ecology and Society* 16 (1): 17. https://www.jstor.org/stable/26268834.

Nagar, Richa, and Amanda Lock Swarr. 2022. "Introduction: Theorizing Transnational Femisit Praxis." In *Critical Transnational Feminist Praxis*, edited by Amanda Lock Swarr and Richa Nagar, 1–22. Albany, NY: SUNY Press.

Narayan, Deepa, and Lant Pritchett. 1999. "Cents and Sociability: Household Income and Social Capital in Rural Tanzania." *Economic Development and Cultural Change* 47 (4):871–897.

Nelson, Ingrid L. 2017. "Interspecies Care and Aging in a Gorilla 2.0 World." *Geoforum* 79:144–152. https://doi.org/10.1016/j.geoforum.2016.02.007.

Neumann, Roderick P. 1998. *Imposing Wilderness: Struggles over Livelihood and Nature Preservation in Africa*. Berkeley: University of California Press.

Nielssen, Hilde. 2011. *Ritual Imagination: A Study of Tromba Possession among the Betsimisaraka in Eastern Madagascar*. Boston: Brill.

Nightingale, Andrea J. 2006. "The Nature of Gender: Work, Gender and Environment." *Environment and Planning D: Society and Space* 24:165–185. https://doi.org/10.1068/d01k.

———. 2011. "Bounding Difference: Intersectionality and the Material Production of Gender, Caste, Class and Environment in Nepal." *Geoforum* 42 (2):153–162. https://doi.org/10.1016/j.geoforum.2010.03.004.

———. 2019. "Commoning for Inclusion? Political Communities, Commons, Exclusion, Property and Socio-Natural Becomings." *International Journal of the Commons* 13 (1):16–35. https://doi.org/10.18352/ijc.927.

Nillos Kleiven, Portia Joy, Sigurd Heiberg Espeland, Esben Moland Olsen, Rene A. Abesamis, Even Moland, and Alf Ring Kleiven. 2019. "Fishing Pressure Impacts the Abundance Gradient of European Lobsters across the Borders of a Newly Established Marine Protected Area." *Proceedings of the Royal Society B: Biological Sciences* 286 (1894):20182455. https://doi.org/10.1098/rspb.2018.2455.

Nirmal, Padini, and Dianne Rocheleau. 2019. "Decolonizing Degrowth in the Post-Development Convergence: Questions, Experiences, and Proposals from Two Indigenous Territories." *Environment and Planning E: Nature and Space* 2 (3):465–492. https://doi.org/10.1177/2514848618819478.

Norse, Elliott A. 2005. "Ending the Range Wars on the Last Frontier: Zoning the Sea." In *Marine Conservation Biology: The Science of Maintaining the Sea's Biodiversity*, edited by Elliott A. Norse and Larry B. Crowder, 422–443. Washington, DC: Island Press.

Noss, Reed F., Andrew P. Dobson, Robert Baldwin, Paul Beier, Cory R. Davis, Dominick A. Dellasala, John Francis, et al. 2012. "Bolder Thinking for Conservation." *Conservation Biology* 26 (1):1–4. https://doi.org/10.1111/j.1523-1739.2011.01738.x.

Nunoo, Francis Kofi Ewusie, and Dogbeda Yao Mawulolo Azumah. 2015. "Selectivity Studies on Beach Seine Deployed in Nearshore Waters near Accra, Ghana."

International Journal of Fisheries and Aquaculture 7 (7):111–126. https://doi. org/10.5897/IJFA14.0458.

Nyamu, Celestine Itumbi. 1998. "Achieving Gender Equality in a Plural Legal Context: Custom and Women's Access to and Control of Land in Kenya." *Third World Legal Studies* 21(15):21–63.

OEC. 2021. "Madagascar." Observatory of Economic Complexity. https://oec.world/en/ profile/country/mdg.

Ogra, Monica V. 2012. "Gender Mainstreaming in Community-Oriented Wildlife Conservation: Experiences from Nongovernmental Conservation Organizations in India." *Society and Natural Resources* 25 (12):1258–1276. https://doi.org/10.1080/0 8941920.2012.677941.

Ohayon, Sarah, Itai Granot, and Jonathan Belmaker. 2021. "A Meta-Analysis Reveals Edge Effects within Marine Protected Areas." *Nature Ecology and Evolution* 5 (9):1301–1308. https://doi.org/10.1038/s41559-021-01502-3.

Ojeda, Diana, Jade S. Sasser, and Elizabeth Lunstrum. 2019. "Malthus's Specter and the Anthropocene." *Gender, Place and Culture* 27 (3):1–17. https://doi.org/10.1080 /0966369X.2018.1553858.

Oliver, Thomas A., Kirsten L. L. Oleson, Hajanaina Ratsimbazafy, Daniel Raberinary, Sophie Benbow, and Alasdair Harris. 2015. "Positive Catch and Economic Benefits of Periodic Octopus Fishery Closures: Do Effective, Narrowly Targeted Actions 'Catalyze' Broader Management?" *PLoS ONE* 10 (6):e0129075. https://doi. org/10.1371/journal.pone.0129075.

Olsen, Wendy. 2004. "Triangulation in Social Research: Qualitative and Quantitative Methods Can Really Be Mixed." *Developments in Sociology* 20:103–118.

Ostrom, Elinor. 1990. *Governing the Commons: The Evolution of Institutions for Collective Action.* New York: Cambridge University Press.

Palmer, Seth. 2019. "In the Image of a Woman: Spirited Identifications and Embodied Interpellations along the Betsiboka Valley." PhD diss., University of Toronto.

Peluso, Nancy Lee. 2012. "What's Nature Got To Do With It? A Situated Historical Perspective on Socio-natural Commodities." *Development and Change* 43 (1):79–104.

Peluso, Nancy Lee, and Michael Watts, eds. 2001. *Violent Environments.* Ithaca, NY: Cornell University Press.

Pendleton, Linwood H., Gabby N. Ahmadia, Howard I. Browman, Ruth H. Thurstan, David M. Kaplan, and Valerio Bartolino. 2017. "Debating the Effectiveness of Marine Protected Areas." *ICES Journal of Marine Science* 75 (3):1156–1159. https://doi.org/10.1093/icesjms/fsx154.

Percy, Jeremy, and Brian O'Riordan. 2020. "The EU Common Fisheries Policy and Small-Scale Fisheries: A Forgotten Fleet Fighting for Recognition." In *Small-Scale Fisheries in Europe: Status, Resilience and Governance,* edited by José J. Pascual-Fernández, Cristina Pita, and Maarten Bavinck, 23–46. Cham, Switzerland: Springer.

Petit, G. 1925. "Protection de certains animaux marins et terrestres de Madagascar: Dugong, tortues, lémuriens." In *Premier congrès international pour la protection de la nature: Faune et flore, sites et monuments naturels, Paris (31 Mai–2 Juin 1923)*, 102–108.

———. 1930. *L'industrie des pêches à Madagascar*. Vol. 2. Paris: Société d'éditions géographiques, maritimes et coloniales.

Pictou, Sherry. 2018. "The Origins and Politics, Campaigns and Demands by the International Fisher Peoples' Movement: An Indigenous Perspective." *Third World Quarterly* 39 (7):1411–1420. https://doi.org/10.1080/01436597.2017.1368384.

Pike, Felicity, Narriman S. Jiddawi, and Maricela de la Torre-Castro. 2022. "Adaptive Capacity within Tropical Marine Protected Areas—Differences between Men- and Women-Headed Households." *Global Environmental Change* 76:102584. https://doi.org/10.1016/j.gloenvcha.2022.102584.

Pilyugin, Sergei S., Jan Medlock, and Patrick De Leenheer. 2016. "The Effectiveness of Marine Protected Areas for Predator and Prey with Varying Mobility." *Theoretical Population Biology* 110:63–77. https://doi.org/10.1016/j.tpb.2016.04.005.

Pimbert, Michel P., and Jules N. Pretty. 1997. "Parks, People and Professionals: Putting 'Participation' into Protected Area Management." *Social Change and Conservation* 16:297–330.

Pinkerton, Evelyn. 2017. "Hegemony and Resistance: Disturbing Patterns and Hopeful Signs in the Impact of Neoliberal Policies on Small-Scale Fisheries around the World." *Marine Policy* 80:1–9. https://doi.org/10.1016/j.marpol.2016.11.012.

Pittman, Simon J., Mark E. Monaco, Alan M. Friedlander, Bryan Legare, Richard S. Nemeth, Matthew S. Kendall, Matthew Poti, et al. 2014. "Fish with Chips: Tracking Reef Fish Movements to Evaluate Size and Connectivity of Caribbean Marine Protected Areas." *PLOS ONE* 9 (5):e96028. https://doi.org/10.1371/journal.pone.0096028.

Plumwood, Val. 1986. "Ecofeminism: An Overview and Discussion of Positions and Arguments." *Australasian Journal of Philosophy* 64:120–138. https://doi.org/10.1080/00048402.1986.9755430.

Pollini, Jacques. 2010. "Environmental Degradation Narratives in Madagascar: From Colonial Hegemonies to Humanist Revisionism." *Geoforum* 41 (5):711–722. https://doi.org/10.1016/j.geoforum.2010.04.001.

Pollini, Jacques, and James P. Lassoie. 2011. "Trapping Farmer Communities within Global Environmental Regimes: The Case of the GELOSE Legislation in Madagascar." *Society and Natural Resources* 24 (8):814–830. https://doi.org/10.1080/08941921003782218.

Ponte, Stefano. 2012. "The Marine Stewardship Council (MSC) and the Making of a Market for 'Sustainable Fish.'" *Journal of Agrarian Change* 12 (2–3):300–315. https://doi.org/10.1111/j.1471-0366.2011.00345.x.

Prakash, Sanjeev. 1998. "Fairness, Social Capital and the Commons: The Societal Foundations of Collective Action in the Himalaya." In *Privatizing Nature: Political*

Struggles for the Global Commons, edited by Michael Goldman, 167–197. London: Pluto Press.

Puig de la Bellacasa, Maria. 2017. *Matters of Care: Speculative Ethics in More Than Human Worlds*. Minneapolis: University of Minnesota Press.

Purcell, Steven W., David H. Williamson, and Poasi Ngaluafe. 2018. "Chinese Market Prices of Beche-de-Mer: Implications for Fisheries and Aquaculture." *Marine Policy* 91:58–65. https://doi.org/10.1016/j.marpol.2018.02.005.

Radcliffe, Sarah A. 2015. *Dilemmas of Difference: Indigenous Women and the Limits of Postcolonial Development Policy*. Durham, NC: Duke University Press.

Raik, Daniela. 2007. "Forest Management in Madagascar: An Historical Overview." *Madagascar Conservation and Development* 2 (1):5–10. http://dx.doi.org/10.4314/mcd.v2i1.44123.

Rakotondrabe, D. Tovorina. 1993. "Beyond the Ethnic Group: Ethnic Groups, Nation-State and Democracy in Madagascar." *Transformation* (22):15–29.

Rakotoson, Lalaina R., and Kathryn Tanner. 2006. "Community-Based Governance of Coastal Zone and Marine Resources in Madagascar." *Ocean and Coastal Management* 49:955–872. http://dx.doi.org/10.1016/j.ocecoaman.2006.08.003.

Ramasindraibe, Paul. 1975. *Fokonolona: Fototry Ny Firenena*. Antananarivo: Nouvelle imprimerie des arts graphiques.

Ramesh, Madhuri, and Nitin D. Rai. 2017. "Trading on Conservation: A Marine Protected Area as an Ecological Fix." *Marine Policy* 82:25–31. https://doi.org/10.1016/j.marpol.2017.04.020.

Ranger, Terence. 1997. "The Invention of Tradition in Colonial Africa." In *Perspectives on Africa: A Reader in Culture, History, and Representation*, edited by Roy Richard Grinker and Christopher B. Steiner, 597–612. Cambridge, MA: Blackwell.

Rasheed, A. Rifaee. 2020. "Marine Protected Areas and Human Well-Being—A Systematic Review and Recommendations." *Ecosystem Services* 41:101048. https://doi.org/10.1016/j.ecoser.2019.101048.

Ratsimbazafy, Hajaniaina, Thierry Lavitra, Marc Kochzius, and Jean Hugé. 2019. "Emergence and Diversity of Marine Protected Areas in Madagascar." *Marine Policy* 105:91–108. https://doi.org/10.1016/j.marpol.2019.03.008.

Raycraft, Justin. 2018. "Marine Protected Areas and Spatial Fetishism: A Viewpoint on Destructive Fishing in Coastal Tanzania." *Marine Pollution Bulletin* 133:478–480. https://doi.org/10.1016/j.marpolbul.2018.06.008.

REBIOMA. 2023. "Atlas Numerique du Système des Aires Protegeés de Madagascar." atlas.rebioma.net.

Reed, Ron, and Sibyl Diver. 2023. "Pathways to Healing: Indigenous Revitalization through Family-Based Land Management in the Klamath Basin." *Ecology and Society* 28 (1). https://doi.org/10.5751/ES-13861-280135.

Reef Doctor. 2023a. "Fisheries." Reef Doctor. https://www.reefdoctor.org/projects/conservation/fisheries/.

———. 2023b. "Issues We Address." Reef Doctor. https://www.reefdoctor.org/about-reef-doctor/issues-we-address/.

Rees, Siân E., Nicola L. Foster, Olivia Langmead, Simon Pittman, and David E. Johnson. 2017. "Defining the Qualitative Elements of Aichi Biodiversity Target 11 with Regard to the Marine and Coastal Environment in Order to Strengthen Global Efforts for Marine Biodiversity Conservation Outlined in the United Nations Sustainable Development Goal 14." *Marine Policy* 93:241–250. https://doi.org/10.1016/j.marpol.2017.05.016.

Reo, Nicholas J. 2019. "Inawendiwin and Relational Accountability in Anishnaabeg Studies: The Crux of the Biscuit." *Journal of Ethnobiology* 39 (1):65–75. https://doi.org/10.2993/0278-0771-39.1.65.

Resurrección, Bernadette P. 2017. "From 'Women, Environment, and Development' to Feminist Political Ecology." In *Routledge Handbook of Gender and Environment*, edited by Sherilyn MacGregor, 71–85. London: Routledge.

Ribot, Jesse. 1999. "Decentralization and Participation in Sahelian Forestry: Legal Instruments of Political-Administrative Control." *Africa* 69 (1):23–65. https://doi.org/10.2307/1161076.

———. 2003. "Democratic Decentralization of Natural Resources." In *Beyond Structural Adjustment: The Institutional Context of African Development*, edited by Nicolas Walle, Nicole Ball, and Vijaya Ramachandran, 159–182. New York: Palgrave Macmillan.

Ribot, Jesse C., and Nancy Lee Peluso. 2003. "A Theory of Access." *Rural Sociology* 68 (2):153–181. https://doi.org/10.1111/j.1549-0831.2003.tb00133.x.

Rio Declaration. 1992. Rio Declaration on Environment and Development. In *Report of the United Nations Conference on Environment and Development*, UN Doc. A/CONF.151/26 (vol. 1), August 12.

Robbins, Paul. 2020. *Political Ecology: A Critical Introduction*. 2nd ed. West Sussex, UK: John Wiley and Sons.

Rocheleau, Dianne E. 2008. "Political Ecology in the Key of Policy: From Chains of Explanation to Webs of Relation." *Geoforum* 39 (2):716–727. https://doi.org/10.1016/j.geoforum.2007.02.005.

Rocheleau, Dianne, Barbara Thomas-Slayter, and Esther Wangari. 2016. "Gender and the Environment: A Feminist Political Ecology Perspective." In *The Environment in Anthropology: A Reader in Ecology, Culture, and Sustainable Living*, 2nd ed., edited by Nora Haenn and Richard Wilk, 34–40. New York: New York University Press.

Rocliffe, Steve, Shawn Peabody, Melita Samoilys, and Julie P. Hawkins. 2014. "Towards a Network of Locally Managed Marine Areas (LMMAs) in the Western Indian Ocean." *PLoS ONE* 9 (7):e103000. https://doi.org/10.1371/journal.pone.0103000.

Rose, Carol M. 1994. *Property and Persuasion: Essays on the History, Theory, and Rhetoric of Ownership*. Boulder, CO: Westview.

Ruppert, Evelyn. 2011. "Population Objects: Interpassive Subjects." *Sociology* 45 (2):218–233. https://doi.org/10.1177/0038038510394027.

Russ, Garry R., Angel C. Alcala, and Aileen P. Maypa. 2003. "Spillover from Marine Reserves: The Case of Naso Vlamingii at Apo Island, the Philippines." *Marine Ecology Progress Series* 264:15–20. http://dx.doi.org/10.3354/meps264015.

Sack, Robert David. 1986. *Human Territoriality: Its Theory and History*. Cambridge: Cambridge University Press.

Said, Alicia, and Douglas MacMillan. 2020. " 'Re-Grabbing' Marine Resources: A Blue Degrowth Agenda for the Resurgence of Small-Scale Fisheries in Malta." *Sustainability Science* 15 (1):91–102. https://doi.org/10.1007/s11625-019-00769-7.

Saito-Jensen, Moeko, Iben Nathan, and Thorsten Treue. 2010. "Beyond Elite Capture? Community-Based Natural Resource Management and Power in Mohammed Nagar Village, Andhra Pradesh, India." *Environmental Conservation* 37 (3):327–335. https://doi.org/10.1017/S0376892910000664.

Sala, Enric, and Sylvaine Giakoumi. 2017. "No-Take Marine Reserves Are the Most Effective Protected Areas in the Ocean." *ICES Journal of Marine Science* 75 (3):1166–1168. https://doi.org/10.1093/icesjms/fsx059.

Sala, Enric, Juan Mayorga, Darcy Bradley, Reniel B. Cabral, Trisha B. Atwood, Arnaud Auber, William Cheung, et al. 2021. "Protecting the Global Ocean for Biodiversity, Food and Climate." *Nature* 592 (7854):397–402. https://doi.org/10.1038/s41586-021-03371-z.

Salafsky, Nick, and Eva Wollenberg. 2000. "Linking Livelihoods and Conservation: A Conceptual Framework and Scale for Assessing the Integration of Human Needs and Biodiversity." *World Development* 28 (8):1421–1438. https://doi.org/10.1016/s0305-750x(00)00031-0.

Salinger, M. J. 2013. "A Brief Introduction to the Issue of Climate and Marine Fisheries." *Climatic Change* 119 (1):23–35. https://doi.org/10.1007/s10584-013-0762-z.

Salo, Ken. 2007. "Contesting Liberal Legality: Informal Legal Cultures in Post-Apartheid South Africa's Privatizing Seafood Fishery." *African Studies Quarterly* 9 (4).

Sammler, Katherine G. 2020. "Kauri and the Whale: Oceanic Matter and Meaning in New Zealand." In *Blue Legalities*, edited by Irus Braverman and Elizabeth Johnson, 63–84. Durham, NC: Duke University Press.

Sand, Peter H. 2012. "Fortress Conservation Trumps Human Rights? The 'Marine Protected Area' in the Chagos Archipelago." *Journal of Environment and Development* 21 (1):36–39. https://doi.org/10.1177/1070496511435666.

SAPM. 2009. *Cadrage général du système des aires protégées de Madagascar*. Edited by Commission SAPM (Système d'Aires Protégées de Madagascar). Antananarivo: Ministère de l'Environnement des Forêts et du Tourisme.

Sasser, Jade. 2014. "From Darkness into Light: Race, Population, and Environmental Advocacy." *Antipode* 46 (5):1240–1257. https://doi.org/10.1111/anti.12029.

———. 2017. "Sexual Stewardship: Environment, Development, and the Gendered Politics of Population." In *Routledge Handbook of Gender and Environment*, edited by Sherilyn MacGregor, 345–356. London: Routledge.

———. 2018. *On Infertile Ground: Population Control and Women's Rights in the Era of Climate Change.* New York: New York University Press.

Saunders, Fred P. 2014. "The Promise of Common Pool Resource Theory and the Reality of Commons Projects." *International Journal of the Commons* 8 (2):636–656. http://doi.org/10.18352/ijc.477.

Scales, Ivan R. 2014a. "A Brief History of the State and the Politics of Natural Resource Use in Madagascar." In *Conservation and Environmental Management in Madagascar,* edited by Ivan R. Scales, 129–145. London: Routledge.

———. 2014b. "Green Consumption, Ecolabelling and Capitalism's Environmental Limits." *Geography Compass* 8 (7):477–489. https://doi.org/10.1111/gec3.12142.

Schroeder, R. 1999. *Shady Practices: Agroforestry and Gender Politics in the Gambia.* Berkeley: University of California Press.

Scott, James C. 1998. *Seeing Like a State: How Certain Schemes to Improve the Human Condition Have Failed.* New Haven: Yale University Press.

Seagle, Caroline. 2012. "Inverting the Impacts: Mining, Conservation and Sustainability Claims near the Rio Tinto/QMM Ilmenite Mine in Southeast Madagascar." *Journal of Peasant Studies* 39 (2):447–477. https://doi.org/10.1080/03066150.2012. 671769.

Shackleton, Sheona, Bruce Campbell, Eva Wollenberg, and David Edmunds. 2002. "Devolution and Community-Based Natural Resource Management: Creating Space for Local People to Participate and Benefit." *Natural Resource Perspectives* 76 (1):1–6.

Sharp, Lesley Alexandra. 2002. *The Sacrificed Generation: Youth, History, and the Colonized Mind in Madagascar.* Berkeley: University of California Press.

Shiva, Vandana. 1989. *Staying Alive: Women, Development and Ecology in India.* London: Zed Books.

———. 1992. "Women's Indigenous Knowledge and Biodiversity Conservation." *India International Centre Quarterly* 19 (1/2):205–214. https://www.jstor.org/stable/23002230.

Shiva, Vandana, and Maria Mies. 1993. *Ecofeminism.* London: Zed Books.

Shore, Cris, and Susan Wright. 2015. "Audit Culture Revisited: Rankings, Ratings, and the Reassembling of Society." *Current Anthropology* 56 (3):421–444. https://www. jstor.org/stable/10.1086/681534.

Sievanen, Leila, Rebecca L. Gruby, and Lisa M. Campbell. 2013. "Fixing Marine Governance in Fiji? The New Scalar Narrative of Ecosystem-Based Management." *Global Environmental Change* 23 (1):206–216. http://dx.doi.org/10.1016/j. gloenvcha.2012.10.004.

Sikor, Thomas, and Christian Lund. 2009. "Access and Property: A Question of Power and Authority." *Development and Change* 40 (1):1–22. https://doi.org/10.1111/ j.1467-7660.2009.01503.x.

Silva, C. N. S., H. S. Macdonald, M. G. Hadfield, M. Cryer, and J. P. A. Gardner. 2019. "Ocean Currents Predict Fine-Scale Genetic Structure and Source-Sink Dynamics in a Marine Invertebrate Coastal Fishery." *ICES Journal of Marine Science* 76 (4):1007–1018. https://doi.org/10.1093/icesjms/fsy201.

Silver, Jennifer J., and Lisa M. Campbell. 2018. "Conservation, Development and the Blue Frontier: The Republic of Seychelles' Debt Restructuring for Marine Conservation and Climate Adaptation Program." *International Social Science Journal* 68 (229–230):241–256. https://doi.org/10.1111/issj.12156.

Simpson, Leanne Betasamosake. 2014. "Land as Pedagogy: Nishnaabeg Intelligence and Rebellious Transformation." *Decolonization: Indigeneity, Education and Society* 3 (3):1–25.

Singh, Neera M. 2019. "Environmental Justice, Degrowth and Post-Capitalist Futures." *Ecological Economics* 163:138–142. https://doi.org/10.1016/j.ecolecon.2019.05.014.

Smith, Hillary, and Xavier Basurto. 2019. "Defining Small-Scale Fisheries and Examining the Role of Science in Shaping Perceptions of Who and What Counts: A Systematic Review." *Frontiers in Marine Science* 6 (236). https://doi.org/10.3389/fmars.2019.00236.

Sodikoff, Genese. 2012. *Forest and Labor in Madagascar: From Colonial Concession to Global Biosphere.* Bloomington: Indiana University Press.

Soliku, Ophelia, and Ulrich Schraml. 2018. "Making Sense of Protected Area Conflicts and Management Approaches: A Review of Causes, Contexts and Conflict Management Strategies." *Biological Conservation* 222:136–145. https://doi.org/10.1016/j.biocon.2018.04.011.

Soto, Cristina G. 2002. "The Potential Impacts of Global Climate Change on Marine Protected Areas." *Reviews in Fish Biology and Fisheries* 11 (3):181–195. https://doi.org/10.1023/A:1020364409616.

Soumy, Mathieu. 2004. "Country Review: Madagascar Review of the State of World Marine Capture Fisheries Management: Indian Ocean." *FAO Technical Paper.* Rome: FAO.

Sowman, Merle, and Jackie Sunde. 2018. "Social Impacts of Marine Protected Areas in South Africa on Coastal Fishing Communities." *Ocean and Coastal Management* 157:168–179. https://doi.org/10.1016/j.ocecoaman.2018.02.013.

Spivak, Gayatri Chakravorty. 1999. *A Critique of Postcolonial Reason: Toward a History of the Vanishing Present.* Cambridge, MA: Harvard University Press.

Starr, Bradley E. 1999. "The Structure of Max Weber's Ethic of Responsibility." *Journal of Religious Ethics* 27 (3):407–434. https://www.jstor.org/stable/40015266.

Steinberg, Philip E. 2018. "The Ocean as Frontier." *International Social Science Journal* 68 (229–230):237–240. https://doi.org/10.1111/issj.12152.

Steinberg, Philip, and Kimberley Peters. 2015 "Wet Ontologies, Fluid Spaces: Giving Depth to Volume through Oceanic Thinking." *Environment and Planning D: Society and Space* 33(2):247–264. https://doi.org/10.1068/d14148p.

Strydom, Hendrik A. 2013. "Environment and Indigenous Peoples." In *Max Planck Encyclopedia of Public International Law*, edited by Rüdiger Wolfrum. Heidelberg: Max Planck Foundation for International Peace and the Rule of Law, 116–132, Oxford, UK: Oxford University Press.

Sultana, Farhana. 2011. "Suffering for Water, Suffering from Water: Emotional Geographies of Resource Access, Control and Conflict." *Geoforum* 42 (2):163–172. https://doi.org/10.1016/j.geoforum.2010.12.002.

——. 2021. "Political Ecology 1: From Margins to Center." *Progress in Human Geography* 45 (1):156–165. https://doi.org/10.1177/0309132520936751.

——. 2022. "The Unbearable Heaviness of Climate Coloniality." *Political Geography* 99:102638. https://doi.org/10.1016/j.polgeo.2022.102638.

Sumaila, U. R., M. Samoilys, E. Allison, J. Cinner, C. DeYoung, and C. Kavanagh. 2014. *Economic Impacts of Ocean Acidification on Fisheries and Aquaculture in the Western Indian Ocean: Current Knowledge and Recommendations*. Indian Ocean and Red Sea (FAO 51, 57), IAEA Report.

Sundberg, Juanita. 2004. "Identities in the Making: Conservation, Gender and Race in the Maya Biosphere Reserve, Guatemala." *Gender, Place and Culture* 11 (1):43–66. http://dx.doi.org/10.1080/0966369042000188549.

——. 2017. "Feminist Political Ecology." In *International Encyclopedia of Geography: People, the Earth, Environment and Technology*, edited by Douglas Richardson et al., 1–12. Wiley-Blackwell and Association of American Geographers.

Swyngedouw, Erik. 2004. "Globalisation or 'Glocalisation'? Networks, Territories and Rescaling." *Cambridge Review of International Affairs* 17 (1):25–48. https://doi.org/10.1080/0955757042000203632.

TallBear, Kim. 2019. "Caretaking Relations, not American Dreaming." *Kalfou* 6 (1):24–41.

Thorburn, Craig C. 2000. "Changing Customary Marine Resource Management Practice and Institutions: The Case of Sasi Lola in the Kei Islands, Indonesia." *World Development* 28 (8):1461–1479. https://doi.org/10.1016/S0305-750X(00)00039-5.

Thorpe, Andy, Maarten Bavink, and Sarah Coulthard. 2011. "Tracking the Debate around Marine Protected Areas: Key Issues and the BEG Framework." *Environmental Management* 47 (4):546–563. https://doi.org/10.1007/s00267-011-9632-5.

Toonen, Robert J., T. 'Aulani Wilhelm, Sara M. Maxwell, Daniel Wagner, Brian W. Bowen, Charles R. C. Sheppard, Sue M. Taei, et al. 2013. "One Size Does Not Fit All: The Emerging Frontier in Large-Scale Marine Conservation." *Marine Pollution Bulletin* 77 (1):7–10. https://doi.org/10.1016/j.marpolbul.2013.10.039.

Topor, Zachary M., Douglas B. Rasher, J. Emmett Duffy, and Simon J. Brandl. 2019. "Marine Protected Areas Enhance Coral Reef Functioning by Promoting Fish Biodiversity." *Conservation Letters* 12 (4):e12638. https://doi.org/10.1111/conl.12638.

Toupin, Louise. 2018. *Wages for Housework: A History of an International Feminist Movement, 1972–77.* Translated by Käthe Roth. Vancouver: UBC Press.

True, Jacqui. 2012. *The Political Economy of Violence against Women.* Oxford: Oxford University Press.

Tsing, Anna Lowenhaupt. 2011. *Friction: An Ethnography of Global Connection.* Princeton, NJ: Princeton University Press.

Tuck, G. N., and H. P. Possingham. 2000. "Marine Protected Areas for Spatially Structured Exploited Stocks." *Marine Ecology Progress Series* 192:89–101. https://www.jstor.org/stable/24855714.

Tucker, Bram, Erik J. Ringen, Tsiazonera, Jaovola Tombo, Patricia Hajasoa, Soanahary Gérard, Rolland Lahiniriko, and Angelah Halatiana Garçon. 2021. "Ethnic Markers without Ethnic Conflict." *Human Nature* 32 (3):529–556. https://doi.org/10.1007/s12110-021-09412-w.

UN Comtrade. 2020. UN Comtrade Database. https://comtradeplus.un.org/.

UNEP-WCMC and IUCN. 2020. Marine Protected Planet. The World Database on Protected Areas (WDPA). Edited by UNEP-WCMC and IUCN. Cambridge. https://www.protectedplanet.net/en/thematic-areas/marine-protected-areas.

UNICEF. 2023. "Birth Registration." UNICEF Data: Monitoring the Situation Of Children and Women. https://data.unicef.org/topic/child-protection/birth-registration/.

UN Women Count. 2019. "Madagascar Country Report." United Nations Women Count. https://data.unwomen.org/country/madagascar.

USAID. 2016. *Marine Biodiversity and Fisheries in Madagascar: A Biodiversity and Extractives Political Economy.* Washington, DC: United States Agency for International Development.

Vandeperre, Frederic, Ruth M. Higgins, Julio Sánchez-Meca, Francesc Maynou, Raquel Goñi, Pablo Martín-Sosa, Angel Pérez-Ruzafa, et al. 2011. "Effects of No-Take Area Size and Age of Marine Protected Areas on Fisheries Yields: A Meta-Analytical Approach." *Fish and Fisheries* 12 (4):412–426. https://doi.org/10.1111/j.1467-2979.2010.00401.x.

Vandergeest, Peter, and Nancy Lee Peluso. 1995. "Territorialization and State Power in Thailand." *Theory and Society* 24 (3):385–426.

Vandergeest, Peter, and Anusorn Unno. 2012. "A New Extraterritoriality? Aquaculture Certification, Sovereignty, and Empire." *Political Geography* 31 (6):358–367. https://doi.org/10.1016/j.polgeo.2012.05.005.

Vannuccini, Stefania. 1999. *Shark Utilization, Marketing and Trade.* Rome Food and Agriculture Organization.

Vaughan, Mehana Blaich. 2018. *Kaiāulu: Gathering Tides.* Corvallis: Oregon State University Press.

Vaughan, Mehana Blaich, Barton Thompson, and Adam L. Ayers. 2017. "Pāwehe Ke Kai aʻo Hāʻena: Creating State Law Based on Customary Indigenous Norms of Coastal Management." *Society and Natural Resources* 30 (1):31–46. https://doi.org/10.1080/08941920.2016.1196406.

Venter, Oscar, Richard A. Fuller, Daniel B. Segan, Josie Carwardine, Thomas Brooks, Stuart H. M. Butchart, Moreno Di Marco, et al. 2014. "Targeting Global Protected Area Expansion for Imperiled Biodiversity." *PLoS Biology* 12 (6):e1001891. https://doi.org/10.1371/journal.pbio.1001891.

Verdery, Katherine. 2003. *The Vanishing Hectare: Property and Value in Postsocialist Transylvania.* Ithaca, NY: Cornell University Press.

Veuthey, Sandra, and Julien-François Gerber. 2012. "Accumulation by Dispossession in Coastal Ecuador: Shrimp Farming, Local Resistance and the Gender Structure of Mobilizations." *Global Environmental Change* 22 (3):611–622. https://doi.org/10.1016/j.gloenvcha.2011.10.010.

Walker, Barbara Louise Endemaño. 2002. "Engendering Ghana's Seascape: Fanti Fishtraders and Marine Property in Colonial History." *Society and Natural Resources* 15 (5):389–407. https://doi.org/10.1080/08941920252866765.

Walker, Barbara Louise Endemaño, and Michael A. Robinson. 2009. "Economic Development, Marine Protected Areas and Gendered Access to Fishing Resources in a Polynesian Lagoon." *Gender, Place and Culture* 16 (4):467–484.

Walker, Cherryl. 2005. "The Limits to Land Reform: Rethinking 'the Land Question.' " *Journal of Southern African Studies* 31 (4):805–824. https://doi.org/10.1080/030 57070500370597.

Wall, Derek. 2014. *The Sustainable Economics of Elinor Ostrom: Commons, Contestation and Craft.* London: Routledge.

Wallerstein, Immanuel Maurice. 1961. *Africa, the Politics of Independence: An Interpretation of Modern African History.* New York: Vintage Books.

Walley, Christine J. 2004. *Rough Waters: Nature and Development in an East African Marine Park.* Princeton, NJ: Princeton University Press.

Walton, A., M. Gomei, and G. Di Carlo. 2013. *Stakeholder Engagement: Participatory Approaches for the Planning and Development of Marine Protected Areas.* Rome: World Wide Fund for Nature and NOAA—National Marine Sanctuary Program.

Watts, Michael. 2017. "Political Ecology." In *A Companion to Economic Geography,* edited by Eric Sheppard and Trevor J. Barnes, 257–274. Oxford: Blackwell.

WCS. 2012. "Formalization of Six New LMMAs." In *WCS Madagascar News,* April 11. https://madagascar.wcs.org/About-Us/News/articleType/ArticleView/articleId/2522.aspx.

———. 2015. "Madagascar Creates Nation's First Community-Led Marine Protected Areas." *WCS Newsroom,* April 22. https://newsroom.wcs.org/News-Releases/articleType/ArticleView/articleId/6709/April-22-Madagascar-Creates-Nations-First-Community-Led-Marine-Protected-Areas.aspx.

———. 2019. "Protecting 1 Million Sq Kms through the $15 Million WCS Marine Protected Area Fund." United Nations Department of Economic and Social Affairs, Sustainable Development, https://sdgs.un.org/partnerships/protecting-1-million-sq-kms-through-15-million-wcs-marine-protected-area-fund.

Weiskopf, Sarah R., Janet A. Cushing, Toni Lyn Morelli, and Bonnie J. E. Myers. 2021. "Climate Change Risks and Adaptation Options for Madagascar." *Ecology and Society* 26 (4). https://doi.org/10.5751/ES-12816-260436.

West, Paige. 2006. *Conservation Is Our Government Now: The Politics of Ecology in Papua New Guinea.* Durham, NC: Duke University Press.

West, Paige, James Igoe, and Dan Brockington. 2006. "Parks and Peoples: The Social Impact of Protected Areas." *Annual Review of Anthropology* 35:251–277.

Westberg, Lotten, and Stina Powell. 2015. "Participate for Women's Sake? A Gender Analysis of a Swedish Collaborative Environmental Management Project." *Society and Natural Resources* 28 (11):1233–1248. https://doi.org/10.1080/08941920.2015.1014594.

Westerman, Kame, and Sophie Benbow. 2014. "The Role of Women in Community-Based Small-Scale Fisheries Management: The Case of the Southern Madagascar Octopus Fishery." *Western Indian Ocean Journal of Marine Science* 12 (2):119–132.

Westermann, Olaf, Jacqueline Ashby, and Jules Pretty. 2005. "Gender and Social Capital: The Importance of Gender Differences for the Maturity and Effectiveness of Natural Resource Management Groups." *World Development* 33 (11):1783–1799. https://doi.org/10.1016/j.worlddev.2005.04.018.

Whitehead, Ann, and Dzodzi Tsikata. 2003. "Policy Discourses on Women's Land Rights in Sub-Saharan Africa: The Implications of the Re-Turn to the Customary." *Journal of Agrarian Change* 3 (1–2):67–112. https://doi.org/10.1111/1471-0366.00051.

Whittlesey, Derwent. 1937. "British and French Colonial Technique in West Africa." *Foreign Affairs* 15 (2):362–373. https://doi.org/10.2307/20028773.

Whyte, Kyle. 2018. "Settler Colonialism, Ecology, and Environmental Injustice." *Environment and Society* 9 (1):125–144. https://doi.org/10.3167/ares.2018.090109.

Whyte, Kyle Powys, and Chris J. Cuomo. 2017. "Ethics of Caring in Environmental Ethics." In *The Oxford Handbook of Environmental Ethics*, edited by Stephen M. Gardiner and Allen Thompson, 234–247. Oxford: Oxford University Press.

Wichterich, Christa. 2015. "Contesting Green Growth, Connecting Care, Commons and Enough." In *Practising Feminist Political Ecologies: Moving beyond the "Green Economy,"* edited by Wendy Harcourt and Ingrid L. Nelson, 67–100. London: Zed Books.

Williams, Meryl J., Nikita Gopal, Rejula K., Carmen Pedroza-Gutiérrez, Arlene Nietes Satapornvanit, Paul Ramirez, P. S. Ananthan, et al. 2019. *GAF7, Expanding the Horizons: Long Report*. https://www.researchgate.net/publication/334954726_Long_Report_GAF7_Expanding_the_Horizons_The_7th_Global_Conference_on_Gender_in_Aquaculture_Fisheries.

Willmann, Rolf, Nicole Franz, Carlos Fuentevilla, Thomas F. McInerney, and Lena Westlund. 2017. "A Human Rights-Based Approach to Securing Small-Scale Fisheries: A Quest for Development as Freedom." In *The Small-Scale Fisheries Guidelines: Global Implementation*, edited by Svein Jentoft, Ratana Chuenpagdee, María José Barragán-Paladines, and Nicole Franz, 15–34. Cham, Switzerland: Springer.

Wilson, Edward O. 2016. *Half-Earth: Our Planet's Fight for Life*. New York: W. W. Norton.

Wilson, Kalpana. 2006. "Who Are the 'Community'? The World Bank and Agrarian Power in Bihar." *Economic and Political Weekly*, 23–27.

——. 2011. " 'Race,' Gender and Neoliberalism: Changing Visual Representations in Development." *Third World Quarterly* 32 (2):315–331. https://doi.org/10.1080/014 36597.2011.560471.

——. 2015. "Towards a Radical Re-appropriation: Gender, Development and Neoliberal Feminism." *Development and Change* 46 (4):803–832. https://doi.org/10.1111/dech. 12176.

Wilson, Kristen L., Derek P. Tittensor, Boris Worm, and Heike K. Lotze. 2020. "Incorporating Climate Change Adaptation into Marine Protected Area planning." *Global Change Biology* 26 (6):3251–3267. https://doi.org/10.1111/gcb.15094.

Winter, Kawika B., Mehana Blaich Vaughan, Natalie Kurashima, Lei Wann, Emily Cadiz, A. Hiʻilei Kawelo, Māhealani Cypher, Leialoha Kaluhiwa, and Hannah Kihalani Springer. 2023. "Indigenous Stewardship through Novel Approaches to Collaborative Management in Hawaiʻi." *Ecology and Society* 28 (1). https://doi. org/10.5751/ES-13662-280126.

World Bank. 2011. On a Proposed Additional IDA Credit from the Global Environment Facility Trust Fund in the Amount of $10.0 Million to the Republic of Madagascar for the Third Environmental Program Support Project (EP3). Washington, DC: World Bank.

——. 2014. "Face of Poverty in Madagascar: Poverty, Gender and Inequality Assessment." In *Poverty Reduction and Economic Management (PREM) Africa Region*. Washington, DC: World Bank.

——. 2016. *Second South West Indian Ocean Fisheries Governance and Shared Growth Project—Region & Madagascar (P153370)*. Washington, DC: World Bank.

——. 2017a. ID4D Country Diagnostic: Madagascar. License: Creative Commons Attribution 3.0 IGO (CC BY 3.0 IGO). Washington, DC: World Bank

——. 2017b. *Madagascar and Indian Ocean Commission Receive $83.15 Million to Improve Management of Fisheries*. Washington, DC: World Bank.

——. 2017c. *The Potential of the Blue Economy: Increasing Long-Term Benefits of the Sustainable Use of Marine Resources for Small Island Developing States and Coastal Least Developed Countries*. Washington, DC: World Bank and United Nations Department of Economic and Social Affairs.

——. 2017d. *Project Appraisal Document on a Proposed Credit in the Amount of US$65 Million to the Republic of Madagascar, a Proposed Grant in the Amount of US$6.42 Million to the Republic of Madagascar for a Second South West Indian Ocean Fisheries Governance and Shared Growth Project*. Washington, DC: World Bank.

——. 2020. *Madagascar: Balancing Conservation and Exploitation of Fisheries Resources*. Washington, DC: World Bank.

Worm, Boris. 2016. "Averting a Global Fisheries Disaster." *Proceedings of the National Academy of Sciences* 113 (18):4895–4897. https://doi.org/10.1073/pnas.1604008113.

Wosu, Adaoma. 2019. "Access and Institutions in a Small-Scale Octopus Fishery: A Gendered Perspective." *Marine Policy* 108:103649. https://doi.org/10.1016/j. marpol.2019.103649.

Wuerthner, George, Eileen Crist, and Tom Butler. 2015. *Protecting the Wild: Parks and Wilderness, the Foundation for Conservation*. Washington, DC: Island Press.

WWF. 2011. *Global Network Policy: Gender Policy Statement*. Gland, Switzerland: World Wildlife Fund.

——. 2016. "Fishery Improvement Projects: A Stepwise Approach to Sustainability." http://seafoodsustainability.org/fisheries/.

——. 2017. "Applying 'Dina' on the Malagasy Coast!" *WWF News*, August 25, 2017. http://wwf.panda.org/wwf_news/?309350/Pour-une-application-du-dina-sur-tout-le-littoral-malgache-.

——. 2018. *Expanding and Consolidating Madagascar's Marine Protected Areas Network*. WWF GEF Project Document G0013. Gland, Switzerland: World Wildlife Fund.

Young, Iris Marion. 1990. *Justice and the Politics of Difference*. Princeton, NJ: Princeton University Press.

Zupan, Mirta, Eliza Fragkopoulou, Joachim Claudet, Karim Erzini, Bárbara Horta e Costa, and Emanuel J. Gonçalves. 2018. "Marine Partially Protected Areas: Drivers of Ecological Effectiveness." *Frontiers in Ecology and the Environment* 16 (7):381–387. https://doi.org/10.1002/fee.1934.